THE

ORGANIC

GREENHOUSE
& CONSERVATORY

THE
ORGANIC
GREENHOUSE
& CONSERVATORY

ROY LACEY

David & Charles

British Library Cataloguing in Publication Data

Lacey, Roy
  The organic greenhouse and conservatory.
  I. Title
  635.9

ISBN 0-7153 9775 3

Typeset by ICON, Exeter
and printed in Germany by Mohndruck GmbH
for David & Charles plc
Brunel House Newton Abbot Devon

CONTENTS

WHY ORGANIC?

By the time you read these pages you will probably either be preparing to invest in a greenhouse or conservatory, or will already own one or other or both.

If you are planning to buy, be assured that your investment will pay handsome dividends. If your plans have already become reality, then you will know that a greenhouse or conservatory adds an extension to the garden that encompasses more than the amount of space it occupies. Gardening under cover means that your activities are not confined to fair weather. It means that the gardener's repertoire of interests can be extended into groups of plants that could not survive without protection, and it offers the opportunity to specialise in one or more of the hobby plants, such as chrysanthemums, carnations, fuchsias, cacti and orchids. It will also give the enormous satisfaction of raising edible crops like tomatoes, cucumbers, melons and peppers.

In its advice on choosing a structure and on the plants to grow in it, this book attempts to be as comprehensive as any other. Where it is different is in the *management* of those crops, because it offers an alternative to dependence on chemicals both in providing food for the plants and in protecting them against pests and diseases within the closed environment of the greenhouse.

The Use of Chemicals

The twentieth century has seen the agrochemical industry grow from an infant prodigy to an almost uncontrollable giant. Many of the post-war promises of the agrochemists have been fulfilled to the great benefit of mankind. At least in the prosperous western world, artificial plant foods have increased crop yields to the point where the problem of shortages has been replaced by mountains of surplus foods, while in less fortunate areas disease-carrying, life-threatening insects have been brought under control.

The aphid is the most commonly encountered garden pest with more than five hundred species in Britain and northern Europe – though this is scarcely in the same category as the major pests of tropical countries. Yet the destruction of greenfly, blackfly and the other members of the aphid family has involved the expenditure by chemical companies of millions of pounds on research and development of aphicides, both systemic and non-systemic, and countless millions by the gardeners who buy the products.

This is an incredibly expensive way of controlling a pest that most organic gardeners keep in check with nothing more toxic or costly than soapy water. Nor is it just the cost in terms of time, effort and resources that is involved. More than two hundred different chemicals are used in a billion gallons of sprays on our food crops every year, yet although government and industry continually assure us that these are safe because they have all passed strict toxicity tests, there has been increasing public disquiet that our health is being affected by residues in the crops, in the soil, in our drinking water, in the sea around us, and in the air we breathe.

There is accumulating evidence that many of the officially declared 'safe' pesticides can cause cancer, allergies (particularly in young children), birth defects and other health problems, and many pesticides long in use by amateur gardeners as well as by farmers and growers have been withdrawn because of concern over the long-term dangers.

The Organic Movement

No wonder, then, that the organic movement, so often derided as the 'muck and mystery brigade', has gained converts in droves. The Soil Association, founded in 1946, has been joined by the Henry Doubleday Research Association in recruiting new members to the organic way of growing plants, to the more humane care of animals and birds raised for food, and to working *with* nature rather than fighting it with an armoury of poisonous sprays, implants and growth promoters. They, in turn, become partners with Friends of the Earth, Greenpeace, the Green Party

and other organisations in a tidal wave of opposition to the destruction of landscape, the pollution of the environment, and generally to agricultural policies that put profit before every other consideration, including the most basic one of ensuring that food is produced to the highest health-giving standards.

A recent British Government survey found pesticide residues in virtually all types of food: in vegetables, fruit, meat, bread, health foods, even mothers' milk. At the same time public opinion polls have found that most people would like either no pesticides used on food crops, or a significant reduction in their use. And the majority wanted to know exactly which pesticides had been used on fresh foods on sale in shops, and on foods which had been processed. More positively, they

An organic garden, however small, makes an important contribution to a cleaner, safer environment.

wanted more opportunity to buy food that hadn't been sprayed or doctored at all with hormones, additives and flavour enhancers.

Grow your Own

Unfortunately the supply of organic food still falls very far short of demand, so for those of us who can do so, the answer is to grow as much as possible of our own food organically, without the use of chemical fertilisers and sprays. And not just food, of course – you can't have a garden operating as an oasis of organic fruit and

vegetable production in a desert of chemically-dependent borders, beds and lawns.

Feeding the Soil

The organic gardener aims to feed the *soil* and so feed the plants, striking a balance between what is given to the soil and what is taken from it by cropping.

Imagine the soil as a bank holding large reserves of nutrients, the accumulated wealth of millions of years, which can be drawn on by intensive cropping until the account is in the red. The inorganic grower has then to replenish the soil constantly with soluble manmade fertilisers that contain the three main plant foods – nitrogen (N), phosphate (P) and potash (K); however, this doesn't always replace the minor ones, or the trace elements that are so vital in determining plant health, or the humus-forming material that is important in maintaining and improving the structure of the soil.

An alternative is to ignore the soil as a growing medium and exploit the ability of plants to take up food in soluble form by feeding them the chemicals in dilute solution, using hydroponics or the nutrient film technique. However, plants grown this way may lack the stamina to resist pests and diseases, cannot compare in flavour with organically grown crops, and would find it impossible to survive outside the controlled environment of the commercial glasshouse.

The Organic Approach

The organic approach to soil management embodies the principle that the grower, whether farmer or gardener, should try to bank more nutrients in the soil than are actually spent on growing crops, so that when the time comes to pass on the patch of land in his or her stewardship it is in rather better heart that when it was taken on.

At first glance, this might seem an impossible objective in the small greenhouse or conservatory, where crops are grown in pots, growing bags or other containers. The principle remains the same, however, and the only difference is basically one of scale. Outside in the garden a fertile, healthy soil is achieved by using animal manures, garden compost, leafmould, green manures and maybe bought-in commercially produced organic composts and manures. Thus owners of greenhouses who wish to use the border soil as the growing medium can give it the same care and management as the soil outside. This is perfectly feasible in a large structure, but in small greenhouses

there may well have to be more dependence on an organic growing medium other than the border soil. In other words, the practice of feeding the soil to feed the plant can be adapted to suit the relatively short-term objective of raising, say, a crop of tomatoes in growing-bags, or some late-flowering chrysanthemums in pots. This involves buying seed, potting or universal organic composts – or making your own – for propagation, and using a growing medium whose relatively short-lived fertility must be maintained for the life of the plants by the addition of organic fertilisers, either solid or liquid.

Safer Environment

It is worth remembering that greenhouse gardening has been practised for many hundreds of years and that it is only relatively recently that artificial fertilisers came on the scene, followed by the fungicides, herbicides and pesticides that derived largely from the efforts of one group of people trying to destroy another group in the 1939-45 war.

However small your garden, when it has been converted to the organic way its contribution to a healthier, safer environment far outweighs its size. Going organic is not just a matter of giving up artificial fertilisers and poisonous sprays: It is a positive, practical technique that gives the gardener a far more intimate understanding of the relationship between himself and the plants he cares for, as compared to the 'force-feeding' methods used by the chemically-dependent gardener.

Even the very small garden that cannot possibly produce enough waste vegetable material to make composting worthwhile need not be denied the benefits of organic gardening: worm-composting is an excellent alternative in such circumstances to aerobic composting, and the output from the 'worm farm' can be supplemented by purchasing organic composts and the necessary organic fertilisers.

Organic Gardening, the companion volume to this one, will, I trust, continue to allay the niggling doubts of the many thousands of people who wish to undertake the conversion to truly 'green' gardening, doubts such as: Will my garden become a haven for all manner of pests and diseases, so that the crops I raise become uneatable? Will yields suffer without the boost from chemical fertilisers? Can I really produce fruit, flowers and vegetables to the highest standards without the help of sprays?

Now, this book takes the organic route indoors, to the greenhouse and conservatory: I hope you enjoy the trip.

PRACTICAL CONSIDERATIONS

Gardening, mankind's longest lasting and best-loved pastime, is experiencing an unparalleled boom as more and more people become homeowners. Gardens are shrinking, but that doesn't prevent a widening of the enjoyment and scope of gardening by the acquisition of a greenhouse or conservatory. There are styles and sizes to suit everyone. Indeed, perhaps the most difficult task is to decide what you want and where you want it. The following pages are designed to help you make a choice by outlining the practical points you should consider. After that, you'll find the pleasure your indoor gardening brings is virtually unlimited.

THE CONSERVATORY: A GARDEN ROOM

In Britain, the large stove-heated winter garden conservatory was a phenomenon of the mid- to late nineteenth century, and a plant room attached to the house was a prerogative of the hereditary landowner, the newly rich industrial tycoon and the upper echelons of the professional classes. Measured by its size, splendour and sheer snob value, the Victorian conservatory probably *is* unmatched by its modern counterpart; but in today's property-owning democracy the dream of having a garden room in the house can quite readily be made to come true. Furthermore a conservatory is a very desirable and marketable product, and there are many merchants whose enthusiasm to part you from your money is unbounded.

Construction methods and materials have moved on from the traditional wood and brick to extruded aluminium and plastic, and the effect with some designs is not so much of an elegant garden room as a lean-to greenhouse; this is further emphasised by greenhouse-type glazing, where the panes of glass are held in place by metal clips.

Choosing a Conservatory

In between the bolt-on DIY job and the traditional turn-of-the-century conservatories are the two main groups of modern structure: those with metal-framed curved eaves, and the rectangular types in either wood or metal. These are undoubtedly more like greenhouses than conservatories, the major distinction being that there is access from within the house or bungalow to which they are attached; they are therefore part of the living space, or should be. There are minor drawbacks: security is one, heating is another – and there may be an additional premium on the property insurance to take into account when budgeting.

But the benefits far outweigh the snags: ask any conservatory owner. And that's probably the best starting point, because a conservatory shouldn't be chosen just by perusing the brochures, any more than a new car is bought without a test drive. Go and see it in the flesh, or if it is being made by a contractor, have a look at similar examples of his work. Check the dimensions of door openings, particularly if they will

 CONSERVATORY CHECKLIST

- Be sure that the conservatory of your choice will fit the site. Take particular care that it will fit round a window or, if a bungalow, under the eaves. The roof slope of the conservatory should be 22 degrees to shed snow.
- The cost of the structure is just the start: even if it is an off-the-shelf model the cost of erecting it is a considerable extra. The foundation and floor have to be prepared, along with provision for heating, shading, plumbing and lighting. Remember to allow for rainwater collection. Special furniture of wicker, iron or plastic will also be needed to withstand the high humidity.
- Is it intended to make maximum use of the conservatory by allowing for an optimum level of heating through the coldest months? The heating can be augmented for personal comfort, but remember too that coolhouse plants need a minimum of 7°C (45°F), warmhouse plants need 13°C (55°F), and hothouse plants need a minimum of 16°C (60°F).
- Building regulations must be observed and followed: as well as the foundations and drainage, they also apply to the roof glass. If the conservatory projects more than 2m (6ft), the correct thickness of toughened glass or polycarbonate must be used.
- Check that the door or doors can be positioned where required, and that they are wide enough for admitting furniture, a wheelchair or wheelbarrow. Check the security fittings to ensure that doors can be locked from both inside and outside.
- Ventilation must be adequate for personal comfort as well as for the well-being of the plants. Automatic vent openers must be totally reliable, but remember that they may function when it is both warm and wet.
- The facility to fit external blinds for shading should be checked.
- Routine maintenance on most modern conservatories should be negligible. Red cedar frames need colour treatment every three years or so, while paint-finished aluminium structures will just need a spring clean with warm soapy water.

be used by a wheelchair or pram. Make sure there will be adequate, leak-free, draught-free ventilation. Consider the method and costs of plumbing, heating, lighting, rainwater collection and drainage. The relevant authority may have to be consulted about planning consent, and a building inspector will certainly want to check that the structure conforms to Building Regulations, to inspect such things as the foundations and drainage, and the quality and strength of the roof glass. A good contractor will take any customer through a checklist of these and other points.

To a certain extent, price will reflect quality, but good quality is not confined to models in the upper end of the market. Most of the complaints that I hear about as a gardening writer come from people who have had shabby services from the manufacturers of nationally-advertised conservatories, greenhouses and home extensions – though this may well be because their jobs far outnumber those of the smaller firms. And while mass production means lower prices, many people prefer to deal with a local craftsman rather than a computer-controlled production line and impersonal sales department.

Heating the Conservatory

Extending the central heating system into the conservatory will be the most effective way of providing heat for frost-tender plants during the winter. This will also add to the enjoyment to be gained from the conservatory because it can then be used for al fresco meals, and as a quiet room for relaxing or studying when the warmth of the day disappears. It could become your favourite room in the house, and your favourite spot in the garden.

 ## MAKE THE BED BEFORE YOU BUILD

If you plan to use your new conservatory to grow shrubs, climbers or small tree in borders or beds for unrestricted root growth, then the time to prepare for this is when the base is being laid. If you are doing the job yourself, simply leave appropriately sized holes in the concrete slab – but remember that a border up against the wall of the house could result in problems with damp. If contractors are doing the work, give them a scale plan of where the beds and/or borders are required. What type of growing medium you fill the beds with depends on the plants you intend to put in it, but on the whole a good loamy soil is far preferable to a peat-based compost. If you want to make a border or beds in an existing conservatory, the best plan is not to interfere with the concrete base but to build up from it using a retaining wall of bricks, logs or rock. A minimum depth of 45cm (18in) is necessary and, of course, you may have to make provision for drainage.

With such a wide choice of designs available, choosing a conservatory can be a bewildering business. A vital requirement is that the structure should blend with the architectural style of the house.

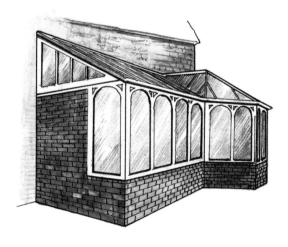

THE IDEAL GREENHOUSE

My love affair with greenhouse gardening began when my wife Margaret, our four children and I, moved from a town house with a minuscule garden into a seventeenth-century cottage on the outskirts of a small village. Our friends and relatives thought we had flipped, because with the dream cottage went just on three acres of highly productive market garden. The intention was that I should continue my career as a journalist and run the market garden in my spare time, with the help of Margaret when she had time to spare from the mounting chores demanded by our new life-style.

At the core of the enterprise were two 40 × 12ft timber-framed greenhouses (which had been out of production for two years), a propagating house, and a rickety shed housing an ancient coal, coke or wood fired boiler that heated the water-filled pipes running round the walls of one of the greenhouses; the other was unheated.

We were not entirely without know-how when we tackled the soft fruit and top fruit areas of the garden, or when planning the least labour intensive methods of production from its vegetable department, because both of us had been brought up in rural households where home grown food was only very occasionally supplemented by shop bought stuff. But the greenhouses were another matter: at the time there was very little literature to give advice on organic growing, and virtually none on organic greenhouse techniques. We were organic not consciously but intuitively. We learned organics the hard way, and it was like rediscovering the wheel.

The growing-bag had yet to be invented, so we grew our tomatoes in a variety of ways and made some appalling mistakes, but enjoyed some soul-stirring successes. The first major mistake was to think we could manage commercial cropping of those two large greenhouses. In early spring the boiler alone

 ## THE SPECIAL NEEDS OF THE DISABLED GARDENER

If you are disabled, or are helping a handicapped friend or relative to choose a greenhouse or conservatory, there are several features to bear in mind.

- For wheelchair users or those with walking aids, a hard surface should be provided up to and inside the greenhouse.
- The doors must be wide enough – say 1.05m (3ft 6in) – to admit a wheelchair, and there should be a ramp to the threshold.
- Consider the height of the staging and width of all working surfaces in relation to the height and reach of the gardener. Most wheelchair gardeners find the best height for staging is about 60cm (24in).
- Siting the greenhouse will have to be a compromise between a situation that provides maximum light and one that gives easiest access for the disabled gardener. The nearer the house the better.
- Watering can be a problem for someone lacking strength or mobility in the arms. A capillary irrigaton system (p23) is the answer, but if watering has to be done by watering can, choose a lightweight one with good balance when full, and with a long spout.

- Shading and ventilation can also be automated (p20). Heating extends the enjoyment of greenhouse gardening throughout the year, but can bump costs up alarmingly. For the disabled, automatically controlled electric heating is preferable to bottled gas or paraffin. But remember that one or more electric propagators will enable many of the functions of the heated greenhouse to be carried out at comparatively little cost. Place the propagator at a suitable working height.
- People with arthritic hands, limited grip or impaired finger mobility find seed sowing a problem, especially with small seeds. Moistening a finger to pick up the seed is a help, while some people use tweezers or special seed dispensers. Spacing the seed evenly is easily done by using a seed-spacing frame or a studded presser board.

  Cover the seed after sowing by shaking a sieve over the tray or pots until the compost is level with the surface. With seed that requires light for germination, use a wooden block to press the seed into close contact with the compost.

demanded hours of ministration, and later in the year, without any automatic ventilation or watering, there was a constant tussle to keep the tomato and cucumber crops contented.

Perhaps the severest lesson of all was to learn the hard way that growing crop after crop of tomatoes in the border soil will inevitably lead to the dreaded soil disease verticillium wilt. So we experimented with alternatives and discovered we could grow magnificent crops in straw bales, planting two tomato plants to each hollowed-out bale, the hollow filled with composted pig muck. It was a method that had a bonus: at the end of the tomato harvest in mid-autumn the partly rotted straw was spread over the

As most small garden greenhouses have to accommodate both edible and ornamental plants, the growing environment is inevitably a compromise between their sometimes conflicting needs.

carrots and parsnips still in the ground to protect them from hard frost, thus enabling us to lift roots as required. Finally in spring what remained of the straw went on the compost heap.

A friend of ours has two identical greenhouses, one of which she fills with flowering ornamental plants, and the other with edible crops – an eminently sensible arrangement, if space and cash allow, because the growing environment that suits one group is seldom right for the other.

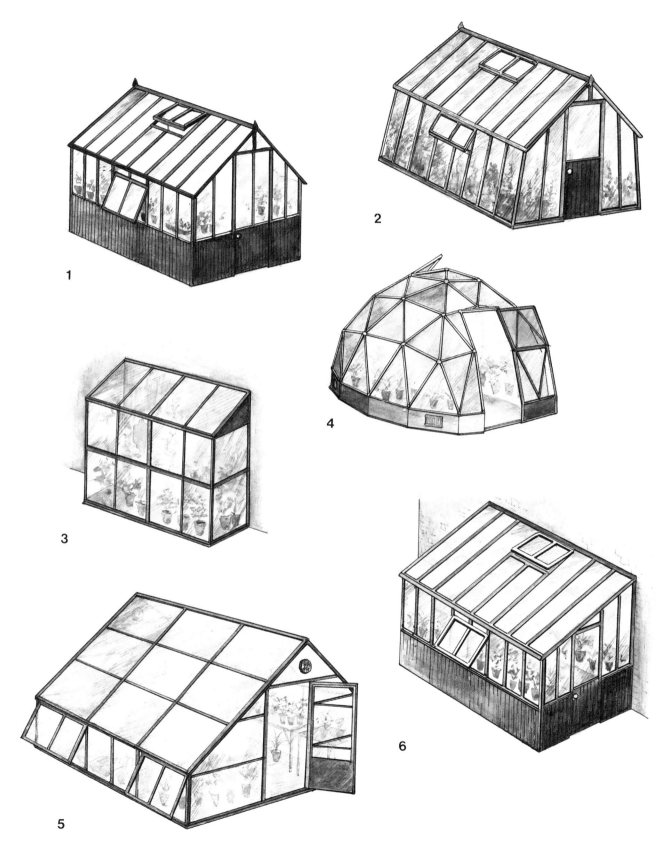

1

2

3

4

5

6

Choosing the Greenhouse

Choice begins with the materials: broadly speaking, you can have metal or wood. The metal is either aluminium, sometimes coated with a special plastic finish, or galvanised steel, while the wood is usually softwood or cedar. Cedar greenhouses cost up to 75 per cent more than aluminium ones, but they have several advantages. They look better, they are far easier to assemble than the metal ones, and they are easier to equip because you can screw fittings into the wood; the metal ones require special fittings that lock into the glazing bars. Timber is a better insulator than metal, so heating is more economical, particularly if the structure is partly clad. Softwood structures are cheaper than cedar but require regular, possibly annual treatment to maintain their durability and their looks, while cedar, being rot-proof, requires only a coat of cedar dressing every three years or so.

As to the relative strength of the structures, it is impossible to be categorical. The violent storms of recent winters were a severe test of robustness. Many greenhouses lost glass, some suffered damage to wind braces, vents and doors, while a few were completely destroyed; yet according to tests by the Consumer Association many of the aluminium greenhouses which were damaged or wrecked by the high winds might have survived had they been better designed. The checklist highlights some of the features to be considered.

GREENHOUSE CHECKLIST

- Buy the biggest and best greenhouse you can, but check that it is possible to add an extension later if required. Width is more important than length.
- If the structure is to be used mainly for plants such as tomatoes, cucumbers, chrysanthemums or carnations, grown from the ground up, vertical fully glazed walls would be preferable to sloping partly clad ones.
- The site for the greenhouse should be large enough and should be free from overhanging tree branches. Remember to make provision for a water butt. Remember also that access to the structure from all sides will be needed for maintenance, such as cleaning and shading the glass.
- The frame should fit snugly without gaps, the doorway should be tall enough to use without hitting your head and wide enough to admit a wheelbarrow or, possibly, a wheelchair (see p14).
- The door should be robust. If opening outwards on a wooden structure, make sure it can be secured firmly. If it is a sliding door, it should move smoothly and be fitted with draught excluders.

- Very few greenhouses are provided with enough ventilators. This can lead to overheating in the summer, while stagnant water and stale air can lead to a build-up of fungal disease. Ensure when ordering that the manufacturer or distributor will supply extra vents, guttering and a downpipe, if necessary.
- Check also that 'safety glass' is available as an optional extra. Normally greenhouses are glazed with standard horticultural glass and this can be a hazard where there are young children. Wooden greenhouses are often supplied ready glazed, so glass of an approved standard of safety should be specified when ordering.
- A base may not be included in the specification, in which case it will have to be ordered as an extra, or made at home. An accurately sized, dead level base is a vital factor in the trouble-free assembly of metal greenhouses.
- On the coast and in areas of industrial pollution, aluminium becomes pockmarked and acquires a white powdery deposit. This should not be disturbed as it serves as a protection.

Illustrated opposite are a few of the many types of greenhouse available from manufacturers: (1) This traditional wooden span-roof type has partly-glazed vertical walls. An alternative would be an all-glass structure; (2) A Dutch light design with sloping walls gives extra growing space; (3) A mini-greenhouse, small enough for a backyard; (4) This dome design makes maximum use of available light and is exceptionally strong; (5) The Serac solar greenhouse is an advanced design embodying principles of solar energy conservation; (6) For a south- or west-facing wall the lean-to is an excellent choice.

MANAGEMENT

In the privacy of the greenhouse or conservatory you can isolate yourself from the world outside and enjoy its protected environment whatever the weather. What you grow depends on you: on the time you can give and your budget. Managing your indoor organic garden should become an absorbing and thoroughly worth-while hobby, but unless you adopt an appropriate management method it could become a time-consuming chore. The following section outlines the options of automating the principal functions of environmental control, plant propagation and maintenance.

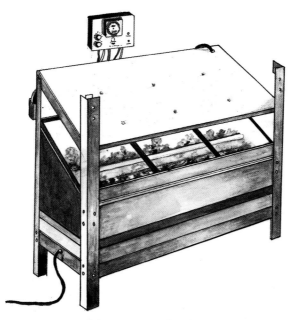

Management Systems 20

MANAGEMENT SYSTEMS

The essential operations of watering, ventilating, shading and heating the greenhouse and conservatory can be automated with a range of equipment that varies from relatively inexpensive low-tech gear to highly sophisticated computer-controlled systems that were originally designed for commercial units and have been scaled down for use by the well-heeled amateur.

VENTILATION

Temperature control is critical. For example greenhouse tomatoes, cucumbers and peppers grow best at 21–24°C (70–75°F), while many pot plants favour slightly lower temperatures. Much above 27°C (80°F), however, and plant growth slows down or stops — and in the height of summer the temperature in the greenhouse can quickly hit 50°C (120°F) if the door and vent are closed. Even in late spring the internal temperature can reach a damaging high for young plants.

Automatic Vent Openers

I can't imagine having to cope from spring to autumn without my solar-powered vent openers; these automatically open both the roof vents and louvres whenever the internal temperature of the greenhouse rises above 13°C (58°F) — the openings get progressively wider as the temperature climbs. Units start at quite modest prices, and with the aid of a screwdriver are easy to fit to both timber and metal framed greenhouses.

The vent openers operate on the following principle: a piston is filled with mineral wax, and as

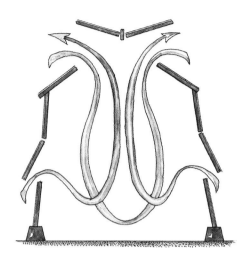

With louvres in the sides and vents in the roof there is maximum air movement in the greenhouse, an important aspect of plant welfare.

the sun heats the wax, so the piston forces up an arm which is attached to the vent. The warmer it gets, the greater the expansion and the wider the vent is opened, to a maximum width of about 45 degrees. The reaction time to changes in temperature is quite fast, and the units are robust enough to give years of trouble-free use.

It is advisable to fit an automatic vent opener to each vent and louvre. They can be set to operate at different temperatures, so that there is greater movement of the air in the greenhouse as the internal temperature rises. This is an important preventive against the fungal diseases that flourish in stale, damp conditions, and against the build-up of red spider mite in a hot, dry environment.

The automatic vent openers will also operate, of course, with conservatory ventilators, but it is important to ensure *before* buying the units that they are man enough for the job. Generally speaking, the more they cost the heavier the task they will do, so a top-priced unit may be capable of lifting a double-glazed conservatory roof ventilator weighing up to 31.7kg (70lb); at the other end of the scale, the lowest-priced model should cope comfortably with a lift of 4.5–6.8kg (10–15lb), which is more than enough for the average roof vent. One small but important point to bear in mind is that when shut, the arm of the automatic opener on the roof vent projects into the greenhouse or conservatory by 20cm (8in) or so — just about head-height!

BUY MORE AIR

Most small aluminium greenhouses overheat at the height of the summer because manufacturers supply them with only one 60×60cm (2×2ft) roof vent – although an extra vent or louvre can be ordered before or after taking delivery. For good ventilation, the total area of roof and side ventilators should be one-sixth of the floor area. If just roof vents are fitted, the ratio should be one-fifth of the floor area.

OPEN THE DOOR WITH CARE

With a small greenhouse on a very hot day, opening the door for several hours is the only way of reducing the temperature to a bearable level. However, it could also be an open invitation to the neighbour's cat or stray birds to move in, so it is advisable to fit netting or a mesh door when the glazed door is open. This is also important if you are using predatory or parasitic insects for pest control. Trials have shown that *Encarsia formosa*, the whitefly parasite, is much more effective when a fine mesh net is placed over the open vents of the greenhouse. The number of adult whitefly entering the greenhouse is reduced, but there is no appreciable effect on temperature or humidity.

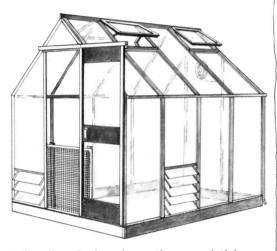

In this well-ventilated greenhouse, ridge vents and side louvres are augmented by an extractor fan. In very hot weather it will be necessary to open the door, day and night. Keep out cats with a firmly secured net screen.

Extractor Fans

It's fair to say that most conservatories are overheated in summer, particularly if they are left to themselves during the day while their owners are at work or for longer periods during the holiday season. This can be extremely uncomfortable, even fatal, for plants left thus to fend for themselves. The answer is to fit a thermostatically controlled extractor fan which will give fairly rapid changes of air. There are units which operate entirely on solar power, but this can be a major disadvantage on sunny days in winter unless there is a facility for a cut-off.

Finally, if you decide to rely on a fan to ventilate a small greenhouse, it is vital to fit one with an adequate extraction rate. For a 1.8×2.4m (6×8ft) greenhouse with a volume of 7.7 cu m (270 cu ft) the fan must have an extraction rate of at least 300 cu m per hour (10,000 cu ft per hour).

SHADING

Direct sunlight can be very harmful to seedlings and to many mature plants, and from late spring to early autumn some form of shading is necessary for the greenhouse and conservatory, both to protect the plants and to help reduce the internal temperature of the structure — large commercial glasshouses have computer-controlled environments in which automatic ventilation is linked to automatic shading. Even the most robust plants can be scorched if exposed to strong, direct sunlight when they have water droplets on their leaves; on the other hand, although overheating can be disastrous, there's a limit to the amount of shading that some plants can tolerate.

How much shading you will need depends on the siting of your greenhouse or conservatory, the geographical location, and what you are growing. The south- and west-facing walls of the structure should be given priority, while the east- and north-facing ones can usually be left unshaded. For example in warmer areas the level of shading needed in a small mixed-cropping greenhouse or conservatory may be up to 50 per cent, and may need to be available from early spring to mid-autumn. In cooler parts the level of shading required may be no more than 30 to 40 per cent from early spring to the end of summer, although much depends on the weather. If you grow shade-loving plants, then their need must be compared with, say, that of cacti, which seldom require more than the bare minimum of shade.

Paint-on Shading

There are two types of shading material: products that you paint onto the glass; or blinds which are fixed to the exterior or inside of the roof and over the side. In tests by the gardening arm of the Consumer Association, one of the least expensive of the opaque washes currently available was also the most effective in cutting down infra-red radiation, while still allowing enough light through for photosynthesis of the plants. This wash is sold as a powder and is mixed with water; it is brushed onto the outside of the glass in the spring and is easily wiped off in the autumn. There is another variant, too, which on rainy days becomes transparent to admit maximum light.

From mid-spring to mid-autumn shading is necessary to protect plants from scorching and to reduce the temperature. This could be in the form of either a liquid solution that is painted on to the glass, or blinds. Roller blinds are best fitted to the outside of the structure, while netting can be secured to the interior framework of aluminium structures using special clips.

However, there are drawbacks to these painted-on products: they are visually unappealing, especially on a conservatory; they are difficult to apply to some structures; and they need to be renewed annually.

On the other hand, liquid shading has the advantage that by early autumn the coating has worn a bit thin so that plants gradually get *more* light as the strength of sunlight decreases.

Blinds

There are several types of blind, ranging from polypropylene netting (in various mesh sizes according to the degree of shading needed) to slatted roller blinds and opaque plastic sheeting. For best effect these should be fitted to the outside of the structure, and in many instances this means that the blinds are in place all year round, so the material used *must* be rot- and frost-proof. Ease of operation is also important because few things are more infuriating than roller blinds that jam partially open and require a ladder to reach them. The hazards of working on a ladder against a greenhouse or conservatory are multiplied considerably if tempers are raised!

WATERING

Saving water makes good sense, and with a greenhouse or conservatory it is easy to catch some of the winter's rainfall with a water butt, gutters and a downpipe. Rainwater is free, it is easily stored so as to

be available when wanted, and it is generally a better product for garden use than tapwater because it has a neutral pH, and does not have chemicals deliberately added to it. In hard-water areas *only* rainwater should be used for watering lime-hating plants in pots or other containers.

Choose your water butt with care, for its eye-appeal as well as its functional convenience. Models which are ribbed for extra strength and have a heavy, black rubberised, fitted lid that accepts all normal size downpipes are ideal. A lid is important to keep the water clean, to reduce evaporation and prevent thirsty birds from drowning — better to install a proper bird bath in the garden than have a lidless rainwater butt.

Watering Cans

From late spring through to the end of summer, watering the plants in the greenhouse or conservatory may be necessary every day, and sometimes twice a day, so a watering can is a basic necessity. Depending on the size of the task, you'll need at least two 9l (2 gal) cans, preferably with long reach spouts and fine spray roses. Galvanised metal cans are much more expensive than plastic ones but will last many times longer because, in time, plastic cans crack. It is well worth looking for secondhand metal cans in local auction sales. In general, the horizontal cans rather than the tall ones are better balanced and easier to

Water trays of seedlings with the rose of the can turned upwards.

when watering so that the water falls on the plants as a gentle shower rather than a thunderstorm.

Drip Systems

From early spring until late autumn plants need access to a reliable water supply. To save having to water in person every day, and also to take care of the task in holiday time, it is quite possible to fit an automatic watering system. Orchids and cacti need special watering techniques, but for the general run of pot plants you can buy either a capillary or a drip system, while for crops in growing bags a self-watering system is also available. For plants in the borders and beds, there are perforated hoses or trickle systems which take tubes and drip nozzles to individual plants; these are operated off the mains water supply. All such equipment, operating off the mains should be fitted with a non-return valve – and of course in times of severe drought, restrictions on the use of hoses would apply to these systems.

Capillary Matting

The simplest automatic watering method uses capillary matting, a felt-like material that acts as a wick in transferring water to potted plants standing on it. The matting holds a large amount of water and can be replenished from a reservoir. There are a few points to bear in mind, however, concerning capillary matting:

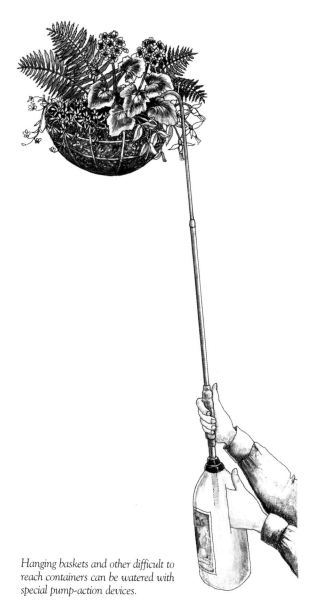

Hanging baskets and other difficult to reach containers can be watered with special pump-action devices.

manage in the sometimes confined space of the greenhouse.

For watering hanging baskets, pots and other containers above about bench height, it is a good idea to invest in a pump-action watering device with a long curved spout that can reach into the plant and place the water precisely.

Whether metal or plastic, watering cans in the greenhouse should be kept filled so that the water is at approximately the same temperature as the atmosphere in the house. Remember, too, that the rose of the watering can should always point upwards

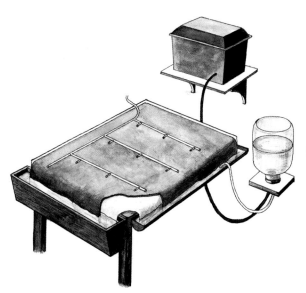

Capillary matting laid over polythene sheeting can be kept moist either by a water-filled gutter fed from a reservoir or cistern, or by a trickle-tube system fed from a header tank.

Capillary matting fed by a wick makes this a simple, semi-automatic watering system for a small greenhouse bench or cold frame.

- The reservoir should be at the lower end of the matting so that the water flows uphill, or should be fed from a mains trickle system or a bag reservoir linked to trickle hoses laid on the matting.
- The matting will lift water vertically about 10cm(4in), but it will only function when the wick is wet.
- While the matting will cope efficiently with trays and small pots placed on it, plants in pots deeper than 13cm(5in) will only have water in the lower part of the pot and the upper surface of the compost will dry out.
- Capillary watering doesn't suit those plants that prefer to dry out between watering; this includes geraniums and many succulents.
- Some water will evaporate from the surface of the mat and this assists humidity, but there is no danger of flooding.

- Some plants if left for too long on the matting without being moved will send roots into the mat.
- Algae will grow on the mat during a season of use. You can turn the mat over and use the other side, but before storing it for use the next season wash it in warm soapy water, rinse and dry.

Bag Reservoirs

An inexpensive alternative to capillary matting, or where a mains water supply is not available in the small greenhouse, is a bag reservoir with trickle tubing to the plants. However, while this will cope effectively with the daily demand of a relatively few plants, it just isn't man enough to handle the needs of the larger units or to manage during a holiday period. For this you will need a mains drip kit, where a pressure regulator controls the water flow to a semi-flexible tube into which drippers are fitted. These can then be located on the capillary matting or, by short lengths of thinner tubing, be directed into pots, growing bags or other containers.

SELF-WATERING DEVICES

Flower-pots that use capillary action to water themselves would seem to answer the problem of how to care for your plants when you go away on holiday. However, self-watering pots are expensive, and in most cases it means repotting your plants; but for a few favourite or moisture-sensitive plants, or when buying new plants, self-watering pots are worth considering. Less expensive, but very effective, is an Austrian watering device which consists of a porous ceramic cone with a long plastic tube attached. The end of the tube goes into a container of water, while the cone is plunged into the compost of the flower-pot. The water is taken from the container through the tube and into the compost by capillary action. When officially tested by the Consumer Association it was found that such a system would keep a plant watered for 'several months' providing the reservoir was kept topped up. It is connected to a mains water supply or is fed from an overhead tank. Kits are available to water twelve hanging baskets or tubs, or four growing bags, or six window boxes.

HEATING

It is a fair bet that most greenhouses and conservatories are underused, either because they have no heating at all, or because the heating over the four or five coldest months of the year is inadequate. Heating a conservatory involves rather different techniques than for the greenhouse, but in fact the same formula can be used for determining the amount of heat needed to maintain a given temperature. Remember that if the conservatory is double-glazed and if the greenhouse is a lean-to, the heat loss is considerably less than that of a free standing structure.

Calculating Heat Loss

To calculate heat loss, the first task is to measure all the external surface areas and find out the square footage of glass. Any parts (other than the house wall of the conservatory) made of timber, brick, breeze block or concrete should be included, but their square footage should be halved. Similarly, if the roof is of polycarbonate or double-walled acrylic and the walls are double-glazed, the total area of these surfaces should also be halved. Bubble polythene insulation can save up to 50 per cent of the heat and so, for this formula, should be regarded as double glazing and the figure for the insulated area halved.

Next step is to multiply the resulting square footage figure by 9.3 to discover the wattage needed to raise the conservatory or greenhouse temperature by 14°C (25°F) above the outside temperature. So, for example, if the greenhouse is a fully-glazed 1.8 × 2.4m (6 × 8ft) one with a height to the eaves of 1.8m (6ft), the total glass area is 21.6m (233sq ft). Multiply this by 9.3 and the wattage needed is 2kw, so a heater giving an output of 2.5 to 3kw will be needed to raise the temperature to 7°C (45°F) at those times when the outside temperature is −7°C (20°F). From this information, plus a knowledge of local temperature patterns, it is possible to calculate the approximate electricity consumption of the heating system, and assess the cost.

Paraffin and Gas Heaters

For the conservatory, paraffin and portable gas heaters should be ruled out because they give off water vapour when burning and so there would have to be adequate ventilation to avoid excessive condensation. This also makes them less than ideal units even for the smallest greenhouse, unless electric power is unavailable.

SAVE ENERGY

- It doesn't make economic sense to heat a greenhouse, however small, merely to overwinter a few plants that could be kept quite safely in a spare room.
- If you want to keep plants frost-free in the greenhouse, try grouping them together and then screening them with, for example, heavy gauge polythene sheeting. Then all that need be heated is the screened area.
- Insulating the greenhouse or conservatory with bubble polythene can save up to 50 per cent of the winter heating requirement.
- Sow bedding plants in early spring rather than late winter.
- Gaps and cracks in the structure and ill-fitting doors, windows and vents all waste heat. Use a sealant to fill cracks and gaps, and replace all broken glass.

SAFETY FIRST

Seek the help of the local electricity company, or contact a member of an electrical contractors association or inspection council. Installing electricity in a greenhouse is no job for the unskilled amateur: leave this to the professional.

POWER-WISE

It takes very little electric current to kill a human being, given the right conditions. If the floor is damp and the hands wet, then just one-tenth of the current taken by a 100 watt light bulb could be a fatal dose, and these are the conditions frequently encountered in the greenhouse or conservatory. For safety, therefore, an electricity supply to the greenhouse should be fitted with a *residual current device* which will speedily cut off the supply if there is a leakage of current. Many amateurs' greenhouses have an electricty supply via a 13 amp socket in the house or garage, and this can easily be fitted with an RCD by using a special 13 amp plug with a built-in RCD, or by fitting an RCD adaptor between the existing plug and the socket. It is important that the RCD is fitted in the house or garage and not in the greenhouse.

Safety precautions are vital if electricity is used in the greenhouse or conservatory. The control unit should be moisture proofed, and the equipment should be protected by a residual current device or power breaker.

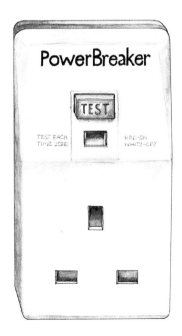

Electric Fan Heaters

In my experience the most useful type of heater for the small to medium size greenhouse is the thermostatically-controlled electric fan heater. A 2kw unit, for example, will keep a 3×2.4m (10×8ft) greenhouse frost free. The internal fan provides gentle air movement and it can be used without the heating element to circulate the air in summer.

Electric Tubular Heaters

For an even spread of radiant heat with the bonus of convective current in the conservatory or greenhouse, perimeter heating by electric tubular heaters is one answer. Depending on the manufacturer, they are rated at 60 or 80 watts per foot (30cm) length and are installed in banks of two or three about 15cm (6in) above ground level. Under staging where there are tubes, there should be a gap of 15cm (6in) between the wall and the staging to allow warm air to circulate. Tubular heaters need thermostatic control, probably of the rod type, located out of direct sunlight.

Greenhouse and conservatory electric heaters should be fully protected for electrical safety, particularly if the system has been added on. A residual current device or power breaker is essential.

For the future, developments to improve solar heating and infra-red heating systems promise even more efficient use of energy for conservatory and greenhouse owners.

PROPAGATION

Auxiliary items of equipment for the greenhouse and conservatory, such as bubble glazing and automatic watering, can be acquired as one's enthusiasm grows. At the top of the list must go staging and shelving, a cold frame for hardening off plants, and an electrically-heated propagator for raising plants from seeds and cuttings; while in the 'highly-desirable but-wait-until-you-can-afford-it' bracket are an electric soil steriliser, mist propagation unit, dewpoint propagation cabinet and, for external use, a shredder to help increase the compost-making material.

Propagators

It is relatively easy to make an electrically-heated, thermostatically-controlled propagator out of a wooden box, a length of soil-warming cable, a thermostat and some polythene sheeting. But this is scarcely worthwhile since commercially produced models are so widely available and competitively priced (unless you are a determined DIY buff).

The advantage of the propagator over propagating trays or heated benches is that it can be moved around for use in the home, greenhouse or conservatory, and afterwards can be stored until pressed into service again. Propagators are available in a wide range of sizes, from small windowsill one-tray units rated at 15 watts to those with three separate chambers each with independent temperature control. However, all are concerned with the primary stage of propagation, and provide the right environment for seed raising and for rooting cuttings. Once the seedlings are strong enough and the cuttings have made roots, they will need to be moved to somewhere with more elbow room and some protection.

The propagator provides bottom heat at a fixed temperature, usually 18°C (65°F) in the least expensive units, or in a range of 7–30°C (45–80°F) in the more advanced units. It also provides humidity, with the plastic dome covering the unit collecting and recycling the moisture given off by the warmed compost. The level of humidity can be varied by vents in the lid.

Remember that even the best propagator can only give a lift of about 10°C (20°F) above the ambient

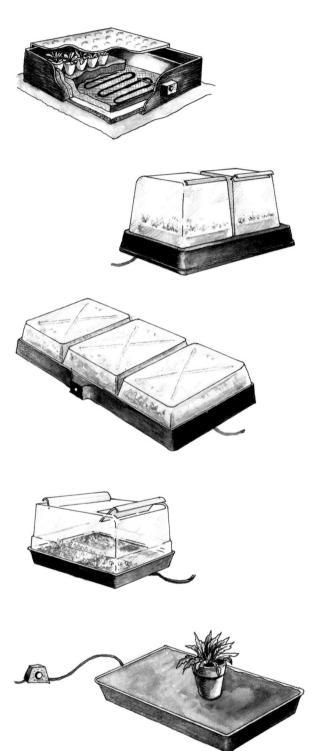

TOP TO BOTTOM: A propagator made from a wooden box and thermostatically controlled soil-warming cable; an electrically-heated propagator which can be used for seed raising and cuttings; a three-tray propagator with adjustable thermostatic control; a single-tray model with fixed output; electrically-heated sheeting with thermostatic control which provides steady bottom heat for propagation.

temperature, so if the temperature in the greenhouse falls below freezing point then the compost temperature when seed raising may be critically low. For this reason alone it is often wise in a severe winter to start raising bedding plants in early spring rather than late winter.

Soil Warming Systems

Mains-operated electric soil-warming cables are an efficient way of heating border soil in the greenhouse, cold frame, propagating trays or the plunge bench used for alpines. Cable can be bought in fully insulated and sheathed form in various lengths. A 6m (20ft) length, for example, giving an output of 75 watts, would be sufficient for a propagating area of 0.9sq m (10sq ft). Alternatively you could buy a kit complete with cable, thermostat and mains connections. This can then be used to make a propagating tray, which should be at least 7.5cm (3in) deep. The cable is placed in a bed of coarse horticultural grade sand about 3.8cm (1½in) deep, then covered with another layer of sand or sand and fine bark mixture, on which trays and pots can be placed for seed-raising or in which cuttings can be grown. Use a dome cloche or polythene sheet supported by wire hoops as a cover.

Mist Propagation Units

A mist propagation unit requires mains water (at a pressure of at least 25 psi), electricity connections into the greenhouse, and a fairly high capital outlay to buy and install the equipment. Nevertheless, for the greenhouse owner who raises large numbers of cuttings it is an invaluable item, giving automatic, frequent fine misting with undersoil thermostatically controlled heating to the rooting area of the cuttings. The warm, damp atmosphere ensures rapid root growth without wilting or scorching. The need for shading is reduced, allowing increased photosynthesis and thus more rapid and even plant growth. Mist propagation units can be bought as a complete installation, including a mains water booster pump if needed, or as items that can be used with existing benches and trays.

Dewpoint Cabinets

Much the same principle as in mist propagation is used in the dewpoint cabinet, for rapid propagation of cuttings and for raising seeds. It is a self-contained unit combining a heated mat, water reservoir and artificial lighting. Fresh air saturated with water vapour cools around the leaves of cuttings and seedlings; transpiration is minimised and so healthy root development is encouraged. Because it has artificial daylight tubes, propagation can be carried out at any time of the year: you decide the day length and set it on a time clock. Two thermostats are provided, one for the daytime temperature, the other for the night.

The unit should be positioned in a garage, spare room or cellar where there is a fairly constant temperature and a mains electricity supply. It should not be located in the greenhouse or conservatory because temperatures can become too high for its efficient operation.

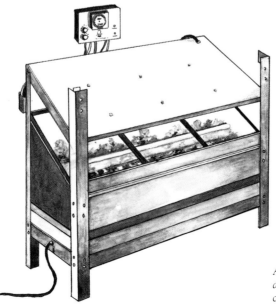

A dewpoint cabinet makes a luxurious accessory for the greenhouse or conservatory.

ORGANIC CULTIVATION

The main elements of successful organic gardening under glass have been practised by many generations of gardeners. They embody the principle that greenhouse and conservatory plants rely totally on the gardener for their needs. Their welfare, therefore, is dependent on adequate time being given to them, with proper attention to feeding and watering, the sensible choice and use of materials and equipment, and a proper understanding of how to cope with pests and diseases without recourse to chemical intervention.

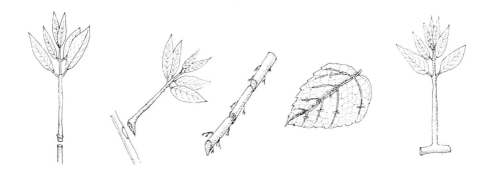

COMPOSTS

PEAT

Several generations of gardeners have come to look on peat as an indispensable part of their gardening, to be used in seed, potting and universal composts, in growing bags and as soil conditioner, mulching material and lawn dressing. It is easy to understand why. Peat is organic. It is free from pests and diseases, chemical contaminants and air pollutants. It is easy to harvest and requires very little preparation to make it marketable. In use it is versatile and adaptable, with high water and air retaining capacity and excellent plasticity for containerised growing, whether in small modules or ultra-large pots. No wonder, then, that peat production in the latter half of the twentieth century became a major horticultural industry and a highly profitable one, too.

The late 1980s, however, brought a challenge to the peat producers from conservationists, their contention being that the natural peat bogs in Britain, home to rare plants, birds and insects, were being destroyed at an alarming rate entirely for commercial gain. It became a hotly contested campaign, particularly when cuts were imposed on government-funded research into peat alternatives. In retaliation, conservationists linked the environmental implications of conserving peatland with the need to recycle organic waste, such as sewage, into compost, and suggested that government funds might be used to buy the most valuable peatlands and designate them as nature reserves, and to compensate the peat producers.

The Henry Doubleday Research Association in its leaflet emphasised that it was unlikely that a single material could be found to fill the various roles played by peat; rather it would be an amalgam of materials such as autumn leaves, municipal wastes, sewage and animal manures. Increasing the use of such materials 'would take the pressure off peat' and would help to reduce wastage and pollution. Ultimately, three products emerged as promising candidates in the effort to find substitutes for peat: composted tree bark, composted straw and sewage, and coir fibre, a waste product of the coconut industry.

DIY COMPOSTS

Composts for seed sowing and potting are essential materials for the greenhouse gardener; as an alternative to the proprietary versions, it is perfectly feasible – though only marginally cheaper – to make your own.

Soil-based composts do have some advantages over the peat-based ones: they are more tolerant of over- or under-watering, they are richer in the minor plant foods and trace elements, and they provide a more secure environment for, say, pot-grown chrysanthemums.

The problem is that you need loam as the main ingredient of soil compost, and loam takes three years to make from scratch, although some very successful organic gardeners make their own version of a peat-less compost using sterilised garden soil enriched with organic fertiliser – a friend of mine has even used the earth spoil thrown up by moles in one of his meadows. The danger of using unsterilised soil, however, particularly for seed compost, is that it could carry the organisms that cause 'damping off', when young seedlings collapse and die quite rapidly or, when the first few leaves have formed, fail to develop satisfactorily.

For sterilising soil in small amounts, you simply have to heat it in the oven at 100°C (212°F) gas Mark 1 for fifteen minutes. Larger amounts will have to be done in a steriliser when perhaps a bucketful – 9 litres (2 gal) – may be dealt with at a time. Such a method sterilises very efficiently using steam that circulates evenly through ordinary garden soil. It usually requires a 1.5kw electric element, the process taking about thirty minutes.

 THE pH SCALE

This measures the balance between hydrogen ions and hydroxyl ions. It is a logarithmic scale so that pH 5.0 is ten times as acid as pH 6.0, and pH 4.0 is 100 times as acid as 6.0.

Below 4.5 extremely acid
4.5–5.0 very strongly acid
5.1–5.5 strongly acid
5.6–6.0 medium acid
6.1–6.5 slightly acid
6.6–7.3 neutral
7.4–8.0 mildly alkaline
8.1–9.0 strongly alkaline
9.1 and over, extremely alkaline

The indigenous nutrients in the soil are not affected by steam sterilisation unless the soil is acidic at pH 5.0 or less, when the recommendation is that you add lime first.

To make loam, you need a supply of surplus turf, free from weeds and couch grass, which can be cut with about 5cm (2in) of soil and stacked grass-side down for at least a year. It then breaks down into a humus-rich crumbly material. If you have land to spare, then by all means sow grass seed specifically to make the turf to cut for loam but it will then have to grow for two years and be stacked for another year.

Compost Recipes

For do-it-yourself composts the following recipes have worked well for me. One type is based on soil, the other on peat or a peat substitute such as leafmould, composted bark or coir fibre.

The following ingredients will be needed for soil-based sowing compost:

> Two parts of loam
> Two parts of peat or substitute
> One part of coarse grit
> Bonemeal
> Dolomitic lime or hydrated lime

To each 9l (2 gal) bucketful of the peat, loam and grit mixture, add 60g(2oz) of bonemeal and 30g(1oz) of lime.

For soil-based potting compost, the following recipe has proved successful:

> Seven parts of loam
> Three parts of peat or substitute
> Two parts of grit
> Blood, fish and bone
> Dolomitic lime, hydrated lime or
> calcified seaweed

Add 150g (5oz) of blood, fish and bone and 30g (1oz) of lime to each 9l (2 gal) bucketful.

The following ingredients will be needed for peat-based sowing compost:

> Twelve parts of peat or peat substitute
> One part of coarse sand
> One part of perlite or vermiculite
> Dolomitic limestone or hydrated lime
> Blood, fish and bone
> Hoof and horn meal or seaweed meal

For each 9l (2 gal) bucketful of the peat, sand and perlite mixture, add 90g (3oz) of blood, fish and bone, 30g (1oz) of hoof and horn or seaweed meal, and 30g (1oz) of lime.

For peat-based potting compost, use the same ratios of peat or peat substitute, sand and perlite or vermiculite, but add three parts of leafmould or composted bark. In place of peat, compost from your bin could be used.

For potting up chrysanthemums and fuchsias, you can make an extremely good potting compost out of worm-worked waste, the product of the worm farm (see p38), using half its volume with half of peat substitute. For other pot plants you will find it beneficial to add about one-eight volume of sharp sand, gravel, perlite or vermiculite. In place of the peat, well-made leafmould or composted tree bark can be used, but with either of these ingredients the volume of sand or perlite or whatever should be increased to open out the texture of the compost.

It is important to mix all composts very thoroughly and to ensure that the fertiliser ingredients and the lime are evenly distributed.

Points to Remember

1: The fertiliser ingredients in these soil and peat-based composts are non-renewable. Once the plants have taken up the nutrients, after four to six weeks, you will have to add more food to the compost as an organic liquid feed.
2: All compost, whether bought or homemade, should be used as fresh as possible and not stored from one year to the next. So only buy or make up as much as you need at one time, even though this might be difficult to judge. Store any surplus ingredients separately, keeping the fertilisers and lime in weatherproof containers and not in the greenhouse or conservatory.

DIY Growing Bags

The potting compost can be used in several ways: for potting on seedlings into modules or cells prior to planting out; for pot plants indoors and outdoors; for outdoor containers such as troughs and hanging baskets; and also to make up your own growing bags. This is especially useful if you want to use a smaller sized bag than the standard 95 × 35cm (38 × 14in).

Simply fill a strong plastic bag to the size you want, then turn over the open end to form a seam and staple or tape it securely. Finally, cut out a square or squares as you would with a commercial bag.

The potting composts already described can be used as a filling for your homemade growing bag; also the half peat, half worm-worked compost, or the half peat half aerobic compost, *as long as* these have been properly made so that there is no possibility of disease or pest carry-over. For the peat content you could substitute composted bark or coconut fibre.

If you can't make your own compost or keep a worm farm for worm-worked compost, don't despair. You'll find the names and addresses of commercial suppliers on p159.

DIY LIQUID FEEDS

One of the best garden plots I have ever seen used only homemade compost. However, this particular gardener also used the dark brown liquid that came from the compost heap during decomposition. This was run off into a container, diluted until it was the colour of bitter beer and then used as a foliar feed.

Liquid Manure

Making liquid manure was standard practice not so long ago, and providing that supplies of stable manure continue to be widely available, there's little reason for the organic gardener not to make up his own. To start with all that's needed is about 40 litres (half a sackful) of rotted horse manure, although pig, sheep, poultry or goat manure can also be used, providing it has been gathered and stacked with straw litter, not wood shavings. The sack should be of hessian, not plastic, and before starting to fill it with the manure put a large stone in the bottom of it to help it to sink.

You will also need a metal or plastic drum such as those used as water butts, and preferably with a draw-off tap. Fill it threequarters full with water. Tie the sack with a double loop of plastic string or rope and dunk it in the drum. Then put the other loop over a length of wood so that the sack is suspended in the drum. The liquid is ready to use after seven days.

HOW MUCH COMPOST?

Manufactured seed, potting or multipurpose composts are sold bagged by volume. The smallest (5l) size works out at approximately twice the price of the largest (40l) size, so it obviously pays to estimate your need for the season and buy the biggest bag or bags to meet that need.

The diagram will help you to estimate how many seed trays and pots of various sizes you can expect to fill from a 40l bag, but remember the precise numbers will depend on the density of the compost and how hard you pack the trays or fill the pots.

The Consumer Association recommends that compost is bought from a shop or garden centre that stores its bags under cover and has a high turnover. Bags that have split and been taped or stapled should be avoided.

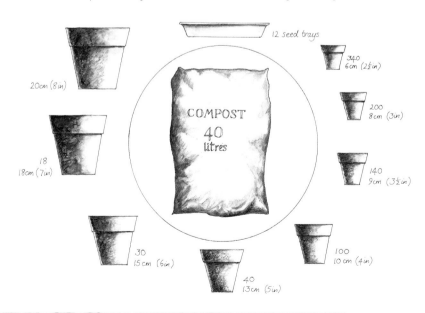

12 seed trays

340 6cm (2½in)

200 8cm (3in)

140 9cm (3½in)

100 10cm (4in)

20cm (8in)

18 18cm (7in)

30 15cm (6in)

40 13cm (5in)

COMPOST 40 litres

An excellent liquid feed can be made by dunking a bag of animal manure in a barrel of water for around seven days, after which it will be ready for use.

The liquid must be diluted; it can then be used on the previously moistened border soil of the greenhouse; on the growing medium of growing-bags or pots; or as a foliar feed for greenhouse and house plants.

If the liquid manure has been made with horse or cow dung, dilute one part of the liquid drawn off with two parts of water; with pig, goat or poultry manure or pigeon droppings, dilute with three parts of water. As you draw off the liquid you can top up the drum with water until the liquid has been replaced twice. After that the old manure in the sack should be added to the compost heap or used for mulching and replaced.

Dried Blood

Dried blood also makes a good liquid feed for leafy pot plants: being high in nitrogen it acts as a spring tonic. Use it at the rate of 30g (1oz) to 9l (2gal) of water.

Comfrey

Comfrey, that wonder plant made famous by the guru of organic gardeners Lawrence Hills is the ingredient of a liquid feed that is particularly rich in phosphorus, potassium, nitrogen and calcium, as compared to one made with farmyard manure. It is especially useful as a feed for tomatoes.

You will first need to grow your comfrey. Offsets or young plants of Russian comfrey can be bought or begged and planted at any time of the year except during hard frost. Set aside a patch of garden that can be spared in perpetuity, and put the plants in about 75cm (30in) apart each way.

Comfrey grows vigorously, and once established, is not easy to keep within bounds. Use the leaves as a mulch or dig them directly into the soil where they will quickly break down without poaching nitrogen as would most other green material.

Concentrated comfrey liquid fertiliser is easily made – but be warned! – the smell is outrageous, and the operation is best carried out well away from any living quarters. Take a container such as a disused plastic dustbin, water butt or large plastic bucket, and fill it threequarters full with comfrey leaves. Then top up with water, cover and allow to ferment for about fourteen days in late spring and summer and up to twice as long in late autumn, early winter.

At the end of the fermenting period, drill a hole in the bottom of the container to allow the foul-smelling black liquid to seep into a container held at the ready. Dilute this concentrate in a ratio of one to twenty parts of water and use it for all the purposes for which you would normally use a proprietary liquid feed.

When the concentrated liquid ceases to seep from the container, use the mushy remains of the comfrey leaves as an activator on your compost heap, and cut some fresh leaves for making more liquid feed.

Points to Remember

1: It is better to use a liquid feed too weak rather than too strong. In fact, plants will benefit more from a dilute feed given twice a week than from a strong feed given once a week.
2: Always moisten the soil or growing medium thoroughly before applying the liquid manure.
3: When giving manure as a foliar feed, use a fine rose in the watering can – or better still – a fine setting on a pressure sprayer and spray thoroughly until the liquid runs off the foliage.

Some people believe that regular liquid feeding of edible crops, such as tomatoes and cucumbers, is all that is needed to guarantee a good yield. Others maintain that liquid feeding is only a short-term answer to the plants' needs and should be supplemented with something more solid, such as blood, fish and bone or seaweed meal or other organic fertiliser, added to the growing medium as a top dressing.

ORGANIC FERTILISERS AND MANURES

There are many organic gardens whose renewable fertility depends entirely on compost made from recycled garden and kitchen waste, perhaps supplemented every two or three years with a dressing of rotted farmyard manure. Certainly in the flower garden and shrubbery this is all the feeding the soil needs, while an annual dressing of finely sifted compost will also look after the needs of the average lawn.

But in the vegetable garden, feeding is more critical because cropping is on a far more intensive scale than in the flower beds and borders; similarly in the organic greenhouse, where we are trying to reduce our dependence on peat: in both of these, therefore, organic manures and fertilisers have a more significant role to play in successful crop management. In fact peat is virtually devoid of plant nutrients, so these have to be added either in chemical form in the case of inorganic composts and growing-bags, or as organic fertilisers in the organic versions. This is also true of some of the peat substitutes, notably coir.

There has been comprehensive research by the agro-chemists to determine the optimum levels of artificial fertilisers in peat-based seed, potting and universal composts, yet very little information seems to have been disseminated on the use of organic fertilisers in growing bags and composts. How much nitrogen (N), phosphates (P) and potash (K) is there in aerobic-made compost, spent mushroom compost or rotted farmyard manure?

The table on p36 gives figures quoted by Elm Farm Research Centre for a range of organic fertilisers and composts.

CARBON/NITROGEN RATIO OF PRINCIPAL COMPOST MATERIALS

Material	Carbon	Nitrogen
Urine		****
Dried blood		****
Bone meal	*	****
Fresh stinging nettles	*	****
Poultry manure		***
Pig manure with straw	*	***
Strawy stable manure	*	***
Pea and bean vines, green	*	***
Spent hops		**
Lawn mowings	**	**
Potato haulms	**	**
Tomato haulms	**	**
Uncooked kitchen waste	**	**
Annual weeds, plant debris	**	**
Cabbage, lettuce leaves	**	**
Fresh seaweed	**	**
Peat	*	*
Coir fibre	*	*
Straw	***	*
Fallen leaves	***	*
Shrub prunings, shredded	***	*
Newspaper, shredded	**	

RELATIVE NPK VALUES OF ORGANIC FERTILISERS AND MANURES

Material	Nitrogen	Phosphorus	Potash
Animal hair	**		
Bone meal	*	***	*
Calcified seaweed	*		*
Dried blood	****	*	
Feathers	**		
Fish meal	**	***	*
Goat manure	**	**	**
Horse manure	*	*	*
Leafmould			*
Manure and peat	Proprietary brands vary		
Municipal compost		*	*
Mushroom compost	*	*	*
Pig manure, rotted	*	*	*
Pigeon manure	**	**	**
Poultry manure	**	***	***
Plant ash		***	
Rabbit droppings	*	**	*
Seaweed meal	**	**	**
Wood ash			***
Worm-worked compost	**	**	**

But perhaps for the amateur gardener, knowing the precise amounts of NPK in home-produced compost or bought-in farmyard manure doesn't matter all that much. With proprietary composts, though, the case for declaring the nutrient content is far stronger, if only to avoid the gardening market's rip-off merchants.

A–Z OF FERTILISERS AND MANURES

Animal hair Save the hair from grooming your dog or cat and add it to the compost bin, mixing it thoroughly with other materials. It is a good source of slow-release nitrogen, and if sufficient quantities are available, it can be spread on the soil and turned in during the winter. It is slow to break down, so don't add it as a fertiliser to greenhouse compost.

Blood fish and bone The organic version of the inorganic Growmore. This gives a well-balanced fertiliser that is added to the base material of home-made composts (see pp30–1). A typical analysis is 5.1 per cent nitrogen, 5 per cent phosphorous and 6.5 per cent potash.

Bone meal An excellent source of phosphates, with some nitrogen and potash. Use it when making your own composts (see p30). If possible, buy the bone flour version because this releases its nutrients rather more quickly than the meal. Outdoors, however, bone meal is a first-rate fertiliser when planting fruit trees and bushes, shrubs and roses, releasing its goodness steadily over two years.

Calcified seaweed Less of a fertiliser, more a soil sweetener and conditioner, this is often used in place of lime to alter the pH of the soil or soil substitute. I use it when making compost and as an ingredient of my worm farm (p 38). In open ground it is effective from two to three years.

Dried blood A rich source of nitrogen and very quick-acting because it is soluble in water. Organic purists frown on those who use this as a quick-acting tonic for leafy vegetables, and its use is restricted by the Soil Association. Compared with its chemical equivalents, however, dried blood does not harm the soil or the helpful bacteria that live in it.

Foliar feeds The practice of feeding plants through their leaves has been followed for centuries, using the liquid derived from dunking a sack of animal manure in a barrel of water. For full details of how to make your own liquid feed, see pp 32–3. There is also a wide choice of proprietary organic foliar feeds available today. Some of the best are based on seaweed extract and contain useful proportions of the main plant foods along with many trace elements, cytokin growth hormones and alginates which act as a wetting agent and have a deterrent effect on sap-sucking insects such as aphids and white fly.

Liquid feeding, whether using organic materials or man-made chemical products, is the most important way of ensuring that container-grown plants are given adequate sustenance. Proprietary inorganic liquid feeds do state the precise amounts of available nutrients in the formula; with many organic preparations, however, particularly the homemade ones, what is available and how soon can only be determined by trial and error. The golden rule with liquid feeding is 'little and often, and always feed after moistening the compost'.

Seaweed extract Foliar feeding with liquid seaweed extract is an important remedy for trace element deficiency: in this case it should be sprayed or watered on the plants every fortnight until the symptoms disappear. Use it also as a supplementary fertiliser for crops in growing bags, and regularly as a source of nutrients for plants in the house and conservatory.

Hoof and horn A medium- to slow-release nitrogen source that can be used with good effect in making up soil-less composts (see p31).

Animal manures Many organic gardeners rely entirely on well-rotted animal manure to secure an optimum level of fertility in their soil, using it both outdoors and in the border soil of the greenhouse. Goat manure and poultry droppings contain a higher proportion of the three main plant foods than horse or pig manure, but in my experience they are best composted with other materials or used as the basis of liquid feeds (see p32).

As well as the plant foods, strawy animal manures provide humus – that invaluable material which helps plants to develop a strong, searching root system, holds nutrients and moisture at a level where the roots can reach them, and gives stability to soil where it is used as the growing medium.

Leafmould There's very little plant food left in autumn's fallen leaves, but they are a good source of humus and can be used in potting composts. Beech and oak leaves are best. How-

Organic fertilisers like these play a vital role in greenhouse crop management.

Leafmould makes a good substitute for peat in potting compost. Stack fallen leaves in a cylinder of wire netting, with a cover to keep the rain out and a weight to keep the stack under pressure. But be patient – it takes a full year before it will be usable.

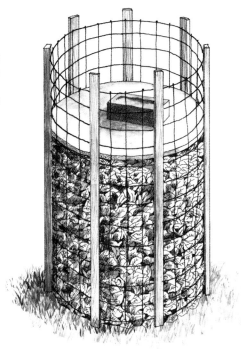

ever, making leafmould (see pp35–6) calls for patience, and if you haven't managed to collect enough leaves in one season, the best way of recycling them is to add what you've got to the compost bin. But *please*, don't burn them!

Processed manures Processed manures are widely advertised as supplements to, or substitutes for, home-made compost or farmyard manure, but because they are classed as soil conditioners, not fertilisers, suppliers do not have to give an analysis of their nutrient content. Nor are they cheap – in fact a bag of super concentrated manure may comprise up to 80 per cent water, and the available nutrients in only minuscule amounts.

In 1990 an extensive survey of these proprietary products was carried out by the Consumer Association to test their cost and effectiveness both as soil conditioners and fertilisers. In cost terms the effective ones were often the cheapest at supplying organic matter, and in fact the report advised people to make as much garden compost as possible or to buy cheap, local sources of stable manure, farmyard manure or spent mushroom compost.

My long-held personal concern has

been the confusion over the use of the terms 'organic-based', 'semi-organic' and 'natural' by the manufacturers of processed manures and fertilisers. The Soil Association is an internationally respected body whose *Standards for Organic Agriculture* are the definitive standards in the UK; these include the following basic definitions:

Organic (biological) agricultural and horticultural systems are designed to produce food of optimum quality and quantity. The principles and methods employed result in practices which coexist with, rather than dominate, natural systems; sustain or build soil fertility; minimise damage to the environment; minimise the use of non-renewable resources.

The enhancement of biological cycles, involving micro-organisms, soil fauna, plants and animals is the basis of organic agriculture. Sound rotation, the extensive and rational use of manure and vegetable wastes, the use of appropriate cultivation techniques, the avoidance of fertilisers in the form of soluble mineral salts, and the prohibition of agrochemical pesticides form the basic characteristics of organic agriculture.

So it seems to me that any product claiming to be organic should match up to the exacting standards of the Soil Association. Having done so successfully, it can then carry the association's symbol which is an internationally respected quality mark for organic products.

Municipal compost Every large town and city should have its own composting plant, as happens in many European countries. Organic waste is collected

NPK ANALYSIS OF ORGANIC FERTILISERS AND MANURES

Material	% Nitrogen	% Phosphorus	% Potash
Strawy cow dung	0.54	0.31	0.67
Rotted cow dung	0.59	0.45	0.49
Farmyard manure	0.65	0.23	0.32
Mushroom compost	0.80	0.63	0.67
Deep litter			
Chicken compost	0.80	0.55	0.48
Comfrey compost	0.77	0.29	0.92
Urine activated compost	0.80	0.29	0.41
Dried blood	9.0–13.0	0.80	
Hoof and horn meal	6.50–13.2	0.20	
Bone meal	0.30–4.60	14.1–33.2	1.0
Fish meal	6.30–8.90	6.0–8.90	1.0
Seaweed meal	2.88	0.22	2.29

SHREDDERS: FOR MORE COMPOST

A lot of garden waste that could become compost for use as a mulch or in the greenhouse is either consigned to the municipal tip or burned, particularly prunings, woody flower stalks, and the stems of cabbages, Brussels sprouts and cauliflowers. All of these, plus newspaper, potato and tomato haulms, potato peelings and leaves, can be chopped up and recycled if you invest in a shredder. There is a range of electrically powered models to suit any size of garden, plus lead-free petrol machines. If your garden doesn't produce a steady supply of suitable material for shredding, instead of buying a shredder you could save the material and hire a machine for a day or half-day.

A word of warning, however: Consumer Association tests on four manufacturers' shredders found that although they all performed reasonably well, there were 'safety drawbacks' though all could be used safely 'if you were careful and followed the instructions'.

All the machines operate in the same way. You feed the raw material into a hopper and the powered cutting blades shred and deliver it as fine chippings; these will decompose more rapidly on the compost heap than in their original state, but can also be used for weed-control mulching.

Safety instructions are issued with the machines, but here are some points to bear in mind:
- Always wear gloves, eye and ear protectors. The machines are noisy, and chips can fly out of the feed hopper.
- Use a residual current device with an electric shredder.
- Switch off and remove the power plug before attempting to clear a blockage or clean the machine.
- Keep children and pets away when using the shredder.
- Take care when feeding weeds into the machine. Surplus soil should be removed beforehand.
- If you are hiring a machine, make sure full instructions are given with it. Check the guards: it should not be possible to touch the cutting blades through the inlet or bottom outlet of the feed hopper.

---

separately from other household waste, and is then recycled and sold as a useful adjunct to homemade compost, saving both money and resources.

Mushroom compost Not so long ago straw was composted with chemical activators and without stable manure to make the mushroom-growing medium. Now, good stable manure and ample supplies of wheat straw make manure-based compost a better deal for mushroom growers, many of whom are switching to entirely organic methods of production. Their spent compost can be bought and used as a supplement to homemade compost; it will be free of pesticide residues, but should be checked for its pH level. You can use it in the greenhouse and conservatory as a constituent of potting compost, too.

Seaweed There aren't many stretches of coastline where seaweed is not available, and what a marvellous bounty of the sea it is – a free, renewable source of fertility for your garden. And even if fresh seaweed is not available to all who would like to use it, there is the dried and powdered version. It is the nearest thing to a complete natural fertiliser, with 2.88

per cent nitrogen, 0.22 per cent phosphorous, and 2.29 per cent potassium. Use it when making composts (p31), as an activator in the compost bin, as well as a general fertiliser anywhere in the garden.

Sewage sludge Millions of tonnes of this organic material are dumped in the sea every year; besides this anomaly, huge amounts of harvest straw are burned – both of which emphasise how wasteful we have become of natural resources. Bring waste straw and sewage sludge together, however, and you have a product that could bring life back to the chemically-dependent arable soils. By controlled composting to remove any potentially harmful pathogens from the sewage while retaining the major plant nutrients and trace elements, the resulting material is a good organic compost that is comparable in nutrient values and humus content to homemade aerobic compost. It can be combined with coir dust to provide a most successful filling for portable growing units, a peat-less organic product with a strong appeal for use in offices, showrooms and other public areas.

Wood ash Ash from wood-burning stoves is rich in potash and should be saved and stored in a damp-proof container, preferably mixed with some pieces of charcoal. It is rich in potash so is a good feed for tomatoes; apply it as a dressing to the moistened surface then lightly tease it in.

Worm-worked compost The earthworm can convert organic waste into a compost with good levels of plant nutrients, a low level of ammonia, good water-holding capacity, high cation exchange capacity and a high microbial population, and this has been exploited by a number of organisations. This compost was first produced on a large commercial scale using pig waste (faeces, urine and straw), when a 6.25cm (2½in) layer of the waste was converted in less than a week into a compost that could be used immediately, or stored without loss of value.

You can buy a ready-made worm farm or produce your own worm compost using quite basic equipment and kitchen scraps that might attract vermin if put into the compost heap. The method is described here.

CREATING A WORM FARM

Every organic garden, however small, should have a compost-making container so that waste fruit and vegetable material can be converted into valuable food for the soil. To avoid the attention of flies, mice and rats, however, any cooked kitchen scraps should be kept out of the compost. Rather than waste such material, it can be put to good use to create compost of another kind by feeding it to brandlings or manure worms – *Eisenia foetida*. No expensive equipment is required to start your own worm farm, just a plastic dustbin with a close-fitting lid, some peat or peat substitute, a couple of kilos of calcified seaweed or ground limestone, about three bucketfuls of food scraps and, of course, the brandlings.

Unlike the aerobic compost-making operation, which relies on a combination of bacterial action and heat, worm-worked compost is produced by the brandlings eating and digesting the waste material fed to them. It is converted into a clean, sweet-smelling material that is rich in plant foods, and can be used in equal quantities with peat or peat substitute as a potting compost for chrysanthemums and fuchsias. It can also be used for a wide range of pot plants with an equal quantity of peat or peat substitute or leafmould or composted bark plus one-eighth volume of sand, gravel, perlite or vermiculite.

Brandlings occur naturally in aerobic compost or any heap of decaying vegetation. They are pink or red and much smaller and thinner than earthworms. To start farming, you will need about a hundred brandlings; if you can't find enough, angling shops are certain to stock them as bait.

The dustbin will need a bit of work on it to prepare it as suitable living quarters. It must be ventilated and this is achieved by boring small holes in the lid using a drill or heated metal skewer. There is bound to be some seepage, but this can be collected in a drip tray and used as liquid manure, so make small drainage holes in the bottom 15cm (6in) of the bin. Fill this bottom 15cm (6in) with a mix of pebbles and sand, then add water until it seeps out of the drainage holes. This provides the right level of humidity. To avoid disturbing this layer of pebbles and sand when you fork out the finished compost, place wooden slats on top.

The next step is to add two bucketfuls of peat (or peat substitute) and well-rotted compost or spent mushroom compost; the peat can be from used growing bags and can include the remains of the root system from the crop. Put the hundred or so brandlings into a plastic cup with either peat or moist breadcrumbs, then sprinkle the entire contents of the cup into the bin on top of this layer; brandlings from an angling shop will probably be in a plastic container already, so just sprinkle them gently over the peat mixture in the bin as soon as possible after buying them.

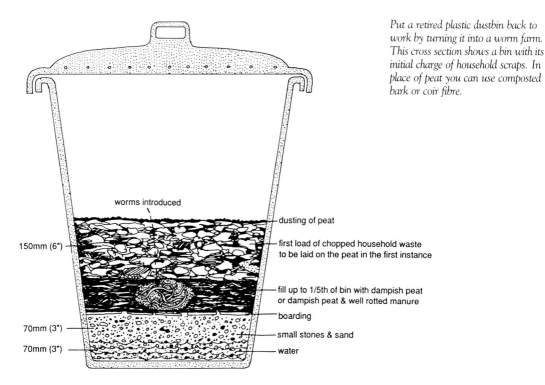

Put a retired plastic dustbin back to work by turning it into a worm farm. This cross section shows a bin with its initial charge of household scraps. In place of peat you can use composted bark or coir fibre.

worms introduced

150mm (6")

70mm (3")

70mm (3")

dusting of peat

first load of chopped household waste to be laid on the peat in the first instance

fill up to 1/5th of bin with dampish peat or dampish peat & well rotted manure

boarding

small stones & sand

water

Dark, friable worm-worked compost can safely be handled, and is used like a concentrated manure. It contains good levels of the main plant nutrients with good moisture holding capacity. Use it particularly for potting up chrysanthemums and fuchsias.

Now add the first layer of food for the worms, chopped as finely as possible because they have tiny mouths. All kitchen scraps are suitable except those that have been saturated in fat or pickled in vinegar. Obviously the worms cannot cope with fish or meat bones, but generally speaking the more varied the diet, the better. You can even add well-shredded, moist newsprint in small quantities, mixed in with other material.

Make the first layer of food about 10–15cm (4–6in) deep; then sprinkle it with about a yoghurt-carton full of the calcified seaweed or ground limestone. The reason for this is that manure worms are very sensitive to acidic conditions, and the calcified seaweed or limestone maintains a neutral pH inside the bin. If the compost dries out the worms cannot survive, so try to ensure that all the material fed to them is moist – though not too wet.

Once you have given the starter colony of worms its first layer of food, don't expect to see results too soon, or add further supplies of food. Each adult worm produces two to five cocoons a week, each containing ten to fifteen hatchings of baby worms which mature in seven to eight weeks. However, such a population explosion is very dependent on the outside temperature; it is fast in late spring, summer and early autumn, while in winter once the temperature falls below about 8°C (45°F) it ceases altogether and the worms simply rest.

About twenty to twenty-five days after adding the first layer of food you should see signs of the tiny worms hatched from the first residents. They are white, thread-like creatures and they *will* benefit from a further helping of food. Try to make this as protein-rich as possible by adding stale bread, stale biscuits soaked in stale milk, scraps of cheese, even the spent yeast from homemade beer. Dog-owners who use one of the whole-meal foods can add the powdery material from the bottom of the bag, though do moisten it first. However, because heat is not involved in the making of worm compost, don't add any garden waste containing weed seeds. And once each layer of food has reached a depth of about 15cm (6in), sprinkle a cartonful of the calcified seaweed or limestone on it. Don't fill the bin right to the top, allow a space of about 15–20cm (6–8in).

The compost is ready to use when it has turned dark and spongy, like friable soil; this takes up to six months from starting. The contents of the bin can be forked into another bin or open-ended sack for use, but keep some in a separate container as the starter for the next colony – and so on, indefinitely.

In the winter, you can encourage the worms to go on working by moving the bin into a shed or garage and wrapping it with an insulating layer of old carpet or thermoplastic.

Worm-worked compost is available as a proprietary product from a number of suppliers.

RAISING PLANTS FROM SEED

Growing plants from seed is the most basic, entertaining and rewarding feature of gardening, for me and I suspect for most other gardeners. It is just about the closest that we come to raw, unpolluted nature. The miracle of creating a new, living thing by bringing together seed, soil, moisture, warmth and light never loses its fascination, and no lifetime is long enough for its thrill to pall. John Kelly in his *Sowing a Better Garden* says: 'To live with a plant from its sowing to its maturity is a deeply fulfilling experience. To buy a plant, nurture it, and see it grow to full-flowering adulthood is to gain a great deal, but to have handled the seed is to have touched creation.'

PLANNING

Raising any plants from seed demands foresight and careful planning. It is easy enough to germinate them in a warm spot in the house, in the airing cupboard or above the central heating boiler, for example; with frost-tender species this was the time-honoured method for countless amateur gardeners. But emergence is just the first phase: what happens to the seedlings once they have entered this brave new world? Is there a warm, light, secure place where they can grow on? These were questions I should have asked myself when I raised my first tomato plants, or rather before I sowed the seed. Tomato seed germinates very readily and my tray above the kitchen stove soon showed a mass of emergent seedlings. They quickly grew lank and straggly, and the problem of what to do with about fifty or sixty seedlings, once they were transplanted into trays or pots, rapidly involved the whole family – there's a limit to sunny windowsills wide enough to accommodate pots of young tomato plants, and we ended up having to give away threequarters of them.

On a later occasion I had some trays of seedlings mostly from pretty expensive half-hardy annual seed just reaching the critical stage of post-emergent growth when I was sent away from home on business for a couple of weeks: unfortunately none of the family was alerted to the mounting crisis in the greenhouse in time to do more than save a pitiful few from death by thirst.

To reiterate, raising plants from seed in a greenhouse or propagator does require particularly careful planning, especially if your commitments put gardening anywhere other than top of the agenda. A sound idea is to start at the end of the production line and work back to the beginning, that's to say, decide on the date you will want to have the plants ready for planting out (with half-hardy varieties that's usually after the last recorded date for a frost in your district), and then time each sequence to arrive at an approximate date for the actual sowing. It works reasonably well once you have gained a bit of experience, but it is always prudent to build belt-and-braces precautions into the technique because germination times will vary from one batch of seed to the next, and weather conditions will obviously have a major effect on the progress of the entire operation.

What you can grow from seed under glass depends on the following factors:

- Your expertise, or information available, because some species are notoriously difficult to germinate.
- Your budget, because it is quite possible to pay a lot of money for just a few seeds, such as hybrid geraniums.
- Equipment: some form of heating is necessary both for germination and for aftercare of the seedlings, and there must be adequate space to accommodate the trays and pots of seedlings when they are pricked out.
- Individual needs: what you intend to do with the plants raised. Also, there is invariably a surplus – one commendable solution is to raise money for charities from the sale of surplus plants.
- Personal schedule: to avoid waste, plan to allow time for the critical phases of seed sowing, pricking-out, potting-on, hardening-off and so on.

The last two items in the list are up to the individual, but I hope this book and others recommended on p151 will extend your expertise. The budget can be stretched by joining a local gardening club, preferably a branch of the Soil Association or HDRA, and taking advantage of the discounts offered to clubs by seed firms, or by sharing seeds among colleagues, friends and relatives. Don't be tempted by bargain basement seed offers. Nowadays, reputable seed companies give quality control a priority place in their marketing strategy. Most seed is sold in vacuum-packed foil for pristine freshness, and its viability is backed by money-back guarantees.

SEED-RAISING EQUIPMENT

Pots

Containers are vital, but relatively inexpensive. For raising just a few seeds small pots, say 8 or 9cm (3 or 3½in) diameter, are ideal, and there are cut-down versions that require less compost to fill them than the ordinary ones. My preference is for clay pots rather than plastic ones because I like the look and the feel of them but they are becoming increasingly expensive. Certainly plastic pots are easier to keep clean, do not dry out quite so quickly, are far lighter in weight and make potting-on easier because the roots of the plant don't cling to the sides.

As well as those for sowing, you will need a range of suitably sized pots for potting-on and, depending on the plants to be raised, adequately sized pots or other containers for those plants that will be resident in the greenhouse or conservatory or raised for transferring to the house. Obviously these containers should be decorative as well as functional; here again, I'd plump for terracotta pots, urns and tubs every time even though they cost several times more than their plastic equivalents.

Trays

Trays are also essential when raising more than just a few plants, and are particularly valuable for bedding plant and vegetable crop production. For some types of seed however, modules can be used where the roles of pot and tray are combined in one unit. These can be bought in two sizes, one with twenty cells, the other with twenty-eight cells, made from thin moulded plastic. The cell section, which can only be used once, fits into the standard seed-tray size of 35 × 20cm (14 × 8in). Otherwise make your own paper pots and stand them shoulder to shoulder in the seed-tray.

Standard seed-trays can be used for sowing large batches of plants and for pricking-out, but it is also advisable to have a stock of half-size trays for raising, say, individual varieties of bedding plants, or fewer plants of a particular species. This is a better technique than growing two or more types of flower or vegetable in the one tray because germination times and growth rates vary to the point where late seedlings may well have to struggle for survival.

Drainage Crocks

Pots and seed-trays have drainage holes, and when soil-based sowing compost is used the drainage holes have to be crocked to allow the water, but not the compost, to drain through. The traditional way of doing this was to use pieces of broken clay-pots, but now that plastic has largely ousted clay for flower-pots, other crocking materials are used. For pots you can use tea bags, still moist, or pieces of discarded tights cut roughly to fit the base of the pot. With trays, you can use a shallow layer of shredded newspaper or a layer of washed gravel, or even pea-sized pebbles collected from a shingly beach.

Labels

Pots, trays and, of course, the compost to fill them, are the essential items for seed sowing, but there are ancillary bits and pieces. Plant labels should be used as you sow to identify the flower or vegetable, the variety and the date sown. You can recycle washing-up liquid bottles and make your own labels.

Plant labels can be made out of plastic containers such as washing-up liquid bottles. All you need is a pair of sharp scissors.

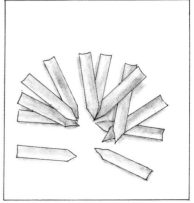

MAKE YOUR OWN POTS

Instead of buying the very expensive terracotta pots or those in cheaper but less long-lasting plastic, it needs only a minimum of equipment to make your own large flower pots out of cement and sand. Good organic pots for raising seedlings can also be made out of newspaper, and used in place of compressed peat pots.

Making paper pots takes very little time, and all you need is a former such as a rolling pin, a few sheets of newspaper preferably tabloid size, and some ordinary flour paste.

Take two sheets of the paper and roll round the former. Paste along the edges and allow the paste to

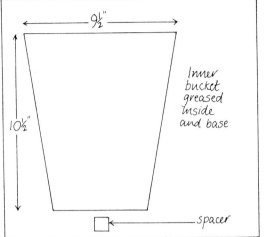

Stand paper pots in a tray before filling them.

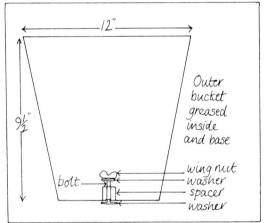

Put bean seedlings outside for hardening off.

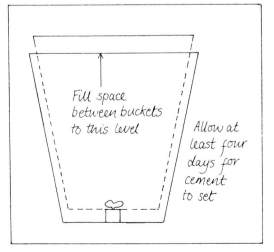

A gardening friend devised this method of making plant pots out of concrete.

MAKE YOUR OWN POTS (continued)

dry. Then slide off and cut the paper tube into suitable lengths. If you plan to use a loam-based compost in the pots, allow for the bottom to be turned in before filling with compost. With peat-based or peat-substitute composts the paper pots can be open-ended, but stand both types in a tray before filling and sowing. Use these paper pots for raising sweet peas, broad beans, French beans, runner beans, courgettes, marrows, peppers, aubergines and cucumbers, sowing one seed to a pot.

When the time comes for transplanting, there's no need to disturb the seedling: simply plant it out, paper pot and all. Keep moist, and the paper will rot down as the roots penetrate through it.

For the concrete pots, you will need two plastic buckets, one about 23cm (9in) deep and 30cm (12in) diameter, the other about 26cm (10½in) deep and 23cm (9in) diameter; also a plastic 35mm film holder or similar plastic cylinder cut down to 3cm (1¼in) deep; a 5mm (¼in) by 6cm (2½in) threaded bolt with wing-nut and washers; some Vaseline or grease; and four parts of sand to one part of cement (the amount will depend on how many pots are to be made).

The idea is that the two buckets are the mould for the pot, with the plastic cap and bolt acting as spacer.

The procedure is first, to drill a hole the same diameter as the bolt through both buckets and the plastic cap. This hole will eventually form the drainage hole in the finished pot. Grease the inside of the larger bucket including the base, also the outside of the smaller bucket, the bolt, wing-nut and washers. Place a washer on the bolt, then push it through the hole of the larger bucket, through the plastic cap and then through the hole of the smaller bucket. Slip on the second washer, then the wing-nut which should be tightened finger-tight.

The two buckets are now joined together by the bolt, but spaced about 3cm (1¼in) apart. This space is filled with the cement, made on the dry side. Feed it down evenly between the buckets, rocking occasionally to remove air gaps. Fill to the rim of the larger bucket and allow to set for four days. Then simply dismantle the mould by releasing the wing-nut and tapping the bolt through the holes. The finished pot will be 23cm (9in) in diameter, 19cm (7½in) deep, with wall and base 3cm (1¼in) thick. As a final touch you can paint the outside of the pot with masonry paint.

The same technique can be used with a variety of containers to make smaller or larger pots and other containers.

Items for Seed Sowing

Two other useful items for seed sowing are a dibber and a pair of tweezers. Careful spacing of the seeds when sowing is sound sense because it saves seed and gives each seedling an equal chance. Large seed, such as sweet pea, can be sown accurately spaced in a tray using a dibber or a plastic template that compresses and marks the surface of the compost. Smaller seeds can be spaced evenly using a dibber to make the indentation in the compost and the tweezers to insert the seed. Tomato seed is slightly woolly and clings to fingers or tweezers when sowing; however, you can use this to advantage because the seed will stick to the end of a moistened matchstick and so is easy to sow one at a time.

Some types of seed should be soaked in lukewarm water for two hours or in cold water overnight before sowing. Moisten the compost, then use a dibber or template to space the seeds evenly. Finally, for seeds that require light to germinate, cover the tray with glass or clear plastic; for seeds that need darkness, add a covering of black polythene or thick brown paper.

SEED-SOWING GUIDELINES

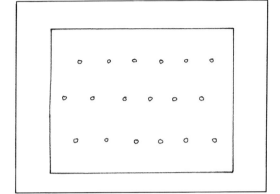

- Make sure the pots and trays are sterile by washing them in disinfectant well before they will need to be used. Check that you have enough for both sowing and pricking-out.
- Use fresh, slightly moist compost – not last year's – and have it in a warm place a few days prior to sowing. After filling the pot or tray, firm it by tapping the bottom of the pot on the bench, and pressing the surface of the compost in the tray with a wooden block.
- Always crock pots and trays if using soil-based compost.
- Water the pots and trays from the bottom by standing them in warm water until the surface of the compost glistens with moisture, then allow to drain.
- Sow the seed as evenly spaced as possible and at the recommended depth, or cover with the correct depth of sifted soil or compost. Sowing too deeply is a frequent cause of failure. Label the tray or pot immediately after sowing.
- Place the pots or trays in the propagator set at the optimum temperature for germination, typically 18–21°C (65–70°F).
- If the compost dries out on the surface before the seeds germinate, gently syringe it with tepid water.
- Once the seedlings emerge, shade from direct sunlight and give some ventilation to minimise the risk of damping off.
- Prick out the seedlings as soon as possible. Prepare the reception tray for the pricked-out seedlings by dibbling holes in the moist compost. Hold the seedling by the seed leaves and use a widger or lolly stick to ease the roots from the compost and to firm it in its planting hole.

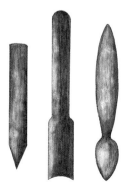

(Left) a sharpened lolly stick is useful for pricking out delicate seedlings; (Centre) a widger of stainless steel and (Right) a plastic dibber are useful propagating aids.

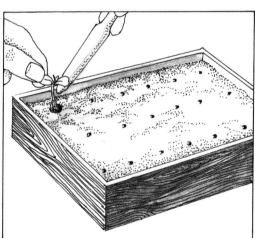

For accurate spacing when pricking out seedlings use a template. Lift the seedling by the seed leaves and a widger. Make the planting hole with a dibber and gently press the compost round the stem.

Very small seeds are difficult to sow thinly and evenly spaced and quite a lot depends on the dexterity of the sower's hands. Small seed tends to be reluctant to leave the seed firm's foil pack, so transfer as much as you will need to a paper cone and then gently tap the cone to transfer the seeds to the surface of the compost. Seed so fine that it is dust-like in the pack needs some silver sand added to it; stir it well to mix it then gently tap it out of the packet. Increasingly, fine seed is being sold in special containers to make sowing less haphazard.

Seed that isn't dibbled or that needs light for germination must be covered after sowing, and nothing does this better than a small sieve. The sifted compost or soil should then be pressed down with a wooden block, made to about a quarter the size of a standard tray.

Temperature

Seed germination trials have demonstrated that where the seed firm gave specific advice on the temperature for germination, it was best to follow it to achieve rapid and even germination. In many instances, however, lowering the temperature slightly brought acceptable results, although this could lengthen the time before emergence by a few days.

For those without a propagator, seed can be germinated successfully in the airing cupboard, although it is wise to check the temperature at various levels in the cupboard because it may be too hot anywhere other than at floor level. Keep a close watch, preferably daily, on progress, and at the first sign of germination move the seed tray to a warm windowsill but out of direct sunlight.

PROPAGATION BY CUTTINGS

A good way to increase your stock of plants is by taking cuttings from those already in the garden, from the gardens of friends and neighbours, or by buying cuttings from specialist growers – this calls for no special skills or expensive equipment and is great fun. There is a widely-held myth that you need green fingers to get cuttings to root; however, many plants, shrubs and trees can be readily propagated by cuttings of one sort or another, and most failures are due to taking the wrong cutting at the wrong time of year. Some cuttings are so eager to root that merely shoving them into a vacant patch of soil is enough.

EQUIPMENT

The greenhouse itself is the single most important bit of equipment needed for success with cuttings, but you will also need something or somewhere to provide the bottom heat and humidity that are necessary conditions for root production.

Plastic Bags

At one end of the scale, a few cuttings can be raised satisfactorily using no more than a plastic bag over a flower-pot; stand these in a warm place until they have rooted, and then transfer them to the greenhouse bench or cold frame.

A pot of compost, a few split canes and a plastic bag make a simple propagating unit for raising cuttings.

PROPAGATING TERMS

Cuttings Many shrubs and trees and some plants are readily propagated from cuttings taken from the parent plant. A leaf, bud, section of stem or root of a living plant is removed and treated in such a way that it becomes a new plant. Softwood cuttings are taken in late spring, hardwood cuttings in autumn and winter, while semi-ripe cuttings are taken from deciduous shrubs in midsummer and from evergreens in early autumn.

Types of cutting include basal, heel, nodal, stem, leaf, leafbud and root. The technique of propagation by cuttings is described on p48.

Hardening off Plants raised in the controlled environment of the greenhouse or indoors and intended for planting outside need to be hardened off. This means introducing them gradually to the climate outdoors. Seedlings raised in a propagator are moved to the greenhouse bench, then to a cold frame and finally to the planting position in the garden.

This procedure is especially important with frost-tender (half-hardy) plants, and even when in the cold frame they will need extra protection, such as sacking or old carpet to cover the glass, when frost is forecast. All young plants, whether half-hardly or hardy, that are raised under cover should be acclimatised in this way.

Before planting out, seedlings should be hardened off in gradual stages. This is especially important with frost-tender plants.

Potting-on When a plant's root system fills the pot with a dense mass of roots it is time to move it to another, larger pot or it will fail to flourish. Always pot on to the next size – from an 8cm (3in) pot to a 13cm (5in) one and then to an 18cm (7in) pot.

Potting-up When a seedling has made enough growth after the pricking-out process it can be transferred to a small pot. This also applies to a cutting that has 'taken' or rooted.

When potting on, put the smaller pot into the larger and fill round it with compost. Then tap the plant out of the pot and drop it into its new home.

PROPAGATING TERMS (continued)

Pricking-out To prevent seedlings from becoming overcrowded, they should be transferred to a larger pot or tray as soon as they are large enough to handle – usually when the first pair of true leaves appears. Ease them gently out of the compost using a widger or pointed lolly stick (p44); hold by the leaves, never by the stem, and set them into trays or pots of potting compost, about 5cm (2in) apart each way – a standard full-size tray measures 33cm (13in) by 23cm (9in) so it should accommodate eighteen seedlings. If you have a fair bit of pricking-out to do a time-saving plan is to make a template of cardboard with evenly spaced holes; place over the filled tray and use a skewer or pencil to mark the holes. Alternatively, you can buy a ready made plastic version.

The trays or pots of seedlings should then be placed in a shaded part of the greenhouse for a couple of days.

Potting up cuttings when they have made a good root system and potting on are basic aspects of plant management.

Re-potting Potting-on means that the plant is put into a larger pot. Re-potting is when the plant is transferred from its existing home to a pot of the same size. This might be necessary because of vine weevil attack (p56), or because the plant – even if grown to its optimum size – has become rootbound and has exhausted the compost.

It will be given a new lease of life by removing it, teasing out the roots and old compost and trimming back the rootball by about a fifth. Re-pot into a fresh pot of the same size and fill with moist compost. If vine weevil was present, ensure the old pot is thoroughly washed in a sterilising solution; the vine weevil grubs should be destroyed and the old compost disposed of in the dustbin rather than the compost heap.

Paraffin Heaters

Next in line for low cost is a paraffin heater used in conjunction with one or more trays; this is cheap to run and doesn't depend on a power supply to the greenhouse. However, there is virtually no control over the operating temperatures and unless the wick is kept trimmed, the oily smoke can be fatal to the plants.

Electrically Heated Propagators

By far the most widely used technique is the electrically heated propagator available in several sizes and degrees of automation. It can best be used where there is an electricity supply to the greenhouse, but this is not essential as it can be positioned indoors for the initial root-forming stage. An electrically heated propagator for bottom heat, with a thermostat to control the operating temperature and a plastic cover to provide warmth and humidity above the compost, should offer ideal conditions for raising cuttings of all kinds. The running costs of a single tray propagator are equivalent to that of a 15 watt lamp, while the three-tray, 'top-of-the-range' unit costs about the same as a 60 watt bulb, so it is understandable why these units are so popular. They are especially suitable for raising plants from seed, and I cannot imagine running my greenhouse without the aid of my propagators. The one drawback is limited space: the one-tray unit when used for raising cuttings can accommodate twelve round 8cm (3in) pots or fifteen 7cm (2½in) square plastic pots, and this may be thought inadequate when a failure rate of fifty per cent is quite normal with many types of cutting.

Soil-warming Cables

Some greenhouse owners have the space and the need to raise a largish number of plants either from seeds or by cuttings, but do not want to heat the whole greenhouse; in this case, soil-warming cables set into a bed on the staging, or an electrically-heated propagating pad (p27) are excellent, and the required level of humidity can be created by covering the heated area with a tent of polythene.

Soil-heating cables used with a specially-made propagating frame and an adjustable thermostat can be bought as a DIY kit, and are the economical answer for those who want to raise a moderate to large number of cuttings and, of course, plants from seed. They can be a permanent feature of the greenhouse or installed in a cold frame, and can be tailor-made to suit the space available. In the greenhouse a cable-warming layout can be upgraded, as experience and enthusiasm grow, to include a misting unit. Cuttings can be rooted into the bed covering the cable, usually a fifty-fifty mixture of sand and peat or peat substitute, with a plastic sheet covering the frame to maintain a good level of humidity.

Electrically Heated Mats

Electrically heated mats or sheets with thermostatic control are more flexible than the soil-warming cable installation because when not in use they can be rolled up and stored. They are available in a choice of lengths and widths. A plastic tent or dome is necessary to cover the trays or pots of cuttings to maintain humidity.

Whatever type of heated propagator is used, it should be capable of giving a compost temperature of 13–15°C (55–60°F) and this should be checked with a soil thermometer (p27).

TAKING CUTTINGS

Softwood, hardwood or semi-ripe cuttings refer to the stage of growth when the cutting is taken. This means that softwood cuttings are taken in spring from young growth, while hardwood or semi-ripe ones are taken in autumn and winter from shoots that have become more woody.

DO'S AND DON'TS OF TAKING CUTTINGS

- Cleanliness is important, so ensure pots and trays are sterile and the compost is fresh. Don't use ordinary garden soil.
- Take the cutting at the right time of the year for the particular plant.
- Try to select only healthy cutting material from healthy plants, preferably young ones.
- Don't let the cutting dry out at any stage.
- Always write out a label when taking the cuttings and keep label and cuttings together.
- Do remember that when the cuttings have rooted they will require potting on and then feeding after about four weeks.

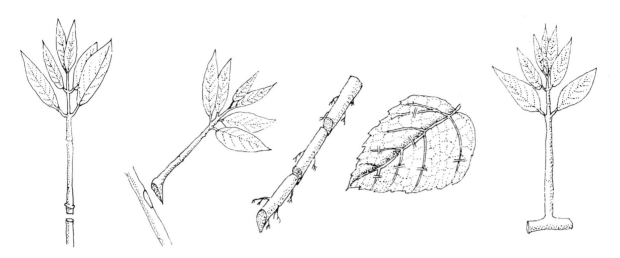

Stem Cuttings

Basal, where the shoot is cut from the parent close to the stem.

Heel, the most widely used way of propagating from stems, whether the cutting is of softwood and taken in spring, or semi-ripe or hardwood taken later in the year. The principle is that you select a side shoot and either pull, or with a sharp knife, cut the shoot off the parent taking a tail or heel of the stem with it. For hardwood cuttings taken in the autumn this is the best insurance against the cutting expiring before roots develop.

A variation is the mallet cutting, in which a short length of the stem of the parent is cut with the side shoot to give a hardwood mallet. This is dipped in the rooting powder and placed in the compost so that all of it and a short length of the shoot are in close contact with the compost.

Nodal, in which the shoot, once cut from the parent, is then cut back to just below a leaf joint.

Internodal, where the cut is made between two leaf joints.

Leafbud, used for camellias and mahonias where pieces of the stem are cut to include a bud.

Softwood cuttings are taken from the immature growth of spring while they are still pliable but turgid. They are cut early in the morning, for preference, from the fast-growing tips of the plants and planted immediately. In late spring these cuttings root very quickly, while those taken in early summer are slower. The cutting type can be nodal, taken just below a leaf joint, or heel.

Leaf Cuttings

Some plants, such as saintpaulia (African violets), begonias except *Begonia rex*, and *Peperomia caperata*

Types of cutting, from the left: basal, heel, internodal, leaf and mallet. Whatever the type of cutting, good healthy material cut from the parent plant is a vital factor in success. Some cuttings root more easily if dipped in hormone rooting powder or liquid.

can be propagated from leaf cuttings. The method is to take a mature leaf complete with its stalk. Push the stalk into a container of compost consisting of half peat substitute and half sand. The leaf should be lying flat against the surface of the compost and roots will form at the joint between the base of the leaf and the stem, followed by new growth of leaves.

Root Cuttings

Several trees and shrubs, such as Aralia and Rhus (sumach), can be propagated from short lengths of root cut during the dormant season and planted horizontally about 5cm (2in) deep in compost.

 ## AN OLD WAY WITH CUTTINGS

Cuttings have always been a favourite way of increasing plants and there are mentions of various ways of taking cuttings as far back as 380BC. A seventeenth-century method was to cut a length of willow branch and bore holes to accept the cuttings. This was then buried in the soil and it is believed the willow gave protection against decay in the cuttings. When they had rooted, the branch was cut off in segments.

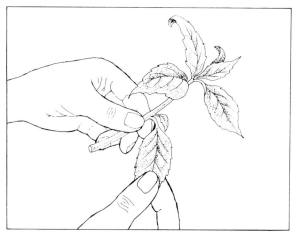

Fuchsias are among many plants that can be propagated by soft stem cuttings taken in spring. Take shoots 10–12.5cm (4–5in) long, cut just below a leaf joint and trim off the lower leaves. Place four cuttings in a 7.5cm (3in) pot of moist compost and cover with a plastic bag. They will root in about three weeks, when more ventilation can be given by making slits in the bag. After potting up, the growing point should be nipped out to encourage bushiness.

Important factors for success with these cuttings are bottom heat of 21–24°C (70–75°F) and adequate humidity. Because the leaves of the shoot are immature they are unable properly to prevent moisture loss through transpiration, so a fairly high degree of humidity is vital. Commercial growers use mist propagation to achieve this. Without misting, the cuttings must never be allowed to wilt, but waterlogging must be avoided. Spraying once a week with dilute copper fungicide solution is recommended by some experts as a precaution against rotting.

When the cuttings have made a good root system they should be hardened off thoroughly before potting-up.

Rooting Hormones

Naturally occurring hormones in plants, called auxins, can stimulate growth. These organic chemicals have been synthesised and are widely used as rooting hormones for cuttings either in powder form or as a liquid. Their use in the organic greenhouse is probably frowned on by the purists, although these products do not seem to be on the restricted or prohibited lists of the Soil Association standards for organic horticulture. I can see no valid objection to using hormones to assist difficult subjects to root. Their routine use, however, is both unnecessary and wasteful because the majority of cuttings will root without intervention.

The base of the rooting powder is finely ground talcum which, in the tiny quantity involved, can surely do no harm in the compost; while the active ingredient – either indole butyric acid (IBA) or napthylacetic acid (NAA) – is virtually identical in composition and effect to the natural hormone in the plant. However, some rooting preparations contain a fungicidal additive which is definitely not organically acceptable. A perfectly satisfactory alternative is to dip

the cutting in dilute copper fungicide solution before inserting it in the compost, and then watering regularly with the same solution.

The correct technique for using hormone powder is to tip a little of the powder into a saucer, then just dip the end of the cutting into water. Touch the powder so that it clings to the cut section only, without any adhering to the outside of the stem. Hormone powder should never be used with leafbud cuttings.

An entirely natural way of stimulating hormone production in hardwood cuttings is called *wounding*, and is particularly successful with cuttings of daphne, juniper and rhododendron. The technique is to cut a slice of bark from the bottom of the cutting, making the cut just deep enough to expose the wood.

CUTTINGS FROM HERBACEOUS PERENNIALS

The following herbaceous perennial plants can be propagated by cuttings taken in spring or autumn, placed in pots in the cold frame. They do not need bottom heat.

Anaphalis (Pearl Everlasting), spring basal cutting, plant out late autumn or following spring.

Anchusa, winter root cutting, plant out early summer.

Artemisia, autumn heel cutting, pot up spring, plant out summer.

Aster (Michaelmas daisy), spring basal cutting, pot up autumn, plant out spring.

Ballota pseudodictamnus (Horehound), autumn heel or nodal cutting. When rooted transfer to frost-free greenhouse.

Brunnera macrophylla, winter root cutting, 8cm (3in) long. Plant out early summer.

Campanula (Bell flower), spring basal cutting, pot up summer, plant out autumn.

Centaurea cineraria, autumn heel cutting, plant out late spring.

Chrysanthemum, hardy types, spring basal cutting, move to nursery bed in summer, plant out autumn.

Diascia, autumn stem cutting, when rooted transfer to frost-free greenhouse.

Dicentra (Bleeding heart), spring basal cutting, pot up when rooted, plant out autumn.

Echinacea purpurea (Purple cone flower), winter root cutting, pot up spring, plant out early summer.

Euphorbia, spring basal cutting, handle with care as milky sap is irritant. Seal stem by passing quickly through a flame. Plant out in summer.

Gypsophila (Baby's breath), spring basal cutting or

summer stem, pot up when rooted, plant out autumn or spring.

Helenium autumnale (Sneezewort), spring stem cutting, pot up when rooted, plant out autumn.

Helichrysum augustifolium (Curry plant), summer heel cutting, pot up when rooted, plant out late spring.

Hesperis matronalis (Sweet rocket), summer basal cutting, pot up when rooted, plant out spring.

Kniphofia (Red hot poker), spring basal cutting, pot up when rooted, plant out autumn.

Lupin, spring basal cutting, transfer to nursery bed when rooted, plant out autumn.

Lythrum (Purple loosestrife), spring basal cutting, transfer to nursery bed when rooted, plant out autumn.

Malva moschata (Musk mallow), spring basal cutting, pot up when rooted, plant out autumn.

Nepeta (Catmint), winter root cutting, 5cm(2in) lengths in pots, pot on when rooted, plant out autumn.

Papaver orientale (Oriental poppy), winter root cutting, 8cm (3in) segments in pots, pot on when rooted, plant out autumn.

Penstemon (Beard tongue), autumn stem cutting, plant out following autumn.

Phlox paniculata, winter root cutting, 8cm(3in) lengths horizontally in trays, plant out in flowering position early summer.

Physotegia (Obedient plant), summer stem cutting, in pots, plant out in spring.

Polygonum (Knotweed), spring basal cutting, plant out late summer.

Potentilla species, spring basal cutting, pot on when rooted, plant out autumn.

Primula denticulata (Drumstick primula), winter root cutting, 5cm (2in) lengths in trays in cool greenhouse, plant out late spring.

Teucrium (Germander), early autumn stem cutting, pot on spring, plant out summer.

 ## IF THE COMPOST DRIES OUT

Check cuttings in pots regularly to make sure the compost hasn't dried out. If it has, stand the pots in a tray of water for fifteen minutes or so until the compost becomes moist again then allow to drain off. The compost should never be waterlogged or the cuttings may rot.

PEST AND DISEASE CONTROL

The cosy interior of the greenhouse or conservatory makes it an almost ideal environment for pests and diseases, and because of the rather tender nature of many greenhouse plants the damage done by rapidly breeding insects such as aphids can be swift and severe. That's the bad news. The good news is that the enclosed structure of the greenhouse makes organic pest control far easier than in the great outdoors.

HYGIENE

The best way to prevent pests and diseases getting a hold in the greenhouse or conservatory is to start a programme of hygiene during the winter and stick to it throughout the year. Diseases can overwinter in the soil, in stale compost and in decaying vegetation, while pests will lurk in pots and trays, in the nooks and crannies of the greenhouse structure, and in shelves and staging. So set aside a couple of days some time before Christmas to give everything a thorough clean.

Spring Cleaning

First, move out any resident plants to a cool frost-free place. And don't forget to remove any dahlia tubers or root vegetables you might have stored in boxes of peat or sand under the staging.

While the greenhouse is empty it is a good time to make any alterations to the layout, and tidy it up generally. Do you really need, for example, all those assorted pots, trays and boxes, some chipped and cracked, left over from previous years? And what about that pile of bamboo canes, rusty secateurs and various objects that you thought might come in useful one day? A clean, tidy greenhouse without surplus bits and pieces is not only more hygienic, it is also more efficient because it is easier to manage.

Also, is the greenhouse really the only place where you can store your summer-flowering bulbs and corms? Certainly those odd part-packets of seed left over from last spring or the one before that should not be there. The fluctuating climatic conditions in the greenhouse will have virtually guaranteed they are no longer fertile; try the germination test described here.

Cleaning Outside

The first major job is to give the entire structure a thorough washing using a solution of household detergent, preferably an environment friendly one. Both for your own comfort and for speed of drying this wash-down is best done on a dry, breezy day. A brisk spraying with the hosepipe will remove surface dust and debris from the exterior of the house, then apply the detergent solution with a soft broom. Clean glass admits more light and reduces heat loss by radiation, so try to find time to give the outside of the glass another going over in the early spring.

THE SAFE PESTICIDES

There are a number of so-called 'safe' pesticides that are approved for use in the organic garden by the Soil Association and Henry Doubleday Research Association. Derris and pyrethrum are naturally occurring substances that are non-systemic and remain active for just a few hours. They are harmless to people and animals, but can kill friendly insects such as bees and ladybirds and are poisonous to fish, frogs and toads.

Derris is derived from the tropical plant *Derris elliptica* and the active ingredient is a powerful alkaline, rotenone. It is used in powder or liquid form to control aphids, red spider mite, weevils and caterpillars. Pyrethrum is prepared from the flowers of *Chrysanthemum cinerariifolium*. It is devoid of phyto-toxicity and is used to control a wide range of pests including aphids, thrips, sawfly, weevils, leaf hoppers and capsids. Ordinary soap has good insecticidal properties, and soapy water, used frequently, is a good control for aphids. Insecticidal soap is less toxic than derris and pyrethrum and doesn't harm friendly insects. It controls aphids, whitefly, red spider mite and scale insects.

GERMINATION TEST

Test seed that has been stored for viability by sowing a sample of, say, ten, twenty or thirty seeds on moist kitchen paper in a saucer. Keep warm and moist and check for germination every day. After three weeks – or longer, depending on the species – count how many seeds have germinated. If there are fewer than 25 per cent, it probably isn't worth sowing the remainder.

JEYES FLUID

Many people swear by Jeyes Fluid as an essential gardening aid, in particular to ward off soil-borne disease and such pests as the carrot fly and cabbage root fly. But is it OK for the green gardener to use? The short answer is, No. Jeyes Fluid contains phenols which will kill not only harmful pests and disease organisms but also those that are important to the soil's health and vitality.

However, Jeyes is certainly a very effective garden disinfectant and can be used, properly diluted, for cleaning the greenhouse, cold frame, glass cloches, trays and pots.

Cleaning Inside

Take extra care when tackling the inside of the greenhouse. If electricity is installed, switch everything off from the source of the supply, not just in the greenhouse. The first chore is to remove as much as possible of the algae, dirt and moss between the panes of glass and the glazing bars, and between the overlaps of the panes.

Loosen as much as you can by pushing a plastic plant label between the overlaps and running it down the sides of each pane. Stubborn areas of algae can be removed with a little household bleach or a proprietary greenhouse glass cleaner, sometimes applied with its own sponge.

Thoroughly clean the glazing bars as well, using a soft brush to penetrate the T-section, and remove assorted insects and debris.

The staging should be removed outside for its wash and brush-up, because this will give easier access inside the house, especially to the lower parts.

The next step is to clean the entire interior of the greenhouse, including the concrete paths and base, using the same detergent solution as that for the outside. If there have been problems the previous season with disease or pests, it might be prudent – though perhaps not entirely acceptable to the organic purist – to use a sterilising solution applied with a brush or spray gun. In this case, wear protective clothing such as an old raincoat, rubber gloves and goggles, and keep the door open.

As an alternative to sterilising solution, the sulphur candle can be used: this is burnt in the greenhouse with all ventilators closed tight. However, it gives off poisonous sulphur dioxide and should never be used except as a desperate measure and then only with extreme caution. In normal circumstances the organic gardener will have no need to use any chemical sterilising agent during the winter cleaning exercise: soap and water or a mild detergent solution and plenty of elbow grease are quite sufficient.

While the greenhouse is clear of all its usual paraphernalia, check it thoroughly for cracked glass and either repair the panes with clear plastic tape or replace them. Check also for leaks and draughts and seal them with waterproof tape. If you are proposing to put up insulation for the winter, such as bubble polythene sheeting, now is the time to do it.

Cleaning the Equipment

Next, deal with all the equipment used in the greenhouse. Clean all the used pots and trays and other containers using a little household detergent, plenty of hot water and a small plastic nail brush. Try to find an alternative home for them because pots and trays not only take up space in the greenhouse that should be put to better use, they also provide cosy quarters for such unwanted creatures as slugs and woodlice.

For example, the area under the staging can be used productively for siting the propagators, for forcing chicory, endive and rhubarb, even for growing mushrooms. Freed of the encumbrance of pots and trays, it can be divided with polythene sheeting into areas for special propagating purposes, such as raising cuttings or starting off salad and vegetable crops. A garden shed or garage makes a better store for many things that usually clutter the average small greenhouse.

Before bringing any plants, bulbs or corms back into the greenhouse, check that they are free from botrytis or mould which is especially prevalent in poorly ventilated plastic-clad structures and in any heated by paraffin heaters. Paraffin produces its own volume in water vapour which condenses and creates just the right conditions in winter, when ventilation is restricted, for the development of fungal troubles.

Inspect each plant carefully and ask the following questions before returning it to the now spick and span greenhouse.

Is it disease and pest free?

Is it worth keeping over the winter, or would it be better to raise new stock from seed or cuttings?

Would it survive the winter without heat?

If not, can you afford to provide the heat without too much concern over the cost?

A TO Z OF PEST CONTROL

Ants These clever insects do not damage plants, but they do 'farm' aphids, mealy bugs and scale insects and, of course, they will make a beeline for any food left in the conservatory. Follow the ant trail back to the nest and use anti-ant dust or boiling water to destroy it.

Aphids The most frequently encountered pests, these suck the sap from almost any plant and in doing so will weaken it and may transmit virus disease. They also excrete honeydew, a sticky substance that falls on to leaves and fruit and this, in turn, attracts a sooty mould. Happily, aphids are easily controlled if spotted early enough.

Small infestations can be controlled simply by wiping with soapy water which will also clean off the sooty mould. For larger areas, spray frequently with soapy water or introduce biological controls – the parasitic wasp *Aphidius* is available all the year round, while the predatory midge *Aphidoletes* is sold in the spring and summer only.

Aphidius is supplied as ready-to-hatch pupae in a sealed tube; just lay the opened tube on its side near to an aphid-infested plant, and the hatched wasps will emerge. Their parasitic activity will soon be made obvious by brown mummified aphids on the plants instead of green sap-sucking ones.

Aphidoletes midges are supplied in larvae form on strips of paper in a sealed tube. Place larvae gently among the colonies of aphids where they will gorge themselves and a few days later drop to the ground to pupate.

Both *Aphidius* and *Aphidoletes* are harmless to humans: the wasp doesn't sting and the midge doesn't bite.

You can also introduce your own biological controllers into the greenhouse. Learn to recognise and catch hoverflies, lacewings and ladybird larvae – although give them their freedom when they have done their job of aphid control.

Capsid bugs Not a common pest in the greenhouse and some species actually do more good than harm by eating aphids and mites. The adults are tiny insects about 6mm (¼in) long with wings fore and aft, and a body colour that varies from yellow to green and bronze. The nymphs look like wingless adults. Capsid bugs seem to favour chrysanthemums more than most other greenhouse plants, and will often take up residence when the plants are outside during late spring and summer. Ragged holes appear in the leaves, while flower buds and shoots may be deformed.

Capsids are not easily sighted: go near the plant and the adults take off. However, repeated spraying with soapy water is a good deterrent.

Caterpillars Rarely a serious pest in the greenhouse, although expect to find them at any time on virtually any plant, where large, ragged holes appear in the leaves. Pick them off by hand or with tweezers and crush underfoot; look for the eggs, too, and crush these between finger and thumb. A really bad infestation can be controlled biologically with *Bacillus thuringiensis*, a bacterium that is sold in sachets; mix the contents in water and then spray on the plants. The effect is to paralyse the gut of the caterpillar without harming other insects.

Earwigs Really only a pest to the ardent chrysanthemum and carnation fancier. It damages leaves, buds and flowers, but can be trapped by placing inverted flower-pots stuffed with straw on the canes supporting the plants. Earwigs are active at night, so shake out the traps in the morning.

Flies House flies are a nuisance in the conservatory rather than a damage-doing pest. Some people swear by Nicandra physaloides, commonly called the shoofly plant, a hardy annual with pale blue flowers.

Froghoppers So called because they have prominent froglike eyes, strong back legs and they jump when disturbed. Although sap-sucking insects, the damage they do is slight, and probably the only indication of their presence

Biological control: a predator in position among greenhouse plants.

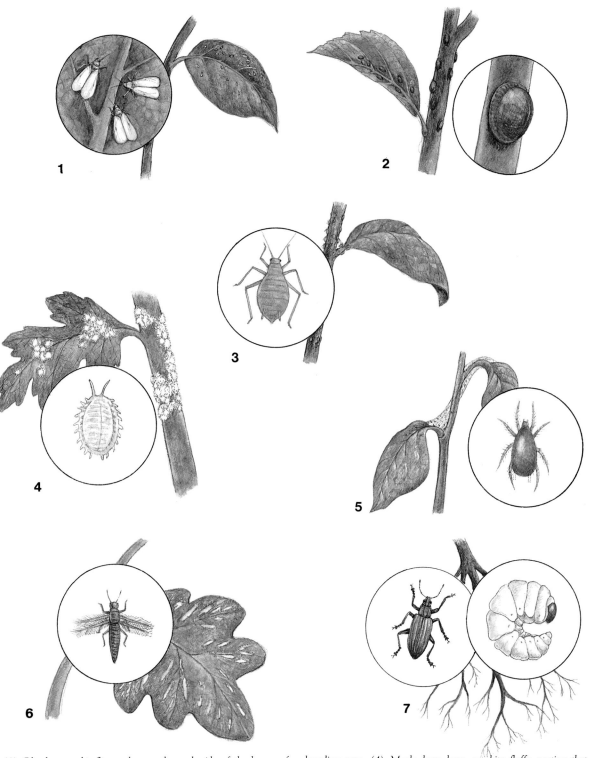

(1) Glasshouse whiteflies gather on the underside of the leaves of many plants. The colony may consist of winged adults, scales and eggs. Like many other sap-sucking insects, the whitefly excretes sticky honeydew; (2) Immobile, hard-shelled and sap-sucking, the scale insects attach themselves to the stems and leaves of pot plants; (3) Aphids come in several colours and more than 500 species, and may be winged or wingless. They are sap-suckers with a phenomenal breeding rate; (4) Mealy bugs have a white fluffy coating that distinguishes them from aphids; (5) The red spider mite is only about 1mm long but is a particularly troublesome greenhouse pest. It is sap-sucking, and large colonies produce fine silky webbing on stems and leaves; (6) Thrips feed on plant tissues, causing mottling and silvering of the leaves; (7) The fat white maggots of the vine weevil live in the compost of pot plants and eat the roots.

will be the frothy deposit of cuckoo spit on the leaves of pot plants, chrysanthemums in particular. If they are not a nuisance, leave them be. Otherwise, a strong jet of water will dislodge them and the cuckoo spit.

Leafhoppers Somewhat similar to the froghoppers; there is a fairly large family of these sap-sucking insects, but happily they do little damage, mainly concerning themselves with the leaves of cucumbers and tomatoes. Remove any leaves that have the tiny white spots which are the eggs and nymphs. Spraying with soapy water is an effective control.

Leaf Miners These are pests of chrysanthemums, tomatoes and cinerarias, and there is no mistaking their presence. The leaves have white winding lines in the tissue which are the tunnels made by the small grubs. Badly affected leaves should be removed and destroyed, others can be squeezed between finger and thumb to kill the grub.

Mealy Bugs These sap-sucking insects are sometimes confused with aphids because they are about the same size and cluster in the same way on stems and on the underside of leaves. Look at them under a magnifying glass, though, and you will see they are white and covered with a powdery fluff. They will attack most greenhouse and indoor plants, and because of that protective coating can be tricky to control. Small infestations can be wiped off with a cotton bud dipped in methylated spirit or liquid derris. Larger colonies can be dealt with by a predacious ladybird beetle called *Cryptolaemus montrouzieri*, a native of Australia, but it is only successful at temperatures above about 18°C (65°F).

Red Spider Mite Hot, dry conditions in the greenhouse or conservatory encourage this tiny, sap-sucking pest. It infests the undersides of the leaves of a wide range of plants, turning them yellow and mottled; there may also be a mass of white webbing. Regular spraying with water to keep the atmosphere humid in hot, dry weather is the best preventive. Minor infestations can be controlled by spraying with liquid derris; major ones are controlled with the predator mite known as *Phytoseiulus persimilis.*

Scale Insects These immobile, hard-shelled insects are like tiny tortoises, and attach themselves to the stems of pot plants and the veins of the leaves and suck the sap. Their shells protect them from spray, but they can be wiped off with a cotton bud dipped in methylated spirit.

Sciarid Flies These tiny flies lay their eggs in the surface of peat-based composts; the eggs hatch into white grubs which then feed on the roots of seedling plants and eat their way into the stalks and caps of mushrooms. Cuttings of chrysanthemums, carnations and geraniums are particularly suceptible to attack, along with young cucumber, sweet pea and freesia plants. However, don't confuse the grubs with the far more damaging vine weevils. Control sciarid fly grubs by removing the compost and replacing with fresh; also, avoid over-and-under-watering plants in peat-based composts.

Slugs Good housekeeping will stop slugs and snails finding a hiding place in the greenhouse and conservatory. Trails of slime and partly eaten leaves will indicate their presence, so seek them out early in the morning or at dusk. Protect plants in border soil or growing bags with special anti-slug tape.

Springtails Tiny jumping insects that haunt soil-less compost where they feed on fungal spores and decaying tissue. They do little or no harm to living plants, so control is unnecessary.

Thrips The adults are commonly called thunder flies, and can fly and jump from plant to plant; there are some 150 species of them in Europe. Both adults and the sedentary larvae feed on plant tissue through mouths like hypodermic needles; this results in silvery discoloration of the leaves, and badly infected plants should be destroyed. Mild infestations can be controlled by spraying with derris.

Vine Weevils The fat white maggots of the vine weevil live in the compost of pot plants and feed on the roots, causing the plants to wilt and die. Cyclamen and tuberous begonias may also be attacked. Keep a watch out for the grubs when re-potting plants: make up a container of liquid derris solution and dunk the entire pot in it; alternatively tease out the compost, grubs and all, into a bucket, wash the roots of the plant and re-pot using fresh compost. Grubs in the old compost can be removed and dealt with. Badly affected plants must be

THRIPS TRAP

A glue trap for thrips in commercial glasshouses has been developed by the biological control company Koppert. It is a glue which is sprayed on to polythene sheeting spread on the floor of the glasshouse. It traps thrips falling to the ground to pupate.

GLUE TRAP FOR WEEVILS

One way of preventing vine weevils damaging pot plants in the greenhouse is to stop them reaching the plants. This is easier said than done, but quite an effective method is to use a sticky barrier of special glue around the legs and around the top edges of the benches and staging. The glue can be applied to strips of sticky tape so that it can be removed readily. Individual pots could also be treated. To help prevent the weevils getting into the greenhouse, the entire base could be treated with a band of glue, particularly across the door.

destroyed and the old compost should not be re-used.

Whitefly A major, common pest of greenhouses and conservatories,. Both the non-flying larvae and the winged adults suck the sap of a wide range of plants, depositing a sticky honeydew on leaves and fruit; this in turn attracts a sooty mould. Sticky yellow cards will help to control the adults, as will a gentle sweep with a vacuum cleaner, having first tapped the foliage of the infested plants to get the whiteflies airborne. However, don't use either of these methods if the biological control *Encarsia formosa* has been introduced, because this tiny wasp is a parasite and lays its eggs in the developing whitefly scales. When the wasp eggs hatch into grubs they eat the young whitefly and the scale turns from white to black. The *Encarsia* are supplied as ready-to-hatch pupae on strips of leaves which should be hung among the greenhouse plants. *Encarsia* will not usually eliminate all whitefly, but will hold down the population at a low level and so avoid the sooty mould problem. Marigolds planted alongside greenhouse crops are said to deter whitefly and other pests, although tests have found that planting French and African marigolds alongside aubergines, peppers and tomatoes in fact had little deterrent effect on whitefly. However, there is scientific evidence that substances released by marigold roots kill nematodes (eelworms) and their cysts, so growing marigolds in greenhouse borders might be advantageous.

Woodlice Not a major pest, but nibbled leaves of young plants are a sign of attack. The best control is a clean, tidy greenhouse.

POINTS ABOUT PREDATORS

Yellow flying insect traps attract and kill whiteflies, leaf miner flies and midges. For best results they are hung just above the plants and are very effective in controlling relatively mild infestations. However, don't use the traps when other flying insects are being used as biological controls, for example the parasitic wasp *Encarsia formosa* for whitefly control, or *Cryptolaemus* for mealy bug control.

Remember that biological control is not instant and will only work if the pest is already in the greenhouse. It may take three or four weeks for the predators to hatch and establish themselves, and during this period the greenhouse needs a daytime temperature of 18°C (65°F) or more. Note the advice offered by one of the firms marketing biological controls, which is still relevant: 'Once introduced to suitable conditions the natural predators and parasites multiply at the expense of the pests to keep them at a low level. If they eliminate the pests completely, they will either disperse in search of more pests outside or will die of starvation. There is no need to worry about them dispersing. As they are attracted to the scent of their prey, you do not need to keep the greenhouse closed while using them.'

PEST MONITOR

It is possible to monitor the presence of some insect pests in the greenhouse with a simple-to-make trap. Use a plastic dish about 20cm (8in) in diameter and 5cm (2in) deep; paint the inside yellow, let it dry thoroughly, then fill it with soapy water. Just as with yellow sticky traps, small flying insects are attracted by the colour and fall in the water. As well as indicating what sort of pests are about, when used with sticky traps the water traps will help to keep numbers under control.

HELP FOR PREDATORS

You can improve the effectiveness of the whitefly predator *Encarsia formosa* in the greenhouse by putting a fine mesh net over the ventilation openings. This reduces very considerably the number of adult whitefly entering the greenhouse but should have no effect on temperature or humidity.

A TO Z OF DISEASE CONTROL

Growing tomatoes and cucumbers in growing bags instead of the border soil in greenhouses has very much reduced the incidence of soil-born diseases such as stem rot and wilts. If you prefer not to use proprietary growing bags, it is quite possible to make your own (p31) using a peat-free compost (p30) or to adopt an alternating cropping programme, for example alternating the tomato crop with cucumbers; the idea is that the risk of soil diseases is minimised by not growing the same crop for more than two years.

Even so, the soil will need sterilising or replacing every two years, and neither is an easy option. It may be best, in fact to regard the soil in the average-size garden greenhouse as unsuitable for raising crops.

In the warm days of late spring and summer, adequate ventilation of the house is a vital factor in successful greenhouse gardening, although it needs to be coupled with a fairly high level of humidity. In the short, cool or cold days of late autumn and winter, open the ventilators whenever possible and keep the humidity low. The phrase 'buoyant atmosphere' is often used to describe the ideal for greenhouses: what it means is, avoid stagnant air, whether hot or cold.

When watering, try to avoid splashing the plants as this can spread ill-health from one plant to its neighbour, and mop up puddles to prevent botrytis and downy mildew.

In recent years hybridists have been successful in breeding disease-resistant varieties of flowers, soft fruit and vegetables, and this work is continuing apace as it offers a sound viable alternative to chemical controls for both commercial and amateur growers. Other things being equal, such as flavour, yield and vigour, choose the disease-resistant variety for preference.

Blackleg A fairly common fungal disease of geranium and pelargonium cuttings. The stem, where it is in contact with the surface of the compost, turns black and quickly rots. Overwatering is believed to be the main cause. Infected plants should be destroyed.

Blossom end rot A disease of tomatoes in which a dark brown corky patch appears on the base of the developing fruit, especially on plants in growing bags. The cause is uneven watering, so always try to keep the growing medium moist but never waterlogged.

Botrytis The dreaded grey mould which appears as a fluffy grey or brown growth on the leaves and stems of soft-leaved plants, particularly during spells of cool, humid weather. Carefully remove all affected leaves, stems and flowers, reduce watering, and try to increase air movement.

Crown, stem or basal rot This affects pot plants as a rotting away of the crown of the plant and is due to overwatering in the cold conditions of winter and early spring. Destroy the affected plant. Stem rot of tomato plants grown in the border soil appears as brown cankers on the stem at soil level. The plant wilts and may collapse. Destroy the affected plant, and sterilise or replace the soil at the end of the season. Better still, avoid growing tomatoes in the border.

Damping off Harmful fungi attack the stems and roots of seedlings causing rot at the surface level of the soil or compost. The baby plants keel over and die. There is no cure, so preventive measures are necessary. Sow seeds thinly; water the growing medium with a permitted copper fungicide; never overwater; and keep the greenhouse temperature within the recommended levels for the flower or vegetable crops you are raising.

Mildew, downy White, downy tufts appear on the underside of the leaves of seedlings, lettuce plants and cinerarias in particular. Remove affected leaves and spray the plants with a solution of bicarbonate of soda (two teaspoonfuls in a litre of water). Sow the seed thinly and improve ventilation as preventive methods.

Mildew, powdery This is quite distinct from downy mildew, although it is sometimes confused with botrytis. However, the white covering on leaves and stems of the plants is a powdery coating rather than a greyish growth. Remove badly affected leaves and spray the plants with the bicarbonate of soda solution (see above), or dust badly affected plants with sulphur. All moulds and mildews are worst in badly ventilated structures.

Rust Sometimes affects carnations, chrysanthemums, fuchsias, lettuces and pelargoniums, appearing as small, raised spots on the underside of the leaves.

The spots range in colour from orange to dark brown. Remove infected leaves and destroy them.

Sooty mould This is a fungus which grows on honeydew, the sticky excretions of many sap-sucking insects, so treat the cause before dealing with the symptom; spray with soapy water or wipe with a damp cloth.

Verticillium A wilt organism that lives in the soil and can survive for many years. It used to be the bane of the tomato grower's life before growing bags appeared. Symptoms are a wilting of the leaves with the lower ones turning yellow prematurely, and the stems, when cut, showing brown streaks. Planting too early into the cold border soil can trigger the organism into life, and raising the greenhouse temperature is a helpful check to its development. Wilt-resistant varieties are available, otherwise graft on to resistant rootstocks (p115).

Viruses Virus infections are spread by insect pests; by handling infected plants and then healthy ones; and by grafting from diseased plants to healthy ones. Luckily, virus-free plants are becoming more readily available, because once infected there is no cure. Symptoms of virus infection vary considerably and can be confused in the early stages with mineral deficiencies (p117). Growth may be stunted or distorted and yellow blotches may appear on the leaves.

DECORATIVE PLANTS

Whether your love of plants is broadly based or crystallises in a passion for carnations, chrysanthemums or one of the other hobby species, the addition of a greenhouse or conservatory to the garden will widen your repertoire. This doesn't mean that as soon as your acquisition is in place there has to be an expense-laden trip to nursery or garden centre. On the contrary, much of the pleasure from your undercover gardening will undoubtedly come from raising your own stock of plants. In this section are described some of the choices the newcomer can make, plus a reminder to those already in thrall of just how versatile this branch of gardening can be.

YEAR-ROUND COLOUR AND INTEREST

Although year-round colour is something most of us seek for our indoor garden, the beauty of foliage and form should not be overshadowed by too much colour – ferns offer a prime example of this.

A conservatory with plants for year-round interest will rely heavily on containers and on planting schemes that take full advantage of the sheltered environment. This means concentrating the winter arrangements on attractively coloured foliage, with highlighted colour coming from berries. Foliage beauties such as codiaeum, abelia, ivy, *Thuja orientalis*, *Choisya ternata* and *Peperomia sandersii* will be accompanied by the winter cherry, *Solanum capsicastrum*, the massed berries of *Skimmia japonica* and, perhaps, the silver leaves of *Senecio maritima*.

Then follow the beautiful colours of early spring, when the scents as well as the sight of massed flowering bulbs fill the indoor garden with the glowing colours and particular fragrances that epitomise spring.

A very effective technique is to plant up pots of bulbs, one variety to a pot – hyacinths, double narcissi and double tulips. When they have come into flower, group them in large containers with auriculas and polyanthus. By careful choice of varieties, the colours of the flowering bulbs can be harmonised with those of the flowering plants.

African violets are unlikely to give of their best in a conservatory that is heated only spasmodically, but a frost-free night time interior and gentle daytime warmth will prove very acceptable to the flamboyant early spring pots of cyclamen, hybrid azaleas, cineraria, *Ranunculus asiaticus* and the elegant crown imperial.

Roses as cut flowers all the year round are possible in a heated greenhouse but scarcely practicable for the amateur. However, it is quite possible to have roses in flower in early spring if a young polyantha or floribunda bush is potted up into a 20cm (8in) pot of ordinary garden soil in early autumn and placed in the greenhouse or conservatory. Prune it in mid-winter and it will come into bloom alongside other spring flowering subjects, such as acacia, the majestic hippeastrum, *Primula kewensis* and *P. malacoides*. After flowering, replant the rose in the garden.

Impatiens that were saved from the summer bedding schemes and potted up can be persuaded by the warmth of spring days under glass that summer is close at hand, and will respond with early flowers, while the Christmas cactus may still be in flower at this time. Also bring in from the spring garden flowering stems of *Berberis darwinii*, forsythia, *Camellia japonica* and *Chaenomeles japonica* to place in vases among the conservatory foliage plants.

Late spring sees the start of the long flowering season of geraniums and regal pelargoniums. Other houseplants in flower could include aphelandra, chloryphytum, African violets, *Saxifraga stolonifera*, *Spathiphyllum wallisii* and schizanthus. From now until the autumn there need be no shortage of colourful interest in the conservatory and ornamental greenhouse, with the rather strident attractions of begonias, gloxinias and streptocarpus offering vivid contrast to the quieter charm of fuchsias in various forms.

As an alternative to pots of chrysanthemums you could try pot dahlias, grown from seed sown in the spring. Choose a dwarfing variety, such as Figaro or Bambino, and pot up several into a large floor-standing container, which should be placed in a cool but well-lit position. When flowering has finished, consign the plant to the compost bin and start again in spring.

Hanging baskets can concentrate on subjects that revel in the light but sheltered conditions under glass. Try, for example, baskets filled with single species and single colours of petunia, nasturtium, verbena or the cascading shell-like flowers of diascias. Don't forget also that the exotic foliage of *Begonia rex* provides a dramatic statement when given a solo position. Not all summer-flowering plants crave the sunlight, however, so choose the shaded parts of the conservatory for tuberous begonias, *Nicotiana alata* and impatiens.

Autumn under glass will see several of the summer showpieces still in flower and they can be joined by *Campanula capensis* and, perhaps, a few pots of late-flowering chrysanthemums.

In the following pages you will find detailed advice on how to gain maximum enjoyment from the many decorative and beautiful plants that can be given a home in your organic conservatory or greenhouse.

A TO Z OF FLOWERS TO SOW FOR PLANTING OUT

HA: Hardy annual
HB: Hardy biennial
HP: Hardy perennial
HHA: Half-hardy annual
HHB: Half-hardy biennial
HHP: Half-hardy perennial

The greenhouse can be used to excellent effect for sowing the seeds of plants that are frost-tender – the large group of half-hardy annuals, and the half-hardy perennials that are treated as HHA: not only will you save money compared with the cost of buying from a nursery, this is also a chance to increase your gardening skills and pleasure.

African Marigold HHA
Magnificent bedding plants in rich yellow, orange and gold shades for an open sunny position. Can also be potted up for summer flowering in the greenhouse or conservatory. Both African and French marigolds are valuable in the organic garden because they attract hoverflies whose larvae devour greenfly.
Recommended varieties: Crackerjack Mixed, Galore F1, Giant Fluffy, Inca F1, Moonbeam, Orange Jubilee, Rhapsody Series, Sierra, Toreador F1. Afro-French varieties include Caribbean Parade F1, Seven Star Red and Solar Series F1 triploids.

Ageratum (Floss Flower) HHA
Summer-flowering carpet subject for front of the borders in tones of blue, pink and white. Prefers full sun, but can also be potted up for the conservatory or sunny windowsill.
Recommended varieties: Adriatic F1 (mid-blue), Bengali F1 (lilac pink), Blue Danube F1 (lavender), Blue Mink (bright blue), Blue Ribbon F1 (mid-blue), North Sea F1 (purple-blue), Seven Seas F1 (mixed blues and pink), Southern Cross (two-tone blue).

Alonsoa (Mask Flower) HHA
Scarlet, crimson, pink and white flowers all summer, suitable for bedding, borders and cutting.

Alyssum HA/HP
Popular dwarf bedding plant in white, pink and lilac for edging. Can also be grown in the cracks of paving and on a rockery.
Recommended varieties: Carpet of Snow, Little Dorrit, Magic Circle, Rosie O'Day, Royal Carpet, Sweet White, Wonderland Series.

Amaranthus (Love Lies Bleeding) HHA
Long-lasting plant with attractive foliage and exotic 45cm (18in) long tassels of blood-red velvety blooms. Ideal as the centrepiece of a formal sunny border or island site, growing to about 90cm (36in) tall. Can also be used as a summer houseplant.

Ammobium alatum graduator (Winged Everlasting Flower) HHA
Silvery-white petals and yellow centres make this an attractive everlasting subject. Cut just after the flowers open and hang upside down in bunches in a cool, dry place until brittle dry.

Antirrhinum (Snapdragon) HHA
Wide colour range. Depending on variety, for use as bedding, edging to borders or patio plants.
Recommended varieties: *Tall*, 60–90cm (24–36in): Bright Butterflies Improved F1, Double Supreme F1, Giant Forerunner F1, Ruffled Super Tetra, Scarlet, Wedding Bells F1. *Medium*, 30–45cm (12–18in): Cheerio F2, Coral Monarch, Crimson Monarch, Coronet F1, Coronette Orchid, Jewelled Sceptre F1, Madame Butterfly F1, Monarch Mixed, Princess Mixed F1, Rust Resistant Mixed, Vanity Fair. *Dwarf*, 15–30cm (6–12in): Floral Carpet F1, Kim F1,

Little Darling F1, Magic Carpet, Royal Carpet F1, Sweetheart F1, Tom Thumb Mixed, Trumpet Serenade.

Arctotis (African Daisy) HHA
Brilliant colours and daisy-like form make this a showy bedder and a popular cut flower.

Aster (See **Callistephus**)

Basil HHA
Not the herb, but the foliage plant *Labiatae ocimum* with very large, shiny, deep purple leaves, often used for contrast in a bedding display.

Begonia, bedding or fibrous-rooted HHP/HHA
A very versatile summer-flowering plant that can be used for bedding, edging, hanging baskets and window-boxes, even as summer houseplants, but does best in humus-rich soil in partial shade.
Recommended varieties: *B. semperflorens* is available in a wide range of both F1 and open-pollinated varieties, with flower colours in shades of red, pink, white and bi-colours. Foliage colours range from brilliant green to shiny bronze. Organdy has red, white and pink flowers with green leaves; Coco, bronze leaves and mixed coloured flowers; Lucia F1, Red and White Picotee F1 and Party Fun F1 are particularly good hybrids.

Begonia, tuberous HHP/HHA
Normally bought as tubers for starting into growth in early to mid-spring at 18°C(64°F), but can be grown from seed using the same technique as for *B. semperflorens*. Tuberous begonias can also be propagated by taking stem cuttings or by division of the tubers (as with dahlias) when young growth appears in mid-spring. Take the cuttings with a heel of the parent tuber

A mass of brilliant colour in the border from plants raised in the greenhouse.

attached and place them in a fifty-fifty mixture of peat (or peat substitute) and sand in a propagator at 18–21°C (64–70°F). They root quite readily and can then be moved on to 8cm (3in) pots.

Raising these beautiful showy greenhouse, bedding, window-box and house-plants from seed is inexpensive compared with buying the tubers, and there is a wide choice of varieties with double and semi-double flowers. Particularly recommended for bedding are the camellia-flowered F1 Pavilion, the non-stop flowering Clips F1, and Pendula Chanson F1, specially bred for use in containers.

Brachycome (Swan River Daisy) HHA
This small, charming, sweet-scented Australian plant is excellent for bedding, window-boxes and hanging baskets. It is a profuse and long-flowering subject that deserves to be more popular.

Busy Lizzie (see **Impatiens**)

Calceolaria (Slipper Flower) HHA
Once a very popular bedding plant, but now mostly used as a winter-flowering pot plant. There has been a moderately successful attempt to re-introduce the bedding version, with a good range of varieties including a dwarf perennial named Goldcrest. Watch out for aphids which are especially attracted to calceolaria: spray repeatedly with soapy water.

Callistephus (China Aster) HHA
This annual aster, with flowers like the big daisy *Bellis perennis*, will give rich, even gaudy colour to the late summer and autumn garden. There are five groups of this big family: single, ball, ostrich plume, chrysanthemum and pompon; and the heights range from

tall at 51–76cm (20–30in), medium at 30–45cm (12–18in), dwarf at 15–30cm (6–12in). The flowering period for all of them is from late summer through to the first frost.

Space the plants according to their height, and for best results give a good mulch of compost or peat, or peat substitute. To avoid the risk of disease, never grow these plants in the same position year after year, and to ensure continuity of bloom, deadhead the plants throughout the flowering period. Recommended varieties: *Dwarf:* Contraster Mixed, fully double, early flowering and selected for resistance to aster wilt; Pinocchio Mixed, a wide range of colours in weather-resistant blooms over a long flowering period; Pixie Princess Mixed and Pot 'n Patio Mixed are good selections for flowering in the conservatory or on a sunny windowsill. *Medium:* Gusford Supreme and Belstead Supreme have contrasting white centres; Early Ostrich Plume

Finest Mixed has large, double feathery recurving petals on long stems, making it a good one for cutting. *Tall:* often grown solely for cutting, these are elegant flowers in a bewildering range of flower forms and colours. Pompon Mixed and Powder Puff Mixed are mid-season varieties, while Californian Giants are late. Famil Silvery Blue and Operetta Mixed are two newish introductions well worth your attention.

Canna HHP
A most attractive border plant from sub-tropical America and the West Indies which,can also be used to grace the greenhouse or conservatory. Broad glossy leaves and brightly coloured flowers are carrried on stems up to 2m (6ft) tall, although there is a 45cm (18in) variety called Seven Dwarfs.

Celosia HHA
Coming from tropical Asia, these plants produce large, vividly coloured plumed or crested flower-heads that are aristocratic subjects for a sheltered sunny border but are miserable in wet, cool conditions. They can also be grown as pot plants and as cut flowers. Outside they require a humus-rich, well-fed, well-drained soil. For growing in pots, choose a small strain such as Lilliput or Dwarf Fairy Fountains, and a peat-based or peat substitute compost preferably enriched with organic fertiliser or worm-worked compost.

Cleome (Spider Flower) HHA
A good choice for those wanting to attract bees to the garden. It has spiralling scented sprays of delicate flowers in shades of rose and lilac, and the plants – which grow to 1m (3.28ft) tall – should be given a position in full sun. Alternatively, they can be grown in 15cm (6in) pots for flowering in the greenhouse or conservatory.
Recommended varieties: Helen Campbell, Cherry Queen, True Rose Queen, Colour Fountain Mixed.

Cobaea scandens (Cathedral Bells, Cup and Saucer Plant) HHP/HHA
A handsome climber with large deep blue flowers that give the plant its common names; these appear in early summer, and it continues flowering until late autumn. It is a vigorous grower, spreading up to 6m (20ft) in a season. It grows vertically first, then spreads fan-shaped. Although grown mostly as a half-hardy annual, it makes a most attractive half-hardy perennial for the large greenhouse or conservatory, or plant it out to cover a pergola, south-facing fence or wall. There is a white form called *C. scandens alba.*

Cosmos HHA
Showy single dahlia-like flowers in radiant colours over a long flowering period make this a great subject for the border and for cutting, while there are dwarf varieties that are excellent in pots or other containers for oudoor or indoor display.
Recommended varieties: Candy Stripe, Gloria, Purity, Sea Shells (this one has fluted petals), Sensation Mixed. For dwarf plants, choose Sunny Gold or Sunny Red.

The colours of cosmos range from palest pink to a radiant carmine.

Dahlias HHP/HHA

Bedding dahlias are grown as annuals from seed, as distinct from border dahlias which are grown from tubers that are lifted and stored over the winter or from cuttings taken from the new growth in spring. Seed is sown in late winter to early spring at a temperature of 18–21°C (65–70°F) using a peat-, or peat substitute-based seed compost, when germination takes about 15–20 days. The seedlings should be pricked off into trays, then into 8cm (3in) pots, and hardened off in mid-spring for planting out after all danger of frost has passed. Planting distances vary according to the height of the variety. Tall kinds, such as Giant Hybrids Mixed and Octopus Series which grow up to 1.5m (5ft) tall, will need 45cm(18in) each way, while the more dwarf varieties such as Bambino Mixed, Coltness Mixed, and the F1 Sunny Series which only grow up to about 37cm (15in) tall, can be set 30cm apart each way.

Dianthus HHA/HB/HP

This covers the big family of carnations, pinks and Sweet William, a mixture of half-hardy annuals, biennials and hardy perennials treated as HHA. It is a very old family, prized over many hundreds of years for the beauty of its flowers and the strength of its scent. The old-fashioned pinks are border and rockery plants which flower in early summer and have a life of four or five years. The modern pinks are hybrids produced from crossing an old fashioned pink with a perpetual-flowering carnation, resulting in *D. x allwoodii*, and it isn't easy to spot the difference between the offspring and the carnation parent. The three species of dianthus usually grown from seed are *D. barbatus* (Sweet William), a hardy biennial; *D. chinensis*, the Indian or annual pink; and *D caryophyllus*, the gilly-flower of Elizabethan times, or annual carnation.
Recommended varieties: *D. barbatus*: Dwarf Double Mixed, Indian Carpet Mixed, Roundabout Mixed, Summer Beauty Mixed. *D. chinensis*: Fire Carpet F1, Princess F1, Snowfire F1, Telstar F1. *D. caryophyllus*: Bambino Mixed, Giant Chabaud Mixed, Knight Series F1.

Eccremocarpus (The Chilean Glory Flower) HHA/HP

A perennnial self-clinging climber that is frost-tender except in the mildest districts. Ralph Gould, the distinguished British hybridiser, has brought this attractive plant into prominence with his Anglia hybrids, which have pink, scarlet, yellow and orange nodding tubular blooms that appear freely from early summer to mid-autumn.

Eustoma (Lisianthus, The Prairie Gentian) HHA/HHB

A cultivated version of a native flower of Texas and Nebraska, available either in its original form of *E. grandiflorum* or as F1 hybrids. These make remarkably good cut flowers, staying fresh in water for up to thirty days.

Gaillardia pulchella (Blanket Flower) HHA

The annual gaillardia, with its yellow and red daisy-like flowers, makes a good border plant and is excellent for cutting. Given a well-drained, sunny position, it will flower from early summer to early autumn. Double Mixed grows to about 60cm (24in) tall, while Lollipops is a dwarf version at about 30cm (12in).

Gazania HHA

These showy, daisy-like flowers that love the sun are perennials, but frost-tender, so except in the mildest of areas are best treated as HHA. The plants are low-growing for good ground cover in the border or rockery; they do particularly well in seaside gardens.
Recommended varieties: Harlequin Hybrids, Mini-Star Mixed, Silver Leaf Carnival F1, Sundance F1.

Geranium HHP/HHA

Geraniums are a wonderfully diverse and versatile family. For a mass of long-lasting summer colour, nothing can match trailing geraniums in hanging baskets, window boxes, tubs and pots. The new F1 hybrids combine attractively zoned, variegated or scal-loped leaves with a wide-ranging palette of colours in single, semi-double and fully-double flowers, while there is a fascinating group of geraniums grown for their scented leaves (see panel).
Recommended varieties: New F1 hybrids appear in the seed catalogues every year and there have been some introductions which at the time were quite startling; for example, Thompson & Morgan's L'Amour series, also their Speckles and Startel series, the British-bred Breakaway series and the richly ranging colours of the Sundance hybrids. All of them are free-flowering and suitable for bedding or as pot plants for porches, windowsills and conservatories. Balcony geraniums are the traditional Continental balcony trailing sorts, while for a genuinely pendulous ivy-leaf geranium look for the F1 Summer Showers. Among the non-F1 varieties there are some good reds in Glacier Crimson, Stadt Bern and Irene, and good pinks in Ivalo and Mrs Parker.

Helichrysum HHA

Known as straw or 'everlasting' this makes a beautiful cut flower and is one of the most popular subjects for drying for winter flower arrangements.
Recommended varieties: Monstrosum Bright Bikini, Hot Bikini, T & M Double Mixed, Golden Star.

Heliotropium (Cherry Pie) HHA

The Victorian gardeners appreciated this plant much more than we do. It is a handsome plant with fragrant royal purple flower heads and deep green foliage, and although it does best in full sun, it is not at all fussy about soil conditions. *H. peruvianum* Marine is the royal purple hybrid, growing about 45cm (18in) tall; Lord Roberts is dark blue; and the white-flowered variety is White Lady.

Hibiscus HA, but treated as HHA

H. trionum from Africa is the 'Flower of an Hour'; the beautiful blooms open for only an hour or so in the morning, but they are produced continuously throughout late summer to early autumn.

SCENTED GERANIUMS

One of the best gardening gifts to come my way was a collection of scented-leaved geraniums. There were half a dozen different sorts in the collection and they opened a window on to a new and intriguing aspect of this astonishing pelargonium family. There are, in fact, dozens of varieties smelling of different fruits, flowers or herbs, making them attractive and functional residents of the conservatory or greenhouse. The scent is released by gently rubbing the leaves, and they can be dried and used in pot-pourri.

The plants are also very easy to grow, only requiring dry, frost-free accommodation for the winter; in summer they can be taken outside with other indoor plants that are grateful for a holiday outdoors. Seed can be bought from specialist firms, and young plants from nurseries specialising in the pelargonium family.

Once your stock plants are established, cuttings can be taken in late summer, just as with zonal geraniums. When the cuttings have rooted, pot on into 8cm (3in) pots of loam-based potting compost. Most of the varieties are happy enough when mature in pots no larger than 13cm (5in), and the size of the more vigorous ones can be controlled by trimming back the roots and then putting them back in the same size pots filled with fresh compost; or cut back the growth quite harshly, allow new shoots to develop, then pinch out the growing points to encourage bushiness.

Like others in the family, scented-leaved geraniums should be given a well-diluted liquid feed every third week. In winter the plants should be kept very dry unless they are in a warm environment. Even then, the water given should be less than generous.

Here are some of the varieties fairly readily available:
Rose-scented: *Pelargonium* Attar of Roses; *P. graveolens.*
Lemon-scented: *P. crispum* Minor; *P. crispum* Major; *P.* Mabel Grey.
Orange-scented: *P.* Prince of Orange.
Peppermint-scented: *P. tomentosum.*
Cedarwood-scented: *P.* Clorinda.

Iberis (Candytuft) HA, but treated as HHA
This lovely old flower is the most tolerant of annuals, and will do well in virtually any soil, and in any site; what a charmer it is, grouped in borders or in dwarf form, as an edging to pathways or in the rockery.
Recommended varieties: Dwarf Fairy, 23cm (9in) tall; Giant Hyacinth, 30–38cm (12–15in); Flash Mixed 30cm (12in).

Impatiens (Busy Lizzie) HHP/HHA
Once just a deservedly popular houseplant, the Busy Lizzie has become one of the most widely used of bedding plants, thanks to the work of hybridists. There is now a well-stocked palette of colours available in brilliant tones, silky pastels and bi-colours, so that extremely effective massed bedding schemes can be carried out, to give colour throughout the summer in sun or shade, wet weather or drought. Furthermore, this versatile plant will settle happily into window-boxes, hanging baskets, tubs or troughs, and indoors it will often flower the whole year round; so it's worth lifting a few plants from the outdoor display to use as flowering houseplants.

Although the modern F1 hybrids are tolerant of most soil conditions, they will respond with extra vigour if the site is enriched with generous amounts of organic matter, dug in over the winter, followed by a dressing of fish, blood and bone or seaweed meal in early spring. When selecting seed from the wide range available today, pay particular attention to the height of the varieties: some are dwarf at only 10–15cm (4–6in), others such as the Camellia Flowered will grow to 60cm (24in).

New varieties appear in the seedsmen's lists every year, usually as F1 series; notable among these are the Accent, Blitz, Super Elfin and Imp series, each with individual named colours or offered as mixtures. Also available are the balsam versions, double F1 hybrids, and open-pollinated hybrids. *I. balfourii* and *I. glandulifera* species are hardy annuals.

Ipomoea (Morning Glory) HHA
An annual climber that surely rivals the clematis in the beauty of its trumpet-shaped flowers and heart-shaped leaves. Unfortunately the flowers only last for a day, although they will be produced continuously throughout the summer. Some varieties are non-climbing and make excellent pot plants for the cool greenhouse, conservatory or patio.

Some varieties grow as tall as 3m (10ft) in a few weeks, while the non-climbing types only make about 30cm (12in). Recommended are Flying Saucers, blue-and-white striped blooms; Scarlet O'Hara, brilliant red flowers; Imperial Japanese varieties; and probably the most popular, Heavenly Blue.

Kochia scoparia (Burning Bush) HHA
K. scoparia is grown for its foliage, which starts as pale green and becomes a dense bush of deep red. It makes an attractive pot plant for the conservatory, but is probably seen to best advantage either en masse as a low-growing summer hedge, or as a solo item in a bedding scheme. For indoor use choose the variety *K. childsii* and grow it in a 13cm (5in) pot. The larger variety is *K. trichophylla*, which makes a plant of 60–90cm (24–36in) tall.

Here are four very popular bedding plants to raise from seed. (Left) gazania; (bottom left) impatiens; (above) ipomeoa; (opposite) lobelia.

SPEEDIER GERMINATION

Some seeds, such as sweet pea, geranium and ipomoea, have hard coats that prevent a ready take-up of moisture. To remedy this, large seed can be nicked with a sharp knife or rubbed with a nail file or sandpaper. Small, hard seed can be held with tweezers and pricked once with a needle. Some seed firms sell hard seeds already treated in this way, so it is worth checking it first, using a magnifying glass. This sort of pre-sowing treatment isn't vital: if it isn't done, germination may simply take longer. Spraying the surface of the compost with liquid copper fungicide is a preventive against damping off and is organically acceptable.

Limonium (Statice) HHA

This is a popular everlasting flower now available in the Fortress strain in a blend of unusual colours including salmon and pink, orange and yellow, pink and carmine, and self-coloured yellows and blues.

Lobelia HHA

A favourite plant for hanging baskets, for the front of the border and the edging of paths and patios, that responds especially well to organic cultivation – it gives the best account of itself in a rich organic soil with an occasional liquid feed of seaweed extract. There is now a wide choice of colours and types, ranging from the classic deep blue white-eyed Mrs Clibran Improved for edging, to the white, carmine, scarlet and purple varieties such as the Cascade series that are particularly successful in hanging baskets. Most sorts, treated well, will flower from early summer to early autumn.

Marigolds HHA

Tagetes, African marigold or French marigold are wrongly named because these extremely popular yellow, orange and bi-coloured plants originally all came from Mexico. Now there are any number of F1 hybrids in giant-flowered double form that bear little resemblance to the original stock. Marigolds are much used by organic gardeners because they work hard for us as companion plants – plant them near roses and the other flowers or crops that are likely targets for aphids and you will benefit from the fact that hoverflies love marigolds and their larvae will eat the aphids in great numbers.

Marigolds fall into three groups: the African, *T. erecta*, are the tallest largest-flowered types; the French *T. patula* are shorter and with carnation-sized blooms; while *T. signata* are dwarf plants with single blooms, but masses of them.

Recommended varieties: African, Inca F1, Galore F1 and Toreador F1 and the open-pollinated Rhapsody series; Afro-French, Solar F1 triploid series; French, Bonita, Boy O'Boy, Holiday Crested, Queen series (all doubles) and for singles the Belle F1 triploids; *T. signata*, Golden Gem, Paprika, Starfire.

Matricaria (Feverfew) HP/HA, treated as HHA

Feverfew, also known as *Chrysanthemum parthenium*, makes an unusual subject for the summer bedding scheme with its small ball-like flowers of white or gold, and its aromatic foliage. Santana Lemon grows only to about 13cm (5in) tall, Tom Thumb White Stars to about 24cm (9in) and Golden Ball to 30cm (12in).

Meconopsis HP, can be treated as HHA

These are the strikingly beautiful blue poppies, although some species have pink, purple and yellow blooms, while Frances Perry, introduced in 1988, is a scarlet form of the Welsh poppy.

Mesembryanthemum (Livingstone Daisy) HHA

A tongue-twisting name for a low-growing spreading plant; it has pale green and purple leaves which glisten as though with dew, and star-shaped flowers that open only in sunlight. Give it a position in full sun and hungry soil and it will flower all summer.

Mimulus (Monkey Flower) HP

A rather short-lived perennial that likes a rich organic soil and some shade, while *M. nanus* is best grown as a conservatory or greenhouse pot plant.

Moluccella (Bells of Ireland) HHA

The deep green, bell-shaped flowers are very decorative when dried and used as part of a winter indoor decoration.

Nemesia HHA

An easy-to-grow, handsome bedding plant that is also a favourite for

SOAKING AND CHILLING

As well as chipping seed to aid germination, other pre-sowing treatments are sometimes necessary. For example, soaking hard-coated seeds is recommended for leaching out any natural chemical inhibitors. Some seeds, such as cytisus and clianthus, absorb water readily, swell up and should be sown immediately after soaking. When pre-chilling of seed is recommended by the supplier a good technique is to sow the seed on moist compost, seal it in a polythene bag and leave it for three days at room temperature 15–18°C (60–65°F). Then place it in the refrigerator for the recommended pre-chilling period. The seed should then be sown with just a light covering of compost.

TRY SOMETHING DIFFERENT

When you grow plants from seed or cuttings to fill your hanging baskets and other containers, you can experiment freely with interesting combinations of foliage and colour. Seed firms offer a far wider selection of species and varieties than bedding plant nurseries. Consider, for instance, combining the striking foliage of variegated nasturtium and coleus with the showy flowers of tuberous begonias in orange and red. Or choose the more muted effect of silver-leaved plants, such as senecio, with the feathery fragrant blooms of schizopetalon. You can enjoy container gardening all year long with winter-hardy plants like the Universal pansies and primulas.

window-boxes and patio containers. Funfair, Fire King and Tapestry are good varieties, while Mello is a striking red-and-white variety.

Nicotiana (Tobacco Plant) HHA
Not, in fact, the cancer-causing weed, but a much-loved, highly fragrant garden plant whose flowers open at dusk to fill the summer evening with intense perfume. Some modern hybrids have flowers that stay open during the day, but their fragrance is less pervasive. Some varieties grow to about 90cm (36in) tall and need staking for support; Domino F1, Dwarf White Bedder and Nicki Mixed are neater with more basal branching, so giving a more bushy effect. Look also for Breakthrough Mixed, Tinkerbelle, Lime Green, Sensation Mixed and Red Devil.

Oenothera (Evening Primrose) HP, treated as HHA
Mississippi Primrose is the variety to be recommended, with lovely ice-white blooms that are produced all summer, a colour that slowly turns to cream then light pink. It makes a good choice for the front of a sunny border or in the rock garden.

Osteospermum (Dimorphotheca, Star of the Veldt) HHA
Also known as Cape marigold or African daisy. A favourite, but sadly the beautifully coloured daisy-like flowers, with a silken sheen to their petals, only open on sunny days, so in some summers their contribution to beds,

borders and window boxes is tantalisingly short. The variety Starshine is one of the longest lasting, and just a few plants will give a good show, being heat-tolerant and not at all fussy over soil conditions.

Pansy HP, treated as HHA
Also classified as Viola, this is a large genus of very popular plants for bedding and for the front of the border; together with the Universal strain, it is therefore possible to have pansies in flower in the garden every day of the year. Some seed catalogues differentiate between the Viola and Pansy; however, may I simply suggest that if you want large-flowered pansies to flower in the spring and summer, sow the seed in winter, while a summer sowing will give flowering plants through a mild winter and well into spring. Recommended varieties: Majestic Giants F1, Crystal Bowl F1, Universal F1, Roggli Giants F1, all sold as mixtures. The best large-flowered individuals or separates are Flame Princess F1, Glacier Ice, the Imperial series, Rippling Waters and Spanish Sun.

Passiflora (Passion Flower) HHP
A very attractive climbing plant that deserves far wider attention from gardeners, because even though it is half-hardy and is cut back by the first hard frosts, new growth will invariably spring from the base. In the large greenhouse or conservatory it offers a multitude of unusual flowers, and also the bonus of edible fruits; in mild winter districts the plants are set out in late spring in a sheltered site in sun or partial shade.

Varieties available include: *P. antioquiensis*, a trailing variety with carmine pink blooms; *P. caerulea*, large blue flowers and orange but non-edible fruit; *P. edulis*, white flowers with a distinctive purple-black corona and egg-shaped edible fruits in late August; *P. ligularis*, white, purple, pink and blue flowers, glossy leaves and sweet aromatic fruit; *P. mollissima* with rose-pink long-tubed flowers, hairy pale green leaves and, erratically, 3in long egg-shaped fruit; and *P. quadrangularis*, the tallest variety which makes up to 9m (25ft), and which is the one grown in the West Indies for its delicious fruit. Moreover, the flowers are particularly beautiful in white and purple. There is also a Passion Fruits of the World mixture.

Penstemon (Beard Tongue Flower) HP/HHP, treated as HHA
There are two groups of this genus: the alpine species, which are hardy

BEST BEDDERS

Every year the seed catalogues clamour for your attention with offers of new, exclusive varieties. Judging their worth before parting with your money can be difficult, but help is at hand from internationally recognised criteria: the awards given by Fleuroselect, the Royal Horticultural Society and the All America Selections. Fleuroselect, a Dutch-based organisation, carries out trials of new varieties at sites throughout Europe and awards a gold medal or quality mark. Similar trials are carried out in Britain, by the RHS, and in the USA, and successful varieties are given the appropriate RHS and AAS awards. All the varieties selected for awards should flourish under a wide range of climatic conditions.

OPPOSITE: *Mesembryanthemum needs a position in full sun while pansies (right) are unfussy over siting and petunias (below) do best in a dry, sunny location.*

perennials propagated from cuttings; and the border species, which can also be propagated from cuttings but are available as mixtures in seed. The flowers are very attractively set on the stem like a hyacinth, and in fact one of the best varieties is Hyacinth Flowered Mixed, growing to about 45cm (18in). In autumn, cut down the stems and cover the plants with a mulch of compost, leafmould or spent peat, or peat substitute from the growing-bags.

Petunia HHP, treated as HHA
This showy bedding plant has had the full treatment from the hybridists: there is now a choice of outstanding F1 hybrids that are absolutely stunning in their massed effect in a sunny summer though often miserably tatty in a wet season. The large, open, trumpet-shaped blooms simply beg for the sun and will give unrivalled brilliant colour to beds, borders, window-boxes and other containers from early summer to mid-autumn.

There are several groups of petunias. The double grandifloras have blooms that look like carnations, while the double multiflora flowers look like pinks. There are also picotees and mini-flowered hybrids. Resisto F1, a multiflora, was bred specifically to stand up to adverse weather, and in gardens only yards from the grey North Sea I've seen Prio Mixed put on a very good show. Other good varieties are Cascade, Super Cascade, Falcon series, Supermagic and Cloud series.

Phlox HP/HHA
The tall perennial species are favourites for the herbaceous border and for cut flowers. The smaller *P. drummondii* varieties are half-hardy annuals. Petticoat grows only 10cm (4in) tall, while Twinkle is a little taller at 15cm (6in).

Portulaca (Sun Plant) HHA
An attractive subject for a sunny border, with narrow bright green leaves and saucer-shaped flowers in a range of colours, all with prominent yellow stamens. This is a rapid grower that hugs the ground.

Primula (Primrose, Polyanthus) HP/HHP
There are hundreds of species in this genus, one of nature's most beautiful, and no garden should be without some members of its ever-growing family. This includes the Common Primrose *P. vulgaris*; *P. variabilis* the Polyanthus with primrose flowers on a stem; *P. denticulata* the Drumstick Primrose; *P. florindae* the Giant Yellow Cowslip; and *P. japonica* the Candelabra Primrose.

Note that *P. obconica* is the species that can cause a nasty allergic reaction to some people with sensitive skins. It is a perennial normally grown as an annual for flowering indoors during the winter months. My particular plea is that every attempt should be made to include some plants of the UK's native cowslip, because modern farming methods and increasing urbanisation have put this lovely member of the primula family at such risk.

Pulsatilla (Pasque Flower) HP
A close relative of the anemone, it is raised from seed quite easily and, given an open position in the rock garden, will flourish for years.

Pyrethrum HP, treated as HHA
A popular border plant with daisy-like flowers that resemble chrysanthemums and are long-lasting as cut flowers.

Rhodochiton atrosanguineum (Purple Bell Vine) HHP, treated as HHA
An extremely attractive, rapidly growing climber with a mass of large, fuchsia-like, crimson and purple flowers. From an early spring sowing it will quickly clothe a sunny wall or porch from early summer onwards until cut down by the first frost of autumn.

Ricinus HHA
A tender shrubby plant from tropical Africa that grows up to 1.5m (5ft) tall and has striking red, purple and bronze foliage and spiny seed pods. It is particularly valued in public park bedding schemes and as a pot-grown conservatory plant. The seeds of this plant are very poisonous, so it is not a suitable subject in a household where there are young children.

Rudbeckia (Cone Flower) HHA
This is the backbone of many borders because the plants are easily grown and produce masses of blooms of bright golden yellow on strong stems that are robust in windy weather and ideal for cutting. It thrives in a sunny open position, but is tolerant of semi-shade. It has a pronounced dark cone which distinguishes it from several other daisy-like flowers. Recommended varie-

PLANTS FOR GROWING ON

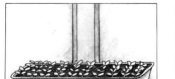

Some bedding plants can be tricky for the inexperienced amateur to raise. Between the choice of sowing the seed (and possible failure) and buying strips or trays of plants from a nursery, is the alternative of plants for growing on. These are baby plants sold by seed firms as Speedplugs, Propaplants, Jiffy Plants, Easiplants, Plantlets or Starter Plants. They are rooted seedlings in cellular trays or Jiffy pots. The idea is to prick them out as soon as possible after their arrival by post. Full instructions on their aftercare are sent with the plants.

ties: Goldilocks, a Fleuroselect (All Europe) Trials bronze medal winner, is an outstanding modern variety, each plant producing up to twenty double and semi-double blooms from mid-summer to the first frosts; its height is about 60cm (24in). Marmalade is slightly less tall, while Nutmeg and Irish Eyes are a little taller, at about 75cm (30in).

Salpiglossis (Painted Tongue) HHA
Trumpet-shaped flowers in rich vibrant colours make this an eye-catching plant for a warm, sheltered sunny bed or border. It also makes an excellent pot plant for the greenhouse, conservatory or a sunny windowsill, but it does need plenty of light to show off its exotic blooms. The modern hybrids such as Ingrid, Splash and Bolero are a good choice, because their hybrid vigour makes them more tolerant of adverse weather; but avoid putting them on to an exposed site.

Salvia (Scarlet Sage) HHA and HP/HHP, treated as HHA
The very popular summer bedding plant is *S. splendens*, a native of Brazil, of which Blaze of Fire, Caribinière and Flarepath are favourite varieties. For an extended flowering period, Splendissima and Torpedo are recommended; alternatively, choose a mixture.

Schizanthus (Butterfly Flower, Poor Man's Orchid) HHA
A lovely plant for showing off in the cool greenhouse or conservatory, or for outdoor bedding in a warm sheltered position. The orchid-like flowers are held above ferny leaves and there is a range of colours from crimson, rose, amber and salmon through to pale pink, all with streaks and spots in contrasting tones or colours.
Recommended varieties: Disco F2 hybrids and Star Parade are particularly compact for pot use, Dwarf Bouquet Mixed, Giant Pansy Flowered Mixed, Morning Mist, Hit Parade. Sweet Lips has very deep colours and the petals are picotee-edged.

Schizopetalon HHA
Something of a rarity, but worth

seeking in a seed list: this delicate little plant is a fine subject for a sunny spot in the rockery, but even better as a container plant. The small white feathery blooms have a room-filling scent of almonds.

Sedum (Stonecrop or Ice Plant) HP/HHA
Most of the sedum family of rock garden and border plants are hardy perennials, but a newish variety *S. caeruleum* Sky Blue is a half-hardy annual. Its bright blue, star-shaped flowers, and green, then deep red foliage, make it a superb alternative to the traditional species. If left undisturbed it will self-seed. It is also suitable for pots and containers.

Senecio HP/HHA
The two varieties *S. maritima Cirrhus* and *S. maritima* are shrubby evergreen plants that can survive a mild winter, but on the whole Senecio are best treated as half-hardy annuals. They are excellent for edges of borders, being low-growing and compact.

Stocks HHA/HA/HB
Most of the strongly scented hybrids of this deservedly popular summer bedding plant originate from the species *Matthiola incana*. There are now six main groups, with sub-divisions in each group; a rule-of-thumb guide is to treat all of them as annuals and to sow any variety marked HHA in the spring for summer flowering. For stocks to flower in the spring, choose a variety marked HB, sow in the summer and give some winter protection in greenhouse or frame and plant out in early spring.
A particularly attractive variety is Dwarf Stockpot. It has a powerful fragrance, grows only about 25cm (10in) tall and has hyacinth-like flower spikes in carmine, rose, purple and white.

Sweet Peas (*Lathyrus odoratus*) HA
The delicate charm and superb fragrance of *Lathyrus odoratus* have captivated gardeners since it was introduced from Sicily; now it is a cult plant like the chrysanthemum, with specialist seed suppliers, hybridisers, totally dedicated

exhibitors and a library of literature. These are climbing plants that relish full sun and an organically fertile soil that is free-draining. If you are not growing for showing, try giving the plants full scope by letting them wander through tall shrubs that finish their flowering in late spring or early summer.

Tacitus (Chihuahua Flower) HHP, treated as HHA
No prizes for guessing where this comes from! It was found in Mexico in 1972 and is still a rarity in Europe. The bright pink blooms will provide a great show in mid-to late summer if given a position in full sun and in a free-draining soil.

Tithonia (Mexican Sunflower) HHA
Vivid orange-scarlet flowers 8cm (3in) across, on strong stems up to 1.2m (4ft) tall – both these qualities make this a good subject for cutting or for the back of a sunny border.

Verbena HHA
A favourite plant for bedding and outdoor containers, with clusters of bright, primrose-like flowers on stems up to 30cm(12in) tall.
Recommended varieties: Amethyst, Dwarf Jewels, Marbella, Showtime, Trinidad and Tropic.

Zinnia (Youth and Old Age) HHA
The flowers are like dahlia, scabious, gaillardia or chrysanthemum blooms, up to 15cm (6in) across on sturdy stems and in vivid colours; consequently this is a most attractive bedding plant, which does well in a rich organic soil and sunny summer. It flowers from mid-summer through to mid-autumn.
Recommended varieties: Tall, up to 75cm(30in): Big Top F1 Mixed, Giant Double Mixed, Envy Double, State Fair Mixed, Peppermint Stick Mixed, Scabious Flowered, Sunshine Mixed, Short, up to 30cm (12in): Fairyland F1, Dwarf Double Mixed, Fantastic Light Pink F1, Parasol Mixed F1, Marvel Mixed, Thumbelina Mixed. Old-fashioned Mexican types: Chippendale, Old Mexico, Persian Carpet, Sombrero.

Modern strains and selections of salvia (above) and schizanthus
(right) have a wider range of colours.

PLANTS FOR THE GREENHOUSE AND CONSERVATORY

There are many hundreds of plants suitable for growing in the greenhouse and conservatory, far too many to include all of them in a book of this size. It can be a bewildering range and your choice will inevitably be influenced by personal preferences and budget, the size of your structure and its location, and whether it is heated in the colder months. The internal layout of the plant house must be planned to accommodate the chosen plants, and the timing of changes to the residents is also important. If, for example, you grow tomatoes in the house in the summer, they must be cleared in time to bring in any frost-tender subjects that have spent the summer outside. You will almost certainly want to have something of interest throughout the year, because a greenhouse that sits empty and idle during late autumn and winter is a sorry place.

In the next few sections of this book I have made a selection of plants under general headings, although it is impossible to categorise too precisely the characteristics of many plants. For example, the fuchsia family contains hardy shrubs and frost-sensitive ones, pot plants, border plants, hanging plants and stately standards. Foliage plants present a similar problem: though grown primarily for their leaves, some also have flowers of great charm.

Then there is *Jasminum polyanthum*, a vigorous climber that blooms in winter and early spring. It isn't so much the small star-shaped flowers that are attractive but their exquisite fragrance that fills the house with sweet freshness in the drab days of winter.

Summer-flowering bulbs, winter-flowering pot plants, chrysanthemums and carnations all have sections to themselves. The bulbs are the easiest to grow – all you need is the money to buy the original stock and advice on their care. Orchids, on the other hand, along with the great family of cacti and succulents, have only relatively brief references because they need more detailed, expert advice that is outside the scope of this book.

Before long, most newcomers to glasshouse gardening reach a compromise on what they would like to do and what the limitations of size, budget and the time available allow them to do. However, the restrictions these factors impose can be too severe and result in a plant-house that is under-utilised. I hope the guidance in the following sections will help to remedy that.

The conservatory layout can be planned to take maximum advantage
of hanging space with a selection of trailing plants, such as the
Emerald Fern Asparagus densiflorus sprengeri (opposite) falling to
meet the climbers. Remember that some will need more shade than
others and all have to be watered and given other attention, so
position them with this in mind.

A TO Z OF CLIMBERS AND HANGING PLANTS

The conservatory and larger greenhouse offer a fine opportunity for the range of plants that grow upward or hang down to follow and thus enrich the architecture of their environment. Some offer the bonus of beautiful blooms, and a few enhance their surroundings with delightful fragrances. Some are relatively easy to grow from seed; others require the propagating skills of the professional, and are best bought as young plants.

Abutilon
One of the mallow family grown for its pendant bell-shaped flowers; it is a very tall plant rather than a climber, and the hybrid A. x suntense, for example, will grow to 3m (10ft). Although best treated as an annual, it can be grown as a container-grown shrub, when it should be stood outside for the summer. Grow from seed.

Araujia sericofera (The Cruel Plant)
A lovely climber with tubular creamy-white flowers, sweetly perfumed, which appear in summer about forty weeks after sowing the seed. The plant continues blooming for up to twelve weeks. It is a vigorous climber that will entwine itself round canes, trellis or any other support. Incidentally, its name of Cruel Plant originates from its native Brazil, where moths attracted to the flowers may have their tongues temporarily glued to the sticky pollen.

Aristolochia elegans (Dutchman's Pipe)
An evergreen climber with quite spectacular blooms in summer, large, urn-shaped and mottled purple and brown. All parts of this plant are poisonous. Grow from seed.

Asarina scandens Violet Glow
A handsome climber for the cold greenhouse or conservatory, it is quick to bloom from a late winter or early spring sowing. The deep blue trumpet-shaped flowers appear from mid-summer onwards, and provide a striking contrast to the fresh green foliage.

A wonderful indoor display of flowering plants, including fuchsias and pelargoniums.

Asparagus densiflorus Sprengeri (Asparagus Fern)
The furry phyllocades that act as leaves will trail down from shelves or raised containers with great delicacy and charm. Easily grown from seed, the plants need to be kept moist and almost pot-bound. A fortnightly feed of an organic liquid fertiliser is advised during the spring and early summer. Keep the plant out of direct sunlight but in a buoyant atmosphere.

Bougainvillea
This vigorous and showy climber is grown for its brilliantly coloured bracts that give the appearance of large paper flowers. It is a plant that needs the

Easily grown from seed, asarina makes a handsome plant for a large pot or tub, which can be put outside for the summer and then brought under cover to continue flowering into late autumn. This is one of the longest flowering of all annual climbers.

space to grow, for it can reach up to 6m (20ft) tall and 1.5m (5ft) wide, and it will need a big tub or other container for its extensive root system. However, given the restriction of a small pot, bougainvillea hybrids will adapt their growth accordingly. Buy a young plant and increase your stock by taking half-ripe heel cuttings in summer. Keep the plants fairly dry during the winter and at a temperature no lower than 7°C(45°F).

Ceropegia woodii (Hearts Entangled)

A hanging plant for the cool greenhouse or frost-free conservatory. Set a mature plant on a shelf or stand 2m (6ft) tall, and its trailing stems will reach the ground. The heart-shaped leaves grow in pairs, and are dark green with silver marbling on the upper surface. Sow seed in spring, or buy the corms and plant just below the surface of the compost. Re-pot every other year, incorporating a little bone meal in the compost. Feed in spring with a liquid seaweed extract.

Chlorophytum elatum (Spider Plant)

This must be one of the most popular of all house plants, the long bi-coloured leaves trailing downwards with plantlets developing at their tip. We had a mature specimen in a sunny porch that grew so vigorously it had to be re-potted twice in a year, and it produced more than twenty plantlets which were potted up and given to a charity plant sale. This is probably the usual way of acquiring one of these plants, but it is also easily grown from seed if you can find a supplier.

Clianthus puniceus (Lobster Claw Plant)

Climbs to 5m (15ft) if given support. It is a native evergreen of New Zealand with fern-like foliage and exotic crimson claw-shaped flowers which grow in large clusters from mid-summer to late autumn. It is grown from seed and given the half-hardy annual treatment, but don't expect to see it flowering for at least two years. In summer it needs plenty of water, but far less over the winter. Re-pot every spring into a soil-based compost, and lightly prune the growth after flowering.

Columnea gloriosa

This beautiful trailing plant belongs to the same family as gloxinias and African violets, and needs some warmth in the winter, when its fiery-red flowers with their yellow throat are at their best. The ovate leaves are covered with brown hairs. Seed is sown in spring, and cuttings can be taken in spring or summer. A mature plant will trail down about 1m (3ft), so it is an excellent subject for hanging baskets positioned at eye level in the conservatory. It needs a lot of water in the summer, far less in the winter.

Datura suaveolens (Angel's Trumpet)

Grows to 4m (13ft) and has richly scented, white, lily-like flowers in summer. It is easily grown from seed. The mature plant needs a pot of at least 25cm (10in) and should be pruned hard in the autumn. All parts of the plant are poisonous.

Fuchsia

As a trailing plant the fuchsia has few rivals. In the cool greenhouse or conservatory the plants will flower all the year through and can reach a ripe old age, although most gardeners prefer to cut back the plant in autumn, re-pot in spring and take cuttings to increase their stock. There are hundreds of varieties to choose from, and once you have sampled the charm of this beautiful plant, you will undoubtedly be hooked for life. See also p50.

Gloriosa (Glory Lily)

A climber with flowers of outstanding beauty; the blooms can be up to 10cm (4in) wide and are of a fluorescent red with orange centres, appearing in mid to late summer all the way up the 1.8m (6ft) stem. The tuber is planted in good compost so that the tip is about 2.5cm (1in) below the surface, in a pot or tub of at least 20cm (8in) diameter. Feed fortnightly with a liquid fertiliser and keep well watered. Tie in the stem to a cane or other support. When re-potting, carefully take off the offsets and grow on to increase stock. When the leaves begin to die off, the tubers should be stored over the winter in a dry, warm place.

Hoya (Wax Flower)

Named after Thomas Hoy, head gardener at Syon House, Isleworth, in the late eighteenth century; it is a big family of climbing and trailing evergreens with star-shaped umbels of waxy flowers which appear from late spring to autumn. The stems of the climbing species attach themselves by aerial roots to suitable supports and will climb to 4.5m (15ft). A miniature version, *H. bella*, is the one recommended for use in a hanging basket. All the hoya family are propagated by cuttings taken in summer. The mature plants need a position in bright light and good humidity, with regular liquid feeding. Water with rainwater only, and do not remove the faded flowers as new buds will take their place for the following season. In winter the plants need a minimum temperature of 7°C (45°F).

Jasminum

A favourite for the conservatory because of the strong perfume of the small star-shaped flowers. *J. officinale* is the summer-flowering species, while *J. polyanthum* will start flowering in winter and continue through to late spring. Both will climb to about 3m (10ft) if given a generous sized pot or container. To induce winter flowering *J. polyanthum* requires a temperature of 15°C (60°F) – lower temperatures merely delay the flowering. Propagate by stem cuttings in late summer with bottom heat.

Lapageria (Chilean Bell Flower)

An evergreen climber and the national flower of Chile, with long, waxy bell-shaped flowers which grow in summer and autumn: it must be the most exciting of all the greenhouse climbing plants. With patience it can be grown from seed. Pot up in large pots or other containers using a soil-less compost free of lime. The stems twine and should be trained, like a vine, up and along wire supports, canes or trellis, to the underside of the roof so that the flowers can hang down. Shade from the summer sun is needed, and a fair degree of humidity. During the winter maintain a minimum temperature of

Philodendron scandens, *the Sweetheart Plant (left) and* Saxifraga sarmentosa, Mother of Thousands, *are deservedly popular house plants needing warmth in the winter. P. scandens does best when trained up a moss stick so that its aerial roots can absorb water. You can make your own with a pole, wire netting and damp sphagnum moss. Wrap the netting loosely round the pole, then pack with the moss.*

7°C (45°F) and in spring, lightly prune to cut out weak shoots and over-vigorous growth.

Passiflora (Passion Flower)

Climbs by its tendrils and is a good subject for the back wall of the conservatory or lean-to greenhouse, although in favourable districts it is grown outdoors as a half-hardy perennial. Seeds of several species are available, including *P. antioquiensis*, *P. ligularis* and *P. mollissima*, which are trailing in habit. The large, showy flowers in summer are followed by sweet, juicy fruit that is edible in most of the species, with *P. ligularis* considered the best of the fruits. Seed is sown in spring; pot on, and give a final pot that restricts root growth. Feed occasionally with liquid seaweed, and water regularly throughout the spring and summer. Heel cuttings can be taken in summer. In winter give protection from frost if grown in an unheated greenhouse, and water very sparingly.

Philodendron scandens (Sweetheart Plant)

A climber grown for its glossy heart-shaped leaves, and *P. melanochryson* for its dark green and coppery leaves with paler veins. Both should preferably be trained up a moss stick to enable the aerial roots to cling and absorb water, although I have seen it grown very successfully tumbling down from a tall shelf. To survive the winter, philodendrons need warmth of 13°C (55°F) and in summer high humidity and some shade are preferred. Propagate in summer by stem sections, air layering or potting-up young plants from the base.

Plumbago auriculata (Cape Leadwort)

Grows to about 3m (10ft) in a large tub or other container. The beautiful pale blue flowers grow in clusters, closely resembling phlox. They appear in late spring and last for months. Seed is sown in spring in a soil-less compost, and potted on gradually until the final pot in the following spring, after which the plant should start flowering. The mature plant needs a cane or trellis for support, and should be cut back to about 15cm (6in) in early spring. Basal cuttings can be taken in spring.

Saxifraga sarmentosa (Mother of Thousands)

Grows wild in China and Japan and is one of the easiest of plants to propagate. Place the mature plant on a shelf or raised container in the conservatory and runners appear at the end of which are plantlets. These are detached from the parent when large enough and potted up into small pots. It's just like taking strawberry runners. This is an unfussy subject, needing just light shade, moderate warmth, regular watering and a feed every now and again with a liquid fertiliser.

Lapageria, with long bell-shaped flowers, is a wonderfully attractive climber for the greenhouse or conservatory. It can be trained along the underside of the roof. Jasmine (opposite) is a vigorous climber, famed for its perfume.

summer. In the second and subsequent season give a top dressing of fish, blood and bone fertiliser in spring, and regular foliar feeding thereafter. Propagate in spring by shoots of previous season's growth with bottom heat of about 21°C (70°F).

Tetrastigma voinierianum (Chestnut Vine)
Given moist conditions in a warm greenhouse and reasonable cultural care, this vine is reckoned to be the fastest growing of all indoor plants. Frequent feeding and regular potting on using a soil-based compost are also requirements. Propagate by stem cuttings in spring with bottom heat at 21°C (70°F).

Thunbergia alata (Black-Eyed Susan)
A superb container plant for the conservatory, climbing to 1.2m (4ft) and flowering within about sixteen weeks after sowing. Give the plant a sunny position, feed and water regularly and dead-head the flowers.

Senecio macroglossus variegata
Looks and grows just like an ivy and makes a fine plant for a hanging basket or placed high on a shelf and allowed to tumble down. Alternatively, it can be given support to climb. It needs a position in good light and plenty of moisture. Propagate by stem cuttings with a pair of leaves and place in a sandy compost with bottom heat at 18°C (65°F). Spray frequently with tepid water in spring and summer and feed fortnightly with liquid fertiliser.

Stephanotis floribunda (Madagascar Jasmine)
Climbs to 5m (16ft) but can be kept far more restrained by restricting the pot size. The white waxy flowers are typically jasmine in form and fragrance, while the leaves are fat and fleshy. Grown from seed germination takes one to three months. Pot on gradually into a final container size of at least 30cm (12in) diameter. Give the plant wire or canes for support and, if space allows, train it under the roof – but give shade during the height of the

Senecio macroglossus variegata, like a small-leaved ivy, needs good light and some support. It grows rapidly and roots readily from stem cuttings.

Tetrastigma voinieranum is another vigorous grower if kept moist and fed well with an organic liquid fertiliser. It also needs regular potting on.

A TO Z OF FOLIAGE AND FLOWERING PLANTS
FOR AUTUMN AND WINTER

Many plants that grow wild in tropical and semi-tropical parts of the world have adapted extremely well to cultivation as greenhouse and conservatory residents in temperate regions. Some, such as the Japanese hybrid azaleas and the African violets, have become dearly-loved houseplants and their propagation a multi-million pound industry. In this section some thirty or so plants have been selected, ones that are at their best in the temperate autumn and winter when indoor gardening always has a special attraction. Some can live in the greenhouse or conservatory for much of the year, and then be taken into the house for flowering. A few, such as fuchsias, bromeliads and saintpaulias, have a range of species or varieties and a fascination that together earn them the title of 'hobby plants'. If you reach that happy state, the brief references here will not satisfy you and I would then suggest joining a local specialist club or furthering your interest with the many books that deal specifically with these plants.

Azalea (*Rhododendron indicum*, Japanese azalea)
A very popular gift plant in winter when it would be quite likely to take pride of place in the warmest room in the house – and that's not the treatment it should have. It will last much longer, and will look better in a cool, light position in the conservatory, especially if kept moist. Dead-head the flowers and place the plant outdoors in late spring and summer, syringing regularly. Bring the plant into the conservatory or cool room in the house before the frosts arrive and, if necessary, re-pot using a compost with extra leafmould. Propagate from cuttings of shoots in early summer. When rooted, pot on at 10°C (50°F), and gradually increase the temperature to 18°C (65°F) to encourage flowering.

Begonia rex
This is one of the finest foliage plants with intricately patterned, multi-coloured leaves. It is readily propagated by leaf cuttings (see p49) in a propagator at 21°C (70°F). The mature plant needs a position of light shade and a temperature range of 15–21°C (60–70°F), although if kept rather dry over the winter it will tolerate a slightly lower night temperature.

Beloperone guttata (Shrimp Plant)
Its common name is from the 'flowers' or pinkish shrimp-like bracts, while *B. lutea* has pale yellow bracts. Most plants are sold in pots that are too

ORCHIDS FOR THE AMATEUR

Orchid growing is too serious and important a hobby to be discussed at any length without a full understanding of the problems and pleasures involved, so no more than a word or two of advice concerning orchids for the amateur's organic greenhouse will be given here.

Having never grown orchids myself, I have the novice's nervousness of them, but have been told that orchids of every kind are ideally suited to organic methods of propagation and management. A good start for the beginner would be the local library and the many excellent books on orchid growing, followed by a visit to a good orchid nursery. As to the conditions for growing, a bare outline of what is necessary would be adequate heating; shading from mid-spring to early autumn preferably by blinds; adequate fresh air with air circulaton by an electric fan; and a relative humidity of from 65 to 85 per cent day and night, preferably provided by an automatic mist spray system.

Adequate heating means winter temperatures for *Cymbidium* and *Odontoglossum* of 10–13°C (50–55°F); *Cattleyas* and *Paphiopedilum* at 13–15°C (55–60°F); *Phalaenopsis* and *Vanda* at 18–21°C (65–70°F).

Beloperone guttata *(left) and* Calathea zebrina *both benefit from regular feeding with liquid seaweed extract and a position out of direct sunlight.*

small, and should be re-potted into a soil-based compost and given fortnightly feeding with liquid seaweed and a light airy position out of direct sunlight. Pinching out the growing tips of the young plant encourages bushiness, and some young shoots can be taken in summer for rooting in a sand-enriched compost at 18°C (65°F). Avoid overwatering at all stages and provide a minimum winter temperature of 13°C (55°F).

Billbergia nutans
This member of the bromeliads is an excellent plant for the conservatory, or a cool room indoors near to a window. The pendulous bracts in late autumn and winter are seen at their best if the plant is at eye-height. Propagate by dividing the clump, and pot into a soil-based compost.

Bouvardia domestica
An evergreen which eventually reaches about 60cm (2ft) tall. The flowers are in white, pink and shades of red on slightly pendulous stems, and are produced in late autumn and winter

when the plant needs sparse watering, but good light and a temperature of 13–18°C (55–65°F). Cuttings can be taken in spring and kept at 10°C (50°F) or suckers can be potted from the base of the mature plant.

Calanthe vestita
An easy-to-grow, winter-flowering orchid which has tall flower spikes with white, pink, or pink-and-white flowers that appear while the plant is resting. Until it sheds its leaves in late autumn, it should be well watered and fed with liquid seaweed. After flowering, the pseudo bulbs should be re-potted in a soil-based compost with extra well-rotted farmyard manure. A warm greenhouse or conservatory, about 18°C (65°F), and a position in good light are needed for best results.

Calathea zebrina
A foliage plant of great beauty growing to about 90cm (3ft) tall; it must have a warm position in the conservatory, but preferably in the shade of a taller plant because it cannot tolerate exposure to

direct sunlight. The bright green leaves with their darker stripes add a definitely exotic touch to the location. Water with rainwater at room temperature, and feed with liquid seaweed during spring and early summer.

Camellia japonica
Flowers in late winter and early spring and is often grown outdoors in mild winter areas, but makes a good subject for the cold greenhouse or conservatory. It can be grown from seed sown in the spring or from cuttings taken in the autumn, using a lime-free compost. Pot on until a final 25cm (10in) pot. Use only rainwater for watering.

Capsicum annuum
(Ornamental Pepper)
Grown for its brightly-coloured fruits that ripen in late autumn and remain on the plant through much of the winter providing it has a position in

good light. Sow the seed in late winter in a propagator at 21°C (70°F) and pot on gradually. A final pot size of 13cm(5in) will give a shrubby plant about 15cm(6in) tall. During the summer the plants can be stood outside, but must be kept moist and given an occasional syringing with tepid rainwater.

Clivia miniata

A stately plant for the cool greenhouse or conservatory which has broad, fleshy, strap-shaped leaves and a thick stem with a cluster of beautiful orange bell-shaped flowers in late winter and early spring. In flower it deserves a solo position on a table or pot stand. Some people raise these plants from seed, while large clumps can be divided to make new ones. To give this lovely subject a long and productive life, re-pot no more frequently than every five years

into a soil-based compost with extra bone meal. The plant should be rested for about three weeks in late autumn; this means keeping it in a cool shaded spot with only a touch of moisture.

Erica (Heather)

Neat little plants with colourful tubular flowers that are produced at almost any time of the year. For winter flowering in the conservatory or cool greenhouse, choose Erica hyemalis with pink flowers. After flowering the plants should be stood outside and trimmed back. They can be brought inside again in late autumn. Propagate from cuttings in late winter in a lime-free compost with bottom heat at 15–18°C(60–65°F). Rooting powder is not advised. Transplant seedlings to 8cm (3in) pots and pot on to a final 10cm (4in) pot of lime-free compost. Feed regularly with liquid fertiliser.

Euphorbia pulcherrima (Poinsettia)

Undoubtedly the most popular winter-flowering indoor plant, with brilliant crimson bracts, as well as pink or cream versions. Hundreds of thousands are bought at Christmas and soon discarded, but with care they can be kept in good condition for many months and propagated from tip cuttings taken from the plant in mid-summer. The sap from the cut end should be rinsed off as it is liable to cause a rash on sensitive skin. Plants can be persuaded to flower for a second winter by light pruning in summer, regular feeding with a seaweed extract fertiliser, natural light and a minimum temperature of 15°C (60°F).

Freesia hybrids

Among the most fragrant of all flowers, freesias are enormously popular as cut flowers. They are grown from corms that, in turn, can be produced from seed such as F. tetraploid Super Giant Hybrid. Germination is erratic and the recommendation is to soak the seed in warm water for twenty-four hours, then sow shallowly in compost at 18°C (65°F). Darkness is necessary for germination and some experts recommend rubbing the seed of the tetraploid with sandpaper to help it along; even so, allow up to thiry days for things to happen. Then, avoid mollycoddling the young plants, but keep them growing steadily and sturdily in a temperature of 13–15°C (55–60°F). Water regularly and feed fortnightly with a liquid fertiliser. The aim is to produce strong stems that will hold the flowers firmly without flopping over, so the pots of young plants can be stood outside for the summer and brought under cover again in early autumn. When the flower buds appear give a cane for support and tie loosely.

Growing from corms is basically similar. They are planted in spring for flowering in late autumn or early winter. After they have flowered, treat the plants as you would a spring-flowering bulb by allowing growth to continue for eight weeks. This will encourage proper development of the corm. After this, the corms can be lifted, dried off and stored. Commercial

growers store the corms for a couple of weeks at 21°C (70°F) to improve flowering the next time around.

Fuchsia

This family is so important and diverse that it is impossible to give it more than a comparatively brief reference. With the proper care, this is possibly the best of all potted plants for flower production and length of season, and certainly a well-grown fuchsia will produce flowers continuously from early spring until early winter. However, they can also prove very disappointing to the indoor plant enthusiast because they need maximum light; plants therefore seem to produce more flowers if grown on the outside windowsill than on the sill inside the room. Also, be careful when introducing them to the possibly drier air conditions in greenhouses and conservatories; some

varieties will drop their flowers immediately they are transferred to an atmosphere drier than that to which they have been accustomed.

Propagation is by cuttings taken from late winter onwards from over-wintered plants that have been started into growth in early to mid-winter. These are good subjects for the flowerpot technique (p50); when rooted they can be potted up into small pots of a soil-based compost and fed fortnightly with diluted seaweed extract. Water sparingly and syringe the plants, especially the undersides of the leaves. Pinch out the growing tips to encourage bushiness, and give shade from direct sunlight. Prune back hard in the late autumn and overwinter the plants in a frost-free place.

Gardenia jasminoides

Usually flowers in the summer, but

some varieties can be persuaded to flower from late autumn onwards. But be warned: growing gardenias for most amateurs means living dangerously because they are notoriously fussy plants. If you succeed, the reward is a magnificent plant with deep green shining leaves and heavily scented double creamy-white blooms. Propagate by cuttings of young shoots in early spring with bottom heat of 21°C (70°F). The plants need a minimum temperature of 18°C (65°F) in light shade, regular misting, and feeding with a liquid seaweed extract. The compost must be lime-free and the water should be rainwater, not from the mains.

Clivia miniata (opposite) has beautiful orange flowers in spring if given a dormant period during late autumn. Fuchsias (below) will, with care, flower from early spring through to winter.

Maranta erythrophylla

A small evergreen plant grown for its attractively coloured and patterned leaves. It needs a warm, humid atmosphere to do well, with frequent spraying and light shade in the summer; its winter temperature must not be allowed to fall below 10°C (50°F). Weak liquid fertiliser should be given from early spring to early summer. Propagation is best done by division when re-potting.

Monstera deliciosa (Swiss Cheese Plant)

One of the most distinctive but badly managed of all houseplants. The problem is that it will carry on growing until it reaches maybe 6m (20ft) tall, if given the space and the right level of warmth. This means a minimum of 10°C (50°F) but an average of 18°C (65°F). It also needs generous watering in summer but a drier compost in the late autumn and winter. It produces aerial roots which need to be guided into the compost; if a moss stick is used

for support they can be allowed to grow into the moss. Re-pot every year in spring until the plant is large enough, then every other year, although this can be a daunting task. It is necessary to sponge the leaves to remove dust, and to provide light shade. Propagation is by stem cutting in summer, taken from the top of the stem below an aerial root.

Musa ensete (Banana)

An interesting and attractive plant for the conservatory that is relatively easy to grow from seed; some will grow into elegant foliage plants only four months after germination. *Musa ensete* can be persuaded to fruit if given a minimum winter temperature of 10°C (50°F), a minimum summer one of 18°C (65°F), and high humidity. The seed should be soaked for seventy-two hours in a saucer of water kept in a warm place. Sow shallowly in a loam-based compost and set the propagator at 24°C (75°F). Germination is erratic: it may happen

in fourteen days or as many weeks. Pot on into a loam potting compost and feed regularly with a liquid fertiliser.

Nephrolepis exaltata (Sword Fern)

The most handsome of the ferns for the conservatory, and one of the easiest to grow; a well looked-after plant will survive for twelve or more years and produce plantlets to carry on the line. A soil-less compost is preferred, along with shade, adequate moisture and a winter temperature not below 10°C (50°F). An occasional foliar feed in spring and summer is appreciated.

Nerine bowdenii

A native of South Africa where it is spring-flowering. In northern Europe the lily-like pink flowers on strong 50cm (20in) stems appear in autumn and last several weeks. There are white, salmon-pink and red varieties, but all are easy to grow from bulbs planted in mid-summer, four or five to a 15cm (6in) pot of soil-based compost

with just the neck of the bulbs protruding. After flowering, allow the foliage to die down and the pots to dry out. Growth re-starts in mid-spring after the bulbs are thoroughly watered. Re-potting is only necessary after four or five years when offsets can be taken and brought on gradually to maturity.

Palms

These are excellent plants for the conservatory as there are species to suit all sorts of locations and they can be grown from seed. *Neanthe bella* is a parlour palm for the smaller conservatory; it is a model houseplant, remaining neat, compact and undemanding throughout its life, and so it tends to get rather negligent treatment. Properly cared for, it has long stems, each with twelve pairs of leaflets. It should be given a well-drained container and not allowed to go short of water, although in winter when growth slows down, watering can be reduced to just enough to keep the compost moist. Seed should be soaked overnight, then

lightly covered with compost and placed in a propagator at 26°C (80°F), when germination takes from thirty days to six months. The advice is to examine the seeds regularly because they can make a root before a shoot appears and will need to be potted up when this happens. The date palm *Phoenix dactylifera* is readily propagated from date stones, often sold at Christmas in the UK (see p137).

Pandanus baptiste and **P. veitchii** (Screw Pines)

These have in-built anti-vandal protection in the form of vicious spines along the edges and central spine of their leaves. This also makes them unwelcome residents in the conservatory used by young children. In other respects, too, these plants are tough customers; they take drought in their stride so could be placed high on a stand, though not too close to the glass. *P. baptiste* is the larger of the two, growing to 1.8m (6ft) tall. The

OPPOSITE: Maranta erythrophylla *has reddish-veined leaves against dark and light green tissue. Monstera deliciosa's glossy green leaves make it a popular house plant.* ABOVE: *(left)* Nephrolepis exalta *needs a shady position and constantly moist compost. Pellionia daveauana can be used as a hanging plant or as a creeper.*

leaves are streaked with bright yellow, while the more compact *P. veitchii* with green and white variegations barely reaches 1m (3ft).

Pellionia daveauana

An attractive foliage plant that can be used very effectively at eye-level, with its oval brown and green leaves trailing from a hanging container. However, I have also seen it creeping horizontally along a shelf in the conservatory. Propagate by stem cuttings about 8cm (3in) long taken in spring; when rooted, these can be potted up into 13cm (5in) pots of soil-less compost, and the growing point pinched out to encourage bushiness.

Peperomia argyreia (Rugby Ball Plant)
Has heart-shaped leaves with dark green stripes on a silvery ground. It is a compact plant that needs light shade and a fairly moist, soil-less compost with regular feeding of a seaweed-type liquid fertiliser. Propagation is by leaf cuttings taken in late spring (p 49). Other good peperomia are *P. caperata*, *P. hederaefolia* and *P. magnoliaefolia.*

Pilea cadierei nana (Aluminium Plant)
Belonging to a large family which includes the common stinging nettle, it is the most widely grown of the pileas. Propagation is by stem cuttings in spring, using the same techniques as for fuchsia cuttings (p50). When rooted, the growing tips are pinched out and the cuttings are potted on to 8cm (3in) pots of loam-based compost. When growing vigorously, the growing points can be nipped out again, and regular liquid feeds will ensure that the bright colours are maintained.

Piper ornatum
This has large, waxy leaves, with silvery markings against a dark, green ground. This plant must have adequate warmth of 18–24°C (65–75°F) and quite high humidity, although water-logging can be fatal. Give it a position in good light, and feed regularly in spring and summer with a good liquid fertiliser. Propagate in spring by a whole leaf with stem (as for African violets) and place in a propagator at 21°C (70°F).

Plectranthus oertendahlii
An attractive plant for a hanging container in the conservatory, it has green and bronze-coloured mottled leaves with spikes of white tubular flowers in the autumn. Propagation is by stem cuttings from the tips, taken in the spring, and given the same treatment as for fuchsia cuttings (p50). Pinch out the growing tips of young plants to encourage a bushy habit. This is an unfussy plant, but does best

ABOVE: *(left)* Musa ensete, *the banana plant, can be grown from seed.*
BELOW: *(left)* Saintpaulia, *or African Violet, requires good light to encourage flowering.*

in good light, plenty of water and regular feeding with dilute liquid fertiliser.

Saintpaulia (African Violet)
Far and away the most popular flowering houseplant, thanks to the specialist producers in the United States and the work of hybridisers in the United Kingdom. Two points worth making

are that successful flowering at virtually any time of the year requires a position in good light, and that over-watering is frequently fatal. On the positive side, propagation is by leaf cuttings taken at any time and is relatively easy (see p49). The cuttings need warmth and humidity and within about ten weeks baby plants appear at the base of the leaf and can be potted on.

ABOVE: *(left)* Peperonia argyreia *has beautiful grey-green striped leaves while* Pilea cadierei *(above right) from Vietnam has silvery foliage with dark green veins.* BELOW: *(left)* Piper ornatum *is another silver-marked foliage plant,* Plectranthus oertendahlii *(right) an attractive subject for a hanging container.*

Sansevieria trifasciata provides a useful vertical form among conservatory plants that may be mostly round-leaved.

Sansevieria trifasciata (Mother-in-law's Tongue)

Has clumps of stiff sword-shaped leaves up to 60cm (2ft) tall, and as a long-lasting plant for the conservatory it is as tough as old boots. Just like mother-in-law, it can outstay its welcome. The most attractive form of the species is *Laurentii* with a yellow margin to the leaves. Propagate by division when the parent plant becomes pot-bound.

Schizocentron elegans

This charming compact plant can be given a position on a shelf close to the glass in the greenhouse or conservatory where it will flower from late spring through to mid-summer. It needs only a small pot of soil-based compost, but regular watering and feeding with a seaweed liquid fertiliser. Propagation is by division of the plant in the autumn or by tip cuttings in late spring or summer, in a sandy compost with bottom heat of about 18°C (65°F).

Schlumbergera x buckleyi (Christmas Cactus)

The most commonly grown cactus, easily raised in a warm environment for flowering at mid-winter or in cooler

conditions for flowering in spring. It needs a compost that is half peat or peat substitute and half soil, and room to develop into a wide 60cm (2ft) plant. There are no leaves, and the fuchsia-like flowers in pink or carmine appear at the ends of the segments which arch over. Propagation is best done after flowering, by potting up individual segments, having first allowed them to dry out for twenty-four hours. Mature plants can be given a summer holiday outdoors, but out of direct sunlight and sheltered from harsh winds. Feeding is not needed until the plant is three years old, when it can be re-potted and fed with a liquid fertiliser every fortnight until early autumn when the flower buds form.

Scindapsus aureus (Devil's Ivy)

A popular foliage plant with heart-shaped leaves in green and pale yellow variegations. It needs light shade and plenty of moisture. Although it is frequently trained to climb or trail, it can be restrained by pinching out the growing tips. It is propagated by stem cuttings or by layering in summer.

Sinningia

A charming miniature version of the gloxinia, with glorious trumpet flowers up to 8cm (3in) across which rise out of neat rosettes of leaves. Available as tubers, or can be grown from seed sown on the surface of the compost. Place in a plastic bag, and then in the propagator at 21°C (70°F), when germination takes 10–21 days. When the young plants are growing vigorously, feed with a dried blood liquid feed until the flower buds appear about six months after sowing; then switch to a liquid seaweed fertiliser. When the foliage dies down in the autumn, allow the compost to dry out and store the tuber as you would a gloxinia.

Solanum capsicastrum (Winter Cherry)

Belongs to the potato family and is a charming plant for winter decoration, the inconspicuous white flowers being followed by bright orange berries that remain on the plant over the winter months. It is easily raised from seed,

sown shallow with the propagator set at 21°C (70°F). Germination takes about fourteen days. Prick out when large enough, and reduce the temperature to 15°C (60°F); pot on when ready to 8cm (3in) pots, and lower the temperature again to 10°C (50°F). The plants can be placed outside throughout the summer, and the growing points should be pinched out to gain bushiness. When the flowers appear, gentle syringing will assist pollination. Keep the berried plants out of reach of children because – like most of the solanum family – the berries are poisonous. Discard the plants after the berries have fallen.

Spathiphyllum Mauna Loa

This elegant plant is from Hawaii; it has a white spathe up to 15cm (6in) long, and needs a humid, warm environment and light shade – it benefits from frequent light syringing with tepid water. Where a minimum temperature of 18°C (65°F) can be maintained, the spathes appear at almost any time. Propagation is by division of mature plants.

Streptocarpus (Cape Primrose)

Like the African violets, this has had a lot of attention from the hybridisers, and most modern hybrids have more flowers, fewer leaves and last much longer than the old favourites. All the same, the long-established blue-flowered Constant Nymph remains one of the longest flowering sorts. Streptocarpus need a good light, moist but not sodden compost, regular feeding with a liquid fertiliser except in the winter, and a temperature of 15–21°C (60–70°F). A good range of hybrids are available as seeds. Sow in early spring at 21°C (70°F) and the resulting plants should be in flower within about twenty weeks. Stock can also be increased by leaf cuttings with bottom heat at about 18°C (65°F).

Tradescantia blossfeldiana

A robust, attractive foliage plant that needs a position in good light to retain the variegations and produce the small purple and white flowers. It is one of the easiest plants to propagate by

cuttings taken in spring and given just gentle bottom heat. It makes a handsome subject for the hanging basket, though it is better to use several young plants at a time so that the effect is of bushiness.

Yucca aloifolia

In the wild this is a smallish tree. In my seaside garden what started as a small pot plant has become a rather overpowering but sturdy specimen 2m (6ft) tall. Short lengths of stem are imported from the West Indies and are rooted at nurseries then sold as pot plants that flourish in good light and if kept on the dry side. Take care when handling, however, as the sword-shaped leaves have toothed margins that can tear sensitive skin. In favourable locations outdoors, tall flower spikes appear in late summer; the seed, when collected and dried, can be used to propagate at 18°C (65°F). Alternatively suckers can be taken in spring and potted on.

ABOVE: *(left)* Schizocentron elegans *has purple flowers in spring and summer;* (right) Tradescantia blossfeldiana *also produces small purple flowers.* BELOW: *(left)* Scindapsus aureus *is one of the most reliable of all foliage plants, rivalled only in popularity, perhaps, by Yucca aloifoilia,* (right).

MORE PLANTS FOR THE WINTER CONSERVATORY

The frost-free yet not overwarm environment of the conservatory in winter is excellent for a range of shrubs, foliage and flowering plants, plus, of course, spring-flowering bulbs. Their common requirements are a maximum amount of light and as much ventilation as possible. Automatic watering systems should not be used.

Spring-flowering shrubs such as *Daphne odora, Forsythia ovata, Hamamelis mollis* the witch hazel, and ribes the flowering currants, can all be container-grown to provide colour and, with some, fragrance, from late winter onwards. All the shrubs should be watered from the rainwater butt, the water at the internal temperature of the conservatory. Arrange the plants at various levels so they can take maximum advantage of the light, and so you can enjoy their beauty.

Universal and other winter-flowering pansies, dwarf primulas, larkspur and phlox, East Lothian stocks, and cinerarias and calceolarias will all give colourful displays in the winter conservatory if sown in early or mid-summer. Add to the flowering plants a range of evergreen foliage plants (pp79–93), grouping them according to size.

As a winter-flowering plant for conservatory or greenhouse, the tender calceolaria has few rivals. The pouch-like flowers come in brilliant colours, marked with blotches and spots.

SPRINGTIME BULBS FOR COLOURFUL DISPLAY

Hyacinths, narcissi, muscari and tulips are deservedly popular bulbs for spring-flowering indoors and, with care, a mass of colour can be had from Christmas through to Easter. Among the more unusual bulbs worth forcing for display in the conservatory are *galanthus* the snowdrop, especially *G. nivalis flore pleno*, the double form; *Brodiaea laxa* the California hyacinth; *Bulbocodium vernum* the Spring Meadow saffron; and *Sprekelia formosissima* the Jacobean lily.

All indoor bulbs should be planted generously in their containers, packing as many together as possible. In bowls it is preferable to keep one variety to one container so that the bulbs are in flower together. Narcissi, such as the double daffodil Tahiti, look extremely effective in large ceramic pots with the flowers so densely packed they are overflowing. They can be planted in two layers, placing a second layer above the gaps of the bottom layer. Tulips can be given the same treatment, choosing either just one striking parrot variety, or two or more varieties whose colours complement each other and that are in flower at the same time.

It is advisable to use special bulb fibre for containers without drainage holes. Those with drainage can be filled with potting compost, having first covered the drainage holes with crocks or pieces of discarded tights or fine mesh netting. Small bulbs should be planted with their tops just below the surface of the compost; large bulbs should have their tops just showing above the rim of the container.

Water the compost after planting the bulbs, then wrap them in sheets of newspaper and place them in a cool dark place, such as a cellar. If this isn't possible, they should be put in a plunge bed: the bowls or pots are wrapped in a sheet of plastic, placed in a hole in a shady part of the garden and covered with 15cm (6in) of soil for 8–12 weeks for the roots to develop. They are then gradually introduced to a lighter, warmer position in the conservatory or indoors.

Springtime in the alpine greenhouse at the Royal Horticultural Society garden at Wisley.

SUMMER BULBS

Hyacinths, tulips and daffodils are the main providers of colour in the home, conservatory and greenhouse during the drab days of winter, and our lives would be the poorer without them. What is far less widely appreciated is that bulbous plants can also make a colourful contribution to indoor gardening in late spring and summer.

These summer bulbs, corms, rhizomes and tubers come from widely different geographical locations and climates and represent no fewer than eighty distinct botanical families, each with individual attributes, habits and requirements for heat, light, water and humidity. However, this doesn't mean that a summer bulb collection for indoors is going to be tiresomely difficult to manage. Surprisingly few require a lot of heat, even those from the hottest habitats, and few of them are greedy for space – though some do produce quite massive flower-heads and others climb with the agility of monkeys, so check on these factors before committing yourself to their upbringing.

The Amaryillidaceae Family

The imperious hippeastrum or amaryllis was a rarity until relatively recently – now it is as familiar an indoor plant as the hyacinth. There are at least seven other members of the same amaryllidaceae family that can be grown just as easily.

Amaryllis belladonna, for example, though fairly widely grown outdoors in sheltered sites, is very happy in the conservatory or on the greenhouse bench. Plant the bulbs in early spring in pots of a rich organic compost (p31) and in late summer its cluster of pale rose trumpet-shaped flowers will appear, followed by the long, strap-shaped deciduous leaves. When the flowers die, the pots can be plunged in the garden to finish ripening, then moved to a frost-free place for storage. There is no need to re-pot for five years: simply top dress with fresh compost when starting the bulbs into growth again in the spring.

Chlidanthus fragrans from South America makes a very attractive conservatory plant, with fragrant, yellow, lily-like flowers on 25cm (10in) stems which appear in early to mid-summer. Plant the bulbs in early to mid-spring, three to a 15cm (6in) pot of compost made of one part peat or peat substitute, one part leafmould, if available, one part loam or sterilised soil with a generous measure of sand. Start into growth in a propagator for bottom heat at about 16°C (61°F). Water sparingly until growth begins, then keep moist. When the flowers appear the plants must be kept in the coolest part of the greenhouse or conservatory. For storing, the bulbs must be dried off by putting the pots on their sides. When quite dry, remove the bulbs and overwinter them in boxes of sand or composted bark.

Haemanthus multiflora, the Blood Lily, Torch Lily or Paint Brush from East Africa, is grown just like the hippeastrum at a preferred temperature of 13°C (55°F). It has dense umbels of many small tubular flowers, surrounded at the base with two or more large brightly coloured bracts instead of petals. Pot in early spring in a loam compost to which an extra part of grit or sand is added. The pot should be twice the circumference of the bulb and this should be set in the compost with just the tip showing. Start into growth in a propagator with the thermostat set at 13°C (55°F) and water sparingly until growth is well established. When the flower buds show colour, move the pot to a cool place in the conservatory and shade from direct sunlight. The plant should be kept moist and given a three-weekly feed of dilute liquid fertiliser. After flowering, continue watering until the long strap-shaped leaves turn yellow. By late autumn the plant will have dried off and the pot should be placed on its side in a frost-free place. Start into growth in spring with a top dressing of fresh compost. *H. multiflora* flowers a little earlier than *H. katherinae* and *H. natalensis.* All three are dramatically beautiful in bloom and grow to about 60cm (2ft) tall.

Hippeastrum or Royal Dutch Amaryllis is truly the emperor of indoor blooms and millions of these very large bulbs are sold every year. From two to eight of the spectacular flowers of the Dutch hybrids are carried on a sturdy leafless stem, and there is a basal fan of strap-shaped leaves which may appear before or with the flowers. The bulbs specially prepared for Christmas are started into growth a few days after potting in mid-autumn. They flower in a few weeks at ordinary room temperature. Ordinary bulbs – the bigger the better – should each have a pot with a drainage hole, the pot being half as large again as the bulb. It is a good plan to soak the lower part of the bulb in water for twenty-four hours before potting in a loam-based compost. Pot bulbs in succession from early winter to mid-spring with only two-thirds of each bulb buried; its top should be about 2.5cm (1in) below the rim of the pot. Start into growth by placing the pot in a shallow dish, such as a pie dish, half-filled with water and placed in a propagator at 21°C (70°F). Add water to the dish to keep the compost just moist.

When the first flowers open, the plant should be placed in a cool, light position; water regularly and feed weekly with a good liquid fertiliser. Remove the anthers to make the bloom last longer, and when flowering has finished, cut off the stems with a sharp knife. Keep the bulb growing until the foliage starts to wither in autumn; then place the pot on its side in a cool, airy place to rest until early

to mid-winter when the bulb can be re-started into growth. Don't transplant it, simply give a top dressing of fresh compost. Hippeastrum relish being pot-bound, so transplanting every four or five years is the rule. Many bulbs, given the proper treatment, will produce a second flowering spike about five weeks after the first.

New varieties of Hippeastrum are constantly appearing, but some of the proven best are: Apple Blossom, pale pink with a lighter throat; Beautiful Lady, light mandarin red, shaded azalea pink; Belinda, dark velvet red; Bermuda, red with a white stripe; Bestseller, deep pink tinged with lilac; Bouquet, deep salmon pink; Firedance, vermilion and dark red; King of the Striped, red flushed and striped white; Orange Sovereign, glowing orange red; Picotee, pure white rimmed with red; Telstar, salmon red; United Nations, pure white with vermilion stripes; White Lady, white with a green tinged throat.

Hymenocallis, the Spider Lily, another amaryllid from South America, has fragrant white or yellow blooms like spidery daffodils. Planted in mid-spring, it will bloom in early summer and grows to about 60cm (2ft).

Pancratium maritimum or Sea Daffodil deserves a place in the summer conservatory for its magnificent perfume. The long trumpet-shaped flowers open in mid-summer on stems up to 60cm (2ft) tall. Somewhat earlier to flower is the equally fragrant *P. illyricum*.

Sprekelia formosissima from Mexico has a strikingly beautiful orchid-like bloom up to 10cm (4in) long on a short, stiff stem surrounded by the typical strap-shaped leaves of the amaryllids.

Stenomesson incarnatum, from tropical America, is well worth looking for in the specialist bulb catalogues. It has long, red funnel-shaped flowers with a dark green stripe in nodding umbels of up to six, which are borne in late summer.

Zephyranthes, or Fairy Lilies, all have solitary upward-facing blooms emerging from sheathing spathes in a colour range from pink to yellow. They

SWEET-SMELLING PLANTS

Some summer-flowering bulbs are fragrant as well as colourful. Examples are the Goldband Lily *L. auratum,* and the various forms of *L. speciosum*, while the Peruvian daffodil *Hymenocallis narcissiflora* is particularly sweet scented. Plant one bulb to an 18cm (7in) pot and it will flower well into summer.

There are many other plants that can be grown in the greenhouse or conservatory mainly for the fragrance of their flowers or foliage, or both. My favourite is the citrus-scented shrub *Daphne odora* with pale purple flowers in winter. The myrtles are also good value for their fragrant white, cream or pink blossom. *M. communis* is probably too tall for the smaller structures, although there is a compact variety *M. communis Tarentina*, while *M. bullata* and *M. ugni* grow only about 1m (3ft) tall. The lemon scent of *Lippia citriodora* is released when the leaves are crushed, and this deciduous shrub can be spring pruned to keep it happy in a 20cm (8in) pot.

Scented-leaved geraniums are described on page 65, and several have strong citrus scents. So, too, has *Eucalyptus citriodora*, the lemon-scented gum. This can be raised from seed grown in spring in a propagator at about 20°C (70°F) and potted on to a final pot size of 13cm (5in). It needs warmth in the winter of not less than 10°C (50°F), plenty of light and reasonable humidity.

bloom from early to late summer and seldom grow taller than 25cm (10in).

All of these *Amaryllidaceae* should be potted keeping the neck of the bulb at or just above the level of the compost. They should be allowed to dry off after the leaves have turned yellow, and can be propagated by offsets taken when potting up.

The Lilaceae Family

The large family of lilies includes many that may be grown in containers in the conservatory throughout the year or given a sheltered position outdoors for part of the summer.

Agapanthus, the African Lily or Lily of the Nile grows to 90cm (3ft) with rosettes of strap-like leaves in spring, and blue and violet trumpet-shaped flowers from mid-summer to early autumn. For best effect, plant three agapanthus together in a large wooden tub filled with a soil/sand growing medium enriched with bone meal.

The roots develop very vigorously, enough to crack terracotta pots. Alternatively grow one plant to an 18cm (7in) pot and re-pot to a size larger after a couple of years. Plenty of water is vital and give a weekly feed of diluted liquid manure in spring and up to flowering.

Brodiaea is a species from North America; the plants are cormous, with starry blue and lilac blooms, and make particularly attractive pot plants for a sunny windowsill or the conservatory. They are readily propagated by taking the cormlets and growing them on.

Convallaria Majus used to provide a Christmas centrepiece in Britain, a pyramid of these lovely, fragrant Lilies of the Valley arranged on the table. Rhizomes would be dug up in early autumn and planted in compost in a propagating frame with bottom heat to force them into bloom for the Christmas festivities. Nowadays it is possible to do much the same using specially treated crowns – given a minimum temperature of 10°C (50°F)

The very popular bulb for winter and spring flowering known as amaryllis is correctly one of the Hippeastrum species. A. belladonna's one to four pink, trumpet-shaped flowers appear in late summer or autumn.

these will come into flower about six weeks after planting. Planted in early spring in large pots of a sand/soil mixture, the crowns will flower a few weeks later.

Gloriosa cultivars from tropical Africa are truly glorious perennial climbers for the conservatory, with their crimson and gold orchid-like flowers in bloom from early summer to early autumn. They are easy to grow and can be trained on to canes, wires or string. The tubers are potted in early spring in potting compost with a generous measure of sharp sand for drainage. The tuber should lie in the pot with the shoot at the end of the tuber upright. It is then covered with about 5cm (2in) of the compost which should be moist, but not sopping wet. Do not water the tubers until growth begins; this will then mean providing a temperature of 13–15°C (55–60°F). Give plenty of water throughout the summer, and a weekly feed of diluted liquid fertiliser up to flowering, with regular mist spraying in the hottest weather. After flowering, and when the leaves have yellowed, the tubers are stored dry over the winter. Offsets can be taken when re-potting in the spring.

Lachenalias are delightful bulbous perennials for the conservatory or indoors. Put five bulbs in a 15cm (6in) pot of soil-based compost in late summer. Water sparingly until plants are growing strongly, then freely and feed with liquid manure every 14 days.

Sandersonia are good conservatory or cool greenhouse climbers, like gloriosa; their golden-orange urn-shaped blooms are normally in flower from midsummer to early autumn. The clinging tendrils protrude from oval leaves and can be trained up canes set in the pot or up a pillar or trellis. The tubers of *Sandersonia aurantiaca* are planted in April, 5cm (2in) deep in a potting compost enriched with well-rotted farmyard manure, allowing one tuber to each 10cm (4in) pot. Bottom heat is not required. Water sparingly until growth is established, then increase the amount given as the temperature rises with the warmer days. Although these are tropical plants they dislike very hot weather, so some shading and plenty of ventilation are needed. After flowering, the stems will die back. Allow the pots to dry and store the tubers in sand in a frost-free place. They can be started into growth again in the spring.

A Selection of Bulbous Plants

Among other bulbous plants for late spring and summer flowering in the conservatory or greenhouse are the freesia-like Babiana hybrids; freesias themselves (p86); the lush and beautiful begonia hybrids, and the equally showy gloxinias; smithiana, the foxglove look-alike or Temple Bells; chincherinchee or *ornithogalum thyrsoides*; and the *Zantedeschia* or Arum lilies in pink, yellow or white.

Achimenes are growing in popularity as summer-flowering pot plants. These perennial hybrids with impatiens-like flowers have a wide range of colours and glossy, fleshy leaves. They were popularly known as Hot Water Plants as it was believed they were better watered with hand-hot water. The plants are propagated from rhizomes, bought dry and started into growth in spring. Some varieties are particularly suitable for hanging baskets.

Babiana is commonly called the Baboon Flower because its fibrous-coated corms are a favourite food of baboons. The corms are planted may-be twelve to a 15cm (6in) pot, in a compost of one part peat or composted fine grade bark, one of loam or clean soil, and one of sharp sand with a little limestone added. Keep the compost moist and feed with dilute liquid manure every three weeks from the time the shoots emerge until the buds show colour. Babiana likes half a day of direct sunlight with a minimum daytime temperature of 13°C (55°F). After flowering, allow the foliage to wither, then store the corms in dry sand over the winter.

Begonia is one of the showiest of pot plants, available as rhizomatous or tuberous species and hybrids in a host of named varieties. Tuberous greenhouse begonias can be grown in pots of a bark-based compost but need regular feeding with a dilute liquid fertiliser every three weeks; they also need a humid atmosphere during hot weather and shading from direct sun-light. After flowering, reduce the watering and allow the compost to dry out gradually. The tubers should be labelled and stored over the winter in sand in a frost-free place.

Freesia, see p86.

Gloxinia hybrids rival the begonias for the exotic beauty of their flowers and velvety foliage. They are actually not gloxinias at all, but derived from *sinningia speciosa* which were mis-named gloxinia and the name has stuck. Anyone with a heated greenhouse or conservatory can grow these magnificent plants from tubers bought by colour, named variety or as mixtures. The plants are compact, not more than 30cm (12in) tall, with trumpet-shaped flowers that can be single, double, waved or ruffled and appear from mid-summer to early autumn. The tubers are potted in a loam-based compost in mid-winter in 15cm (6in) pots, with the top of the tuber just level with the surface of the compost. Water thoroughly and place in a propagator, or provide alternative bottom heat of 18–21°C (65–70°F) to get them going. A minimum night temperature of 15°C (61°F) is vital. When growth gets under way, give protection from strong sunlight, water liberally and spray with tepid water until the flower buds appear. Be careful not to let water become trapped in the centre of the plant, as this will cause rotting. After flowering the leaves will start to die back and watering should be discon-tinued. Over the winter lay the pots on their sides under the greenhouse staging or in another frost-free place. Before starting into growth again give a top dressing of fresh compost. Tubers more than three years old should be discarded.

Ornithogalum thyrsoides, the chincherinchee has a longer life as a cut flower than any other, and if cut in bud the blooms will last at least six weeks. They can, of course, be grown outdoors, but are good subjects for a cool greenhouse. Planted in late winter or early spring they will flower in early summer. The round, white bulbs should be planted 7.5cm (3in) deep and 5cm (2in) apart in deep pots or boxes of potting compost which are then placed under the greenhouse bench. Water sparingly until growth is well established, and then the pots or boxes can be moved to a light position and given a minimum temperature of 7°C (45°F).

Oxalis make attractive little plants for the conservatory. Plant the tubers in early spring 2.5cm (1in) deep and 5cm (2in) apart in loam-based compost, and without heat they will flower for most of the summer, with masses of bell-shaped rose-opal blooms above a rosette of clover-type leaves. Shade the plants from direct sunlight, but give them plenty of air and water and a monthly feed of liquid fertiliser.

Smithiana, the foxglove look-alike or Temple Bells, are handsome plants for the conservatory or indoors. Rhizomes can be potted at monthly intervals from late winter to late spring and grown at 18–21°C (65–70°F). Divide the rhizomes into 5cm (2in) pieces, each with one shoot, at potting time.

Zantedeschia or Arum Lilies in pink, yellow or white are grown individually in 15cm (6in) pots of soil-based compost. Plant 5cm (2in) deep in early spring and keep moist, until growth starts, then water sparingly until plants are in full leaf, then water generously and feed weekly with liquid manure.

CARNATIONS AS HOBBY PLANTS

Two types of this beautiful flower are grown under glass: perennial carnations grown as annuals from seed, and perpetual carnations grown from cuttings. Though the cultivation of perpetuals can become an absorbing hobby, they are not the ideal partners to share a small greenhouse with other plants because they require a drier, sunnier atmosphere – just the sort of condition, in fact, that favours thrips and red spider mite infestation.

Another rather off-putting need is a minimum winter temperature of 5°C (40°F), and although carnations can be grown with no more than a frost-free level of heat, for winter flowering a minimum of 10°C (50°F) is essential. Having said that, they are not difficult plants to grow and bring enormous pleasure with a truly bewildering number of varieties to choose from and readily available expertise from many books. Cuttings are almost always available from local nurseries or specialist raisers – note that cuttings should come from stock plants kept solely for this purpose, because these are more vigorous than cuttings taken from flowering plants.

At one time it was accepted practice to plant directly into the greenhouse border after it had been enriched with well-rotted farmyard manure or home-made compost plus a dressing of fish, blood and bone fertiliser; however, this option is less popular today than planting in pots.

on as soon as a rooting system has developed. Bottom heat isn't vital, but rooting is quicker if gentle heat of about 10°C (50°F) is provided. Successional cuttings can be taken at virtually any time to give a long period of flowering, and for established plants, lower shoots can be layered to increase stock.

As soon as possible the winter cuttings should be put into 8cm (3in) pots of a loam-based compost (see p31) with added lime, then in mid-spring transplanted into 13cm (5in) pots, and finally, in early or mid-summer, into 18 or 20cm (7 or 8in) pots that must be scrupulously cleaned. Watering is fairly critical at this stage. The cutting should leave a moist compost and go into a drier compost for at least a couple of days before being given more moisture, because the danger is stem rot.

As to the composition of the compost for potting on and final potting, the author G.W. Robinson recommends a mixture of loam with sand and mortar rubble or limestone chips:

> If the loam is of good quality, the proportion is four loam to one of the other materials, with a proprietary carnation fertiliser added as recommended by the manufacturers. For rooted cuttings a higher proportion of sand should be used for the first potting; if the loam is heavy it may be as much as half and half. Lime in some form is essential, as the parent species are lime-lovers and will not tolerate acid soil conditions. Where it can be obtained, lime rubble, broken up and screened, is probably the best way of incorporating lime, as it improves drainage at the same time.

Cuttings

Carnation cuttings are taken from early winter onwards to give flowering plants the following winter. They root quite readily in sharp sand, but need potting

Feeding and Care

Opinions differ widely on what sort of feeding regime is required. Hoof and horn with its slow-release nitrogen was considered the ideal feed, but some think

Border carnations are best propagated by layering. Choose a vigorous side shoot and strip off leaves below the top four to six pairs. Make a slit with a very sharp knife in the stem just below a joint. Then open it out and gently press the tongue into the soil, which has been specially prepared with a generous quantity of sand. Hold the layer in place with an opened-out paper clip, The layer should root in around six to eight weeks, when it can be severed from its parent.

this could stimulate the growth of foliage at the expense of flowers and lead to soft growth. My choice has always been seaweed meal applied as a top dressing in mid-summer gently teased into the compost at the rate of about 25g (1oz) to a 20cm (8in) pot, followed by foliar feeding with a liquid manure at fortnightly intervals through to early autumn.

Stopping and disbudding are the techniques used to produce fine quality blooms. Stopping means taking out the growing point to encourage the development of lateral shoots. It starts in early spring when the top of the young plant is broken off – not pinched out – to leave about 15cm (6in) of stem. When the plant goes into its final pot a cane of up to 2m (6ft) tall should go with it and as the bushy growth develops it can be loosely tied in to it. The side shoots are stopped a few at a time until early mid-summer. As the flowering stems develop, lateral buds are formed, and just as with chrysanthemums, these have to be removed carefully to allow the crown bud to form properly.

Cutting the flower stem is about the only pruning needed for perpetual carnations, and the mature plants can be kept in production for as long as they remain vigorous and healthy. In the third year it is advisable to re-pot from a 20cm (8in) pot into a 23cm (9in) one, or to re-pot into the same size pot by reducing the rootball and providing fresh compost.

With modern F1 hybrid carnations such as the Knight Series, growing from seed to have flowering plants within about twenty weeks is entirely feasible. Sow early in the year in a propagator at about 15°C (60°F); prick out into trays of a loam-based compost, and reduce the temperature. Pot on as for cuttings.

Problems

Red spider mite and thrips relish the sunny, dry atmosphere of the carnation house, so regular syringing is a preventive. A mild attack by either pest can be controlled by spraying with derris, three times at six-day intervals. The biological control technique for red spider mite is to introduce the parasitic mite *Phytoseiulus persimilis* (p56).

Carnation rust starts at the base of a plant as small yellow blisters, usually appearing from late autumn to late winter. During the warmer days of spring and summer the blisters burst to become brown pustules. Most modern varieties of carnation are either resistant to, or tolerant of the disease. Any affected leaves should be picked off and destroyed, and care should be taken when watering that spores from stem pustules are not washed on to healthy growth.

CHRYSANTHEMUMS AS HOBBY PLANTS

For many years vases of crimson, yellow, bronze and white chrysanthemums have been a feature of winter decorations: not the bunches of spray chrysanths, but the big blooms that come from disbudding the plants. They are a joy to grow, and give such long-lasting pleasure as cut flowers that they alone justify the cost of buying a greenhouse.

Of course, these late-flowering chrysanthemums are not everyone's idea of floral beauty, being so bold that some people consider them too ostentatious – while advice on raising them is often shrouded in mystery. Sometimes gardeners who have never tried their hand at it are put off by the experts' talk of the right time to stop the plants and secure the buds.

There is no doubt that the chrysanthemum is one of the oldest flowers in continuous cultivation. It came to Britain in about 1754 from China where chrysanthemums had been treasured flowers for more than two thousand years. Europe and America then 'discovered' them and took to them with zest, and in no time at all they had become an indispensable feature of every superior garden.

Now they are deservedly the most popular of all the specialist flowers, with hundreds of thousands of devotees in specialist chrysanthemum societies and associations throughout the world.

As far as many enthusiasts are concerned, a great plus point is that the best-grown chrysanthemum plants are those raised entirely in pots and therefore, because they stand outside for the summer and most of the autumn, they leave the greenhouse free for growing edible crops.

With a formidable choice of plant types, the newcomer can be perplexed at the outset: anyone who intends to take up the hobby as an exhibitor would be well counselled to join a regional specialist group. In the UK's National Chrysanthemum Society there are thirty sections in its system of classification. For late flowering in the greenhouse, usually late autumn and early winter, there are twelve sections: Large Exhibition usually grown as one bloom on one plant; Medium Exhibition grown as one or two blooms on a plant; Incurved, two or three blooms on a plant; Reflexed, two or three blooms; Intermediate, two or three blooms; Anemones, four to six blooms; Singles, four to six or ten to twelve blooms, depending on flower size; Pompons, ten to twelve blooms or sprays; Spiders, Quills and Spoons, grown as single blooms or several to each plant; any other types; and Charms

and Cascades, grown as dense small-leaved domes covered in small, scented flowers.

Cuttings

Making a start with chrysanthemums in the greenhouse means buying rooted cuttings. From then on it is usual to take cuttings from one's own stock plants, occasionally buying in new material when you want a change in type or variety. Which varieties should be grown, and how many? Perhaps the best advice for the newcomer is to send for a catalogue from a chrysanthemum nursery and to choose from one of the late-flowering collections of eight, ten or a dozen cuttings. The exact number chosen will obviously depend on the space available in the greenhouse during the final weeks up to full flowering. As an example, in a 2.4 x 1.8m (8 x 6ft) greenhouse without benches or staging, ten plants in 23cm (9in) or 25cm(10in) pots can be accommodated on either side. For particulary tall-growing plants you might have to dig trenches in the border so that the blooms are not forced against the glass in the eaves.

Always go to a specialist nursery for cuttings to avoid disappointment. Advice on raising them will also be given and after a while you will be able to adapt the technique of cultivation to suit your particular requirements. In my case this means choosing a few of the very beautiful reflexed and intermediate varieties and allowing each plant to produce six or so blooms that can be cut for use in the house, not for exhibition purposes. They don't reach quite the proportions of those on plants restricted to two or three blooms, but they are an ideal size for cutting and, in vases, will remain in fine condition indoors from late autumn right through the Christmas period.

The cuttings are taken from the plants or stools that have flowered and have been overwintered in boxes of peat, or peat substitute. Either take off the cutting with a knife, or simply break it off when it is about 5–8cm (2–3in) long; remove all but two pairs of leaves, and insert each cutting singly into an 8cm (3in) pot of compost or put three or four cuttings round the rim.

The cuttings should be taken as early in the year as possible and kept at a temperature of about 10°C (50°F), although a night temperature of 8°C (45°F) will not harm them. The time taken for a good root system to develop depends on the warmth provided: gentle bottom heat, say 15.5°C (60°F) in a propagator, will have roots forming in about fourteen days, while at 10°C (50°F) the process takes seven to ten days longer. Once the cuttings have rooted, they can be removed from the propagator and given a cool, light position to encourage short, sturdy plants with a big root system.

In early spring the young plants should be ready to move into 13cm (5in) pots, and can be grown on in unheated conditions in the cold greenhouse or cold frame. Towards late spring the cuttings have to be stopped by pinching out the growing tip to encourage the development of shoots at the leaf axils.

The second and final potting on is done in late spring, when 20cm (8in), 23cm (9in) or 25cm (10in) pots will be required, depending on the vigour of the variety. If you are doubtful about vigour, go for 23cm (9in) pots and a good multipurpose compost. Two or three 1.5m (5ft) canes will also be needed for each pot, some fillis string and enough space outside to stand the pots throughout the summer and early autumn.

The final potting exercise should be carried out with extra care. First, put some crocks or pebbles in the bottom of the pot to ensure that the drainage hole functions properly. Then fill the pot with the compost, firming it thoroughly as you do so; some gardeners only fill the pot half full to allow for top dressing with fresh compost over the growing period.

THE CHRYSANTHEMUM TIMETABLE

This is the seasonal schedule which should be followed in order to produce late-flowering chrysanthemums in an unheated greenhouse. The timings are approximate.

Mid-/late winter. Order plants or take cuttings from overwintered plants or stools.
Early spring. Pot up cuttings into 13cm (5in) pots.
Mid-spring. Stop the cuttings and stand the pots outside.
Late spring. Final potting into 20cm (8in), 23cm (9in) or 25cm (10in) pots.
Early summer. Second stopping and start feeding.
Mid-summer. Surface dress pots with compost.
Late summer. Second surface dressing.
Early autumn. Secure the buds.
Mid-autumn. Take pots into the greenhouse.
Late autumn/early winter. Blooms are ready for cutting.

Late-flowering chrysanthemums can be stood outside the green-house for the summer and early autumn, then taken inside before the first frosts.

STORING STOCK CHRYSANTHEMUMS

Once a stock of chrysanthemum plants has been bought, both the garden (the early flowering types) and the greenhouse ones can be used for propagating plants for the subsequent season. The parent plants or 'stools' are used to take cuttings as described on p102 as early in the year as possible, although many commercial growers and expert amateurs start to take cuttings of late-flowering specimens in late autumn, and cuttings of the outdoor varieties between late winter and early spring.

The stools in the garden, and those of the late-flowering type in their pots, are prepared for the winter by stripping off all the foliage above ground level and then cutting the main stem down to about 15cm (6in) with secateurs. Tie a label securely to the stem with the name of the variety written on it, along with any other information you might wish to record.

Next, lift the stools carefully from the soil with a garden fork or ease them from their pots and tease away as much of the growing medium from the rootball as possible. To rid the plants of any slugs that might have taken up residence, as well as their eggs, dunk the roots in warm water, to which a mild garden disinfectant can be added. This will remove a lot more of the soil or compost and spread the roots which can then be trimmed back.

The stools are now ready for their winter quarters, preferably in boxes under the staging in the greenhouse, in a light, airy shed or garage. They can be packed quite closely together in wooden boxes with just enough peat or peat substitute to cushion the roots. They need not be considered very tender subjects because they will survive two or three degrees of frost (down to −2°C (28°F), but they must have adequate ventilation. Damp air is more dangerous than dry air, so on foggy days keep the ventilator closed, and on very cold windy days use leeward ventilation, if possible.

The stools should be kept on the dry side up to the turn of the year: just give a little water if the peat or compost shows signs of drying out. Too much moisture can cause the shoots to rot at or just below soil level. If this happens, remove the affected shoot and lightly dust the stools with flowers of sulphur. From mid-winter onwards the new shoots should develop quite rapidly and more water can be given, particularly in the week before the cuttings are taken.

My technique is to fill the pot to within 5cm (2in) of the rim with compost, firming it with the handle of a hammer. Place an empty 13cm(5in) pot in position in the larger pot as you fill it, and it makes a planting hole for the transplant; this is made even easier if the compost is well moistened before you start filling.

Next step is to place canes round the plant, with string holding the plant securely to the canes. The shoots which will carry the blooms are tied into the canes as growth develops.

After this final potting, water sparingly for about ten days to encourage the rootball to break out into the new compost. This stage often seems to coincide with a hot, dry spell; if there are signs of flagging, give a gentle foliar spraying first thing in the morning and again in the evening.

The plants in their pots rapidly make a lot of growth and become somewhat top-heavy; they are therefore liable to damage from wind and thundery rain, so it is essential to give thought to where you can stand them that will offer them full sunlight, if possible, and sufficient elbow-room, but will also shelter them from the wind. Regular watering and liquid feeding will be needed, with the occasional gentle spraying from a hosepipe or spray gun. Also, at the end of their summer holiday outdoors, the plants will have to be manhandled into the greenhouse – and that can be a tricky operation! It can be very embarrassing to discover that they just won't fit back in to the greenhouse when the first frost of autumn is forecast.

So where you site the pots should be selected carefully. If it isn't on a concrete or tarmac surface, a plastic sheet or slates must be put down to keep out the worms. Stakes must be positioned at both ends of the site, to which you can attach horizontal wires; the canes in the pots can then be tied into the wires to hold them firm.

Where there isn't much room to spare, a standing-out method can be improvised by removing the wooden staging from the greenhouse – turned upside down, this accommodates the pots of chrysanthemums very neatly. It is returned to the greenhouse when the tomato and cucumber plants have finished in late autumn; this is just the right time, too, for taking the chrysanthemums into the greenhouse.

Feeding and Care

Watering and liquid feeding are the two regular chores which are essential if your chrysanthemum plants are to give of their best. So don't go away on holiday without making proper provision for these tasks to be

done by someone you can trust.

Feeding with bought-in or homemade organic fertiliser need not start until six weeks after the final potting, and then the rule is feed a little and often.

Towards mid-summer the late-flowering chrysanthemums have to have a second stopping to enable further branches to develop. In fact, pinching out the growing tips of the three or four main branches will result in a final eight, ten or more branches, each of which will carry a single bloom. How many you allow to develop is entirely up to you.

When the time comes, feed once a week at normal strength, then feed twice a week at half strength, then three times a week at one-third strength. Towards the end of mid-summer, maybe sooner, feeding roots will appear on the surface of the compost and this is the signal to add fresh compost to the pot. A further top dressing will probably be necessary in late summer or early autumn.

At about this time the first buds will appear, and the final act of pruning takes place. This is called 'taking' or 'securing the bud', and involves carefully taking off all the small buds and shoots to leave just one selected bud per branch to develop. Left to its own devices, the plant would produce a lot of little blooms in a spray.

Continue regular feeding until the buds begin to show colour, then ease off and finish feeding about three weeks later. The flower stems will need to be tied securely to the canes, and this is especially important before the plants are moved back into the greenhouse, because the branches are very easily snapped away from the main stem.

Problems

Blind shoots. This is when the growing tip of a cutting or shoot fails to develop. The cause could be frost damage but is more likely to be due to capsid damage. These are small green or brown insects about 5mm (¼in) long which can be picked off with tweezers and destroyed.

Buds eaten. Capsids, caterpillars and earwigs can cause this damage, but are easily located and can be picked off by hand or tweezers.

Foliage troubles. Mottling of the leaves in mature plants is almost certainly due to a virus disease and the plants should be destroyed. On young plants, speckled leaves are an indication of too rapid hardening off, but they should recover. Yellowing of the leaves on more mature plants is a sign of over-watering, even waterlogging, and the plants should be allowed to dry out. Yellowing of the lower leaves could be due to magnesium deficiency, while in the upper leaves it could be iron deficiency. Foliar feeding should correct the deficiencies. Distorted leaves at the growing point often indicate aphid attack. Spray with soft soap solution or soapy water (p52).

Over-feeding. This is unlikely to happen to organically-grown plants. Symptoms are buds rotting and generally coarse blooms. Powdery deposit on leaves. Spray with Bordeaux mixture.

Tunnelling of leaves. White pathways in the leaves indicate the presence of leaf miner grubs: crush them with your fingernail. If there is severe infestation, the egg-laying flies must be controlled using the parasites *Opius pallipes* and *Dacnusa sibirica*.

EDIBLE CROPS

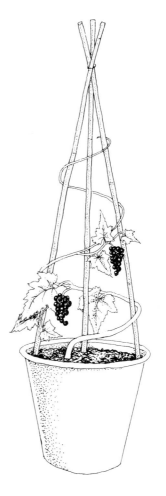

In the weather-protected environment of the greenhouse a good range of crops can be grown almost all the year round. Salad crops, rich in vitamins and minerals, are especially suitable for cropping either in growing bags or in the border soil. There are varieties of lettuce, for example, that are excellent for this purpose and have been specially bred for the short-day conditions of late autumn and winter.

Tomatoes are the most popular choice for the amateur's greenhouse, and deservedly so. Top flavour varieties can be grown and enjoyed straight from the plants. A frost-free interior, careful selection of varieties and special attention to pest and disease control are the key elements in successfully raising the crops described in the following section.

YEAR-ROUND FOOD FROM THE GREENHOUSE

Making the best use of the greenhouse means planning to keep it productive all through the year, even though it may be unheated over the winter.

As well as providing a home for overwintering chrysanthemum and fuchsia plants (see p101), it can also be used to stretch the season for salads; to give early supplies of sweet, young carrots; to produce plants for the vegetable patch (sowing details are on pages 142–50) and, of course, to provide rich pickings from the summer cropping of tomatoes, cucumbers, peppers and melons.

The only restricting factors are the time you can give to year-round production; whether or not you can provide frost protection either by insulation or a minimum of heating or both, using the greenhouse in conjunction with a heated propagator; and your geographical location. In northern England and Scotland, for example, a lack of light in late winter and early spring is somewhat restrictive unless natural light is augmented with artificial lighting.

To raise half-hardy and early-season edible crops a heated propagator is invaluable, because it can be used to speed germination before the internal temperature of the greenhouse reaches the necessary level.

Plan on paper what you would like your greenhouse to do and then put the plan into action, with the proviso that it should be flexible enough to take minor alterations in its stride. Major setbacks have to be borne with fortitude. In the severe weather of February 1991 my greenhouse was cut off for a week by a four-foot snow drift. Night temperatures dipped as low as −10°C, and I feared for the boxes of seed potatoes set

---

UNDER THE STAGING

There's no reason why the area under the greenhouse staging should not be used all the year round. In winter, as well as forcing crops such as rhubarb and chicory, it can be the place where you store dormant plants like chrysanthemum stools, dahlia tubers and summer-flowering greenhouse bulbs.

If there is a reasonably good level of light, as with glass-to-ground structures, you can use the space for growing bags sown with winter lettuce and carrots (page 109). Many flowering pot plants can successfully be grown on under the staging. For example, after pricking out into small pots, calceolaria, cineraria, cyclamen, polyanthus and primula can all be grown on to the final potting stage.

The shaded light is very much appreciated, too, by many houseplants being propagated by cuttings – even well-established houseplants benefit from a few weeks' spell under the staging. But plants below bench level are very easily overlooked. Don't forget that they will need watering, and, perhaps, feeding. If any show signs of becoming drawn and spindly move them to a lighter position, but still out of direct sunlight. Remember also that sub-stage plants will be vulnerable to splashes or worse from watering operations *on* the staging and these can lead to fungal disease, particularly in lettuces.

Some greenhouse gardeners install soil-warming equipment in the border soil under the staging and use it for raising early salad crops, for seed propagation and for starting dahlias and begonias into growth. This area can readily be curtained off to give zone heating, and a refinement is to add artificial lighting. In early spring it is a useful plan to locate an electrically-heated propagator under the staging for the germination of seeds. This leaves the staging free to carry trays and pots of seedlings after pricking out.

for chitting (sprouting) and half trays of tomato seedlings in the propagator. In the event, bubble polythene insulation proved a godsend and just about everything survived, apart from half a dozen of the potatoes. Under the thick blanket of snow that darkened the greenhouse, however, the tomato seedlings became drawn and weak, and I had to start all over again with a second sowing. However, since such severe conditions are seldom encountered more than one year in seven or eight in the British Isles, it really isn't worth the expense of making special provision to counter them; it is best to adopt a management-by-exception philosophy.

The checklists for the seasons provide summaries of what could be happening in your greenhouse and conservatory throughout the year. Here are suggestions on how to make a small greenhouse an all-seasons one for food production, by using it to raise vegetables for planting outside as well as crops to mature in situ.

Winter

In early winter sow a row of an early carrot such as Amsterdam Forcing, Gregory F1 or Suko in a used growing bag, ready for harvesting in the spring. Bring in a few roots of mint to pot up in 15cm (6in) pots of soil to provide fresh-cut mint from the start of the year onwards.

In mid-winter sow a second row of early carrots in the growing bag for harvesting in late spring. In another used growing bag sow a pinch of Winter Density lettuce and French Breakfast radish for harvesting in the spring.

Seed potatoes can be set out for chitting in wooden trays or egg cartons, but be prepared to protect them from frost. In a heated propagator sow broad beans in paper pots (p42), and in mid-winter sow half trays or modules of Brussels sprouts, early cabbage such as Hispi or Pixie, leeks, onions, summer cauliflowers, and lettuce such as Little Gem, Bubbles or Erthel, for planting out in spring.

Spring

Shallots and onion sets can be started into growth on shallow trays of moist soil. Plant out when they have made about an inch of roots. Harvest any salad crops as they become ready. In pots or modules in a propagator, sow seeds of greenhouse tomatoes in late winter. Sow those for outdoor growing in early spring.

Sow half-trays of summer cabbage, calabrese and more lettuce. In mid-spring sow courgettes, cucumbers,

An egg carton is useful when setting out seed potatoes for chitting (sprouting).

marrows, melons, peppers and sweet corn, in pots.

Prick out the tomato seedlings as soon as they are large enough to handle. Sow French beans and runner beans in paper pots in mid-spring for planting out in late spring.

Summer

The greenhouse is in full production with tomatoes, cucumbers, peppers and all the other crops you have chosen. All the early-sown vegetables should have been moved out to the kitchen garden or allotment.

At midsummer, sow half trays of herbs, including parsley, for over-wintering. See p126 for how to produce new potatoes at Christmas.

Autumn

As the tomatoes, cucumbers and other plants reach the end of their cropping, put the remnants in the compost bin, but save one or two growing bags for winter sowings of salads.

For out-of-season strawberries follow the advice on p125.

CROPS TO GROW UNDER GLASS

TOMATOES

Tomatoes are the most widely grown greenhouse edible crop and deservedly so. The tangy perfume of a freshly-picked, still sun warm tomato is surely just as much the smell of summer as sweet peas and newly-cut grass. Flavour is a matter of opinion, but in my view, nothing the commercial producer can offer compares with organically-grown, home-produced Gardener's Delight, Ailsa Craig, Sonata or the handsome Tigerella.

Tomatoes under glass are relatively easy for the amateur to raise from seed, with a wide choice of varieties that offer a rich return for a small outlay. In fact six plants will keep a family of four well supplied with fresh tomatoes throughout the summer, with a fair few to give to friends besides.

Since inexpensive growing-bags have become widely available, the problem of the soil diseases which used to plague tomato growers, both amateur and professional, has been overcome. Growing-bags are just one way of raising this worthwhile crop. You can also grow direct into the greenhouse soil using a proprietary compost or your own mix; or you can grow the plants in straw bales or chunks of straw bale. Ring culture, using bottomless pots or fibre cylinders placed

over a layer of gravel, is yet another widely-used technique. Hydroponics is a method of growing plants in water containing the main plant foods, although this has been largely superseded by other systems – and in any event, because it relies on artificial fertilisers, it cannot be considered an organic cultivation technique.

Tomatoes come in two types: bush, and standard or upright. The bush types are generally more suitable for growing outdoors than in the greenhouse, although the plants can be raised under glass and then transplanted. However, gardeners may grow a crop of bush tomatoes at ground level in the greenhouse in company with either cucumbers or melons, trained up and over.

Biological control of the two major pests of greenhouse tomatoes – spider mite and whitefly – is now a practical and economical proposition for the amateur grower. Even so, these and other problems of tomato growing are easier to prevent than to cure, and advice on this is given in the troubleshooting section on p117. Recognising a potential problem before it becomes too troublesome is the key to successful management of any greenhouse.

Tomato Checklist

Before embarking on the exciting and profitable task of raising your own tomato plants and growing them on in your greenhouse or conservatory, go through this list of requirements.

First, a heated propagator, seed tray, and peat-based or peat substitute compost (see diagram on p32 for the amount required). For reliable germination a temperature of 15–20°C (60–68°F) is necessary; a warm place indoors, such as above the boiler or in the airing cupboard, could be used if you don't have a heated propagator.

Decide on how many plants can be accommodated; allow for three plants for each standard size growing bag, or for about 1m (3ft) between plants if using the greenhouse border, ring culture, large pots or straw bale methods.

Each plant, properly grown and managed, should produce 2–3kg (5–9lb) of edible fruit over a cropping period of 60–80 days, depending on when the plants start bearing, the sort of summer it is, and the region.

From the seed tray the seedlings are transplanted into 8cm (3in) pots, so you will need a pot for each seedling.

RIPEN YOUR GREEN TOMATOES

If you prefer to have ripe tomatoes rather than green tomato chutney, the way to ripen the last of the greenhouse crop is either to pick them and put them in a tray or drawer in a cool, airy but frost-free place, or to hang up the tomato plant, complete with fruit but minus its leaves, in a shed, garage or cellar.

Take the green fruit in stages, as needed, and allow about fourteen days for the ripening process. This is achieved by popping the green tomatoes into a clear plastic bag along with a ripe banana or ripe tomato. The ripe fruit gives off ethylene gas naturally – and this is the gas used commercially to start the ripening process of fruit picked 'green' for market. By timing the procedure carefully you can have ripe tomatoes right up to Christmas.

Tigerella, a tomato with orange stripes on red, has both good looks and an excellent flavour. Raise it from seed, as it is seldom available as commercially-grown plants.

Once into their final positions, tomato plants grow rapidly and need support. The best technique for plants in growing bags is to use soft string, such as fillis, for this. Make sure there is a horizontal support under the eaves at about head-height to which to tie the lengths of string. Fitments are available for aluminium-framed greenhouses for this job of running wires from one end to the other.

For pots, ring culture and straw bales you will need tall canes for the plants.

The developing plants will have to be fed regularly with a liquid organic fertiliser such as Maxicrop. The 500ml size will be more than adequate to feed six plants through a whole season, but remember that the larger sizes are cheaper in the long run and the product doesn't deteriorate if properly stored from one year to the next.

Shading for the plants when young and adequate ventilation are necessary, along with a rigid regime of watering. A fully grown tomato plant needs up to 2 litres (3½ pints) of water a day.

Remember, too, that if you go away on holiday, somebody must care for your plants until you return.

Finally, what can be done with the green tomatoes that cannot be ripened at the end of the cropping period? Homemade green tomato chutney is delicious!

Choosing the Variety

Certain varieties are dual purpose, so that you can grow some of the plants under glass and the others outside. Suitable varieties for this dual role are Ailsa Craig, Alicante, Gardener's Delight, Golden Sunrise, Harbinger, Moneymaker, Outdoor Girl, Shirley, Sungold, Sweet 100 and Tigerella.

The plants that will grow on in the unheated greenhouse can be put into their final position in mid-spring in warmer regions, and late spring where the climate is colder. From flowering until the first ripe fruit takes 10–12 weeks, so the first ripe tomatoes should be ready to pick from mid-summer in those warmer areas, and probably three to four weeks later elsewhere.

Go on picking the tomatoes until the first sharp frost is forecast, then clear the entire crop.

Tomato Varieties for the Greenhouse

Variety	Flavour rating	Comments
Ailsa Craig	G	Good yield medium fruit
Alicante	G	Good all-rounder
Celebrity	M	Moderate disease resistance
Curabel F1	M	Good disease resistance
Dombito F1	G	Beefsteak type
Estrella F1	M	Good for border growing
Eurocross F1	M	Heavy cropper
Gardener's Delight	E	Cherry size, superb flavour but low yield
Golden Sunrise	G	Yellow fruit, tangy
Grenadier F1	M	Moderate disease resistance
Harbinger	G	Ripens early
Herald	G	Sweet, medium size fruit
Ida F1	M	Good disease resistance
Jumbo Tom	M	Very large fruits
Moneymaker	P	Old favourite, but why?
Outdoor Girl	G	Good all-rounder
Piranto	M	Good for borders
Red Ensign F1	G	Firm fruit, good cropper
Seville Cross F1	M	Early cropper
Shirley F1	M	Good disease resistance
Sonata	M	Good disease resistance
Sungold	E	Good disease resistance
Sweet 100 F1	E	Cherry size, low yield
Tigerella	E	Fine flavour, handsome
Ultra Boy F1	G	Very large fruits

Key to flavour: P poor, M moderate, G good, E excellent. But note: this is a personal choice, and what suits my palate may not suit yours.

Raising the Plants

It is important to work out exactly when to sow the tomato seed because unless you can provide some warmth when the seedlings are pricked out, there is little advantage in sowing too early.

Sow from late winter in warmer regions, and from early spring in colder areas. For just a few plants, the seed can be sown onto moist compost in a 12cm (5in) pot, allowing three seeds to each pot. Then cover the seed with about 3mm (¼in) of compost. For more than, say, half-a-dozen plants use a half tray which will happily accommodate 15–20 seeds.

The seedlings will need to be pricked out 8–12 days after sowing and be grown on at a minimum temperature of 10°C (50°F). The aim is to produce short, sturdy plants with dark stems.

A Choice of Growing Methods

Growing bags The standard size growing bag is approximately 96cm (38in) long by 35cm (14in) wide. So in an 8ft by 6ft greenhouse without staging it is possible to accommodate twelve plants in four growing bags, or with staging along one side only there would be room for two growing bags.

Organic growing bags are not always readily available; in this case many of us have to compromise by using conventional bags but organic techniques of feeding and management. This means feeding the crop with an organic liquid fertiliser and controlling pests and diseases without the use of pesticides.

Whichever type of bag is used, these should be bought well in advance of planting-out time for the young tomato plants, and placed in the greenhouse so that they warm up. Give them a thorough shaking to loosen the compacted compost and place them on a flat surface free from stones. If placed directly on to the border soil, it is wise to put down a sheet of plastic first to avoid possible contamination by pests and diseases from the soil.

When planting out the tomatoes into the growing bag, have the supporting strings already in position so that the loose end can be tucked under the root ball of the plant as it goes into the bag. Alternatively, tie the string loosely round the bottom of the stem of the plant. Either way, as the plant grows it will have to be gently encouraged to entwine with the string – though take the string round the plant, not the plant round the string.

Follow the growing bag instructions about watering before planting the tomatoes. And as already mentioned, always use water from a container in the greenhouse so that it is at about the same temperature as the compost.

There are two danger periods when watering growing bags. Firstly, when the plants are still young, early in the season, it is easy to overwater. This can be fatal, causing the immature root systems quite literally to drown. To prevent this, make slits in the bag about 5cm (2in) long on each side and about 2.5cm (1in) above ground level. A simple check to determine whether or not the bag needs watering is to take a handful of compost and squeeze it gently. If water comes out before you have completed squeezing, don't water.

Later on the problem is the reverse: attention to adequate watering is crucial to the successful development of the fruit. The problem becomes acute, of course, if you go away on holiday or even for a weekend break. Then you must either go to the expense of installing automatic watering and ventilating, or rely on the help of friends or neighbours to give twice-daily attention to your greenhouse plants.

Another important point to bear in mind is that growing bags contain only enough nutrients to see the plants through the first few weeks after transplanting.

Fisons is the firm which invented the growing bag. Initially this met a need expressed by the professional growers, and among the first major users were the tomato growers in the UK island of Guernsey. The company recommends that tomato plants in growing bags should be given liquid feed 'when fruit on the first truss are the size of peas'.

I use a liquid seaweed-based feed; in addition to the main plant foods, these seaweed extracts contain minor plant nutrients and trace elements (see p35). They can be used, suitably diluted, both for root application and as foliar sprays. To supply the roots with both water and liquid feed it is a good idea to make holes in the base of plastic cups, and then sink them into the bags alongside the plants; in this way both water and feed will get quickly to the roots of the plants.

Used as a fine mist spray before and during the flowering stage, seaweed extract assists pollination and ensures a good set of the fruit. Seaweed foliar sprays also help the plants to resist attacks by sap-sucking insects and to slow down the ageing process so that they stay in production longer. It's a wonder there isn't a version suitable for human consumption.

Growing in pots For this you will need a large pot

for each plant. I prefer clay pots to plastic ones, but either way they should be 30cm (12in) in diameter for preference, although the 25cm (10in) size can be used with the less vigorous varieties, such as Gardener's Delight, Ida and Herald. Pots that aren't brand-new should be given a thorough washing in soapy water before being filled with compost.

Stand the pots on plastic sheeting or flagstones, ensuring that the drainage holes operate effectively. The plants can be supported by string, like those in growing bags, but I prefer to use tall bamboo canes firmly tied to horizontal supports under the eaves and to which the plants are tied with fillis, raffia or patent clips every 30cm (12in) or so.

The watering and feeding requirements for plants in pots are the same as for those in growing bags.

Ring culture This method is easier to manage in terms of watering, but it does take a bit of trouble to set up, and it requires more in the way of equipment.

A large sheet of clear or black polythene will be needed, to line a trench about 15cm (6in) deep, 30cm (12in) wide and long enough to take your plants at about 1m (3ft) spacing.

Each plant will need a ring or bottomless pot 23cm (9in) in diameter; these can be bought as 'whalehide' or fibre cylinders. The trench has to be filled with an inert material such as clean, washed gravel or peat/peat substitute, and on this the rings are placed, filled with compost and, of course, the tomato plants supported by strings or canes.

The idea is that the plant roots work through the compost in the rings and into the material in the trench, making watering and feeding very simple. For the first few weeks after transplanting only the compost in the rings is watered. Then, as the roots extend into the trench, only the trench is watered as often as necessary to keep it moist not sodden. Liquid feed the rings, however, not the trench.

At the end of the season the gravel will have to be disposed of or cleaned for future use. If you have filled the trench with peat/peat substitute it can be dug out and used elsewhere in the garden.

Straw bale growing For this method you will need farm-baled straw or one-third bale size wads of straw, preferably wheat straw, that is guaranteed free from chemical contamination, probably from an organic arable farm nearby.

The straw is first thoroughly soaked in the greenhouse for several days until it is wet through to running-off point, then it is treated with a high

nitrogen liquid fertiliser to start the fermentation process that will generate heat and decompose the straw.

Dried blood reconstituted in liquid form can be used, or a seaweed-based liquid fertiliser; alternatively, make up your own liquid by steeping a sack of stinging nettles in water for a week or ten days until they are mushy and the liquid is the colour of strong tea and rather evil-smelling.

When the straw has been doctored with this liquid, decomposition soon starts and the internal temperature of the bale starts climbing, reaching maybe 54°C (130°F) at its peak. If you put a metal rod as a probe into the centre of the bale, the end will be too hot to handle. Wait until it drops to about 32°C (90°F) before planting. If after a week the temperature shows no sign of falling, give the bale another dose of water, but don't overdo it.

Whether wads or bales are used, holes must be cut out about 23cm (9in) in diameter and 15cm (6in) deep to accommodate the plants, three to a bale. Fill with compost and firm thoroughly before planting the young tomato plants. Use canes or string for support.

The straw provides a cosy, warm environment for the plants, and watering and feeding with liquid fertiliser are carried out as for growing bag culture.

In earlier days, gardeners would steep a bag of animal manure in a barrel of rainwater to make a weak liquid feed that was ideal for tomato growing.

One interesting feature of straw-bale growing is that the tomato plants relish the opportunity of letting their roots run through the open texture of the straw. Gradually decomposition of the straw gets under way, releasing nitrogen to the plants and giving the environment a degree of carbon dioxide enrichment.

When the crop has been harvested the straw can be added, bit by bit, to the compost heap.

Border culture and grafted stock Don't attempt to grow tomatoes direct into the greenhouse soil if it has been in use for many years for growing crops. The chances are it carries the spores of soil-borne diseases, such as verticillium wilt.

In disease-free soil that has been carefully prepared – that is, by adding a plentiful amount of organic material such as well-rotted farmyard manure, garden compost or a composted proprietary organic fertiliser – very good crops of tomatoes can be grown for several seasons. Aim for a pH level of 6 to 6.5, and use ground limestone or calcified seaweed to adjust it.

Direct planting into the border can be done in the same way as for growing bags.

After, say, three years it is advisable either to turn to one of the other methods of growing described here, or to use rootstock and grafts. This is easier than digging out and replacing the border soil. The alternative is to grow only those varieties that are reasonably resistant to wilt and other soil-borne diseases.

However, a word of warning. Grafting is a tedious and costly way of growing tomatoes and it is still no guarantee of avoiding the spread of virus diseases. Grafted stocks are prepared with a simple tongue graft. The stock and graft are taped together and potted up into an 8cm(3in) pot. The top of the scion is cut back to just one leaf. In about sixteen days or so when the graft has taken, the scion roots are severed and removed.

Management

Plants grown as standards up strings or with canes for support should have side shoots removed. This is simply a matter of pinching out the shoots between thumb and finger, although a smoker would be advised to wear surgical gloves or to disinfect his hands thoroughly before touching the tomato plants, to prevent them becoming infected with tobacco mosaic virus.

As the plants grow, twist the supporting string gently around the stem of the plant or tie the stem to the cane using fillis or raffia.

Yellowing leaves should also be removed by a sharp upward jerk. Take off only the leaves below the first truss. If the foliage becomes too heavy and dense, don't go in for wholesale removal of leaves. Cut half a leaf at a time of no more than a third of the leaves of each plant. Remember that the leaves are vital to the plant's healthy development all through its life.

Removing the side shoots and yellowing leaves is best done early in the morning when the plants are turgid. Sometimes shoots develop from the end of the fruit trusses and these should also be pinched out.

When the plants reach the top of the string or cane supports, the tops can be pinched out so that as much of the fruit as possible will mature and ripen; on the other hand, if all that is required is to have a quantity of smallish, green fruit, the plants can be trained along horizontal wires and the unripe crop picked for chutney.

Whichever method of growing tomatoes you choose, standard plants must be given support from canes or strings and have the sideshoots removed.

 REMOVING THE LEAVES

To strip or not to strip the leaves off the greenhouse tomato plants? That's a question frequently asked and only recently answered definitively. The theory is that stripping off the leaves, once the trusses have set, hastens ripening, makes picking easier and reduces the risk of pest and disease. However, research has discovered that removing the leaves above the level of the ripening fruit actually reduces the yield. There's no harm, apparently, in snapping off the lower leaves as they turn yellow, and if there is too much foliage it can be reduced gradually, below the level of the ripening truss, preferably early in the morning when the plants are turgid.

Concerning plant vigour, there is the story of one amateur gardener who bought four tomato plants in early spring and set them out in a polythene tunnel. The tops of each were cut off and rooted in small pots in mid-spring, as were the side shoots which were grown on in 18cm (7in) pots on a greenhouse shelf and allowed to produce just one truss. The result was, that from just four plants this thrifty gardener filled a polytunnel.

It is possible to propagate from just one plant, and why not ask gardening friends for any spare side shoots – tomato cuttings or side shoots up to 15cm (6in) root very easily in a couple of weeks in moist compost.

The number of trusses of fruit that develop varies with the variety grown, how well the flowers were pollinated, and how early the seed was sown and the plants encouraged into production. It can be as few as five trusses, or as many as twelve.

The number of fruit that develop to maturity on each truss also varies considerably. With a cherry-size tomato such as Gardener's Delight or Sweet 100, there may be scores of fruit on each truss; while on other standard fruited varieties there may be just half-a-dozen or so fruit. My personal record is a truss of Gardener's Delight with fifty-eight ripe tomatoes.

Pollination of the flowers to achieve a good set is assisted by foliar sprays of water or liquid feed, and you can further assist the transfer of pollen by gently tapping the supporting string or cane each day. Cold weather, poor ventialtion and lack of water also have an effect on successful pollination.

NATURAL BEE POLLINATION

When a considerable number of tomato plants are grown in a greenhouse, ensuring proper pollination can be a problem. Tapping the plants has been the traditional practice but in very large commercial houses it is boring for the staff and not altogether effective.

A solution is to use bumble bees, a method which has two advantages: it offers potentially better pollination, and since bees can only thrive in virtually insecticide-free environments, using them is tantamount to a public declaration that the nursery is environmentally friendly.

The bees are not just any old bumbles. They are specially hired from a Belgian company which is very secretive about them altogether and they arrive in sealed containers. Because tomato flowers do not produce nectar, a separate feed of sugar syrup is provided; the only maintenance needed is twice-daily checking of the sugar syrup dispenser.

Watering, Feeding and Ventilating

Tomato plants growing in pots and growing bags need watering as often as three times a day during the hottest summer weather, and this aspect of crop management is vital to success.

Capillary matting and automatic watering systems, as described on pp23–4, are valuable if regular daily attention cannot be given to the plants, but only if the watering system is allied to foolproof automatic ventilation (see p20). The requirement is to keep the compost or soil moist but not waterlogged, and the air buoyant, never stagnant. Stale, hot air can lead to the rapid build-up of pests, such as the spider mite. Don't forget that as well as the roof vent, you can also use the door as a ventilator, leaving it open when necessary.

Don't shut everything down at night, particularly on hot, humid nights. Aim for a maximum daytime temperature of 23°C (75°F) and a night temperature of 15°C (60°F). If the day readings consistently exceed the recommended maximum, shading will help to lower the temperature, providing it doesn't interfere with the ventilation (see p21). Temporary relief from too high a temperature can be achieved by damping down the paving stones in the greenhouse.

When watering by can, keep two or three full two-gallon (p101) cans in the greenhouse for at least forty-eight hours before you intend to use them, so that the water temperature is approximately that of the compost. Whether or not this is appreciated by the plants is difficult to say, but I have a feeling it is. Similarly, when spraying with water or using a foliar feed, try to ensure there isn't too wide a difference in temperature.

Picking the Crop

Organic fruit and vegetables should naturally taste better than chemically-induced crops in my opinion, but you can prove for yourself that they are not only healthier for you, but also have superior flavour. The flavour guide on p111 is based on the personal preference of myself and my family; you will have to experiment to find out the varieties which suit your taste and style of growing. Having done that, there are a few other things to consider that have a bearing on flavour.

Don't overwater the crop. Most commercial varieties of tomato in use today have been bred to respond to soluble chemical fertilisers and high intakes of water, a combination that puts high yield above flavour. Generally speaking, the more water the crop takes up, the less pronounced the flavour of the fruit.

Another flavour factor is ripeness. The commercial grower picks his tomatoes in an unripe condition, timing it so they gain colour in transit from him to the retail outlet, but in doing this he sacrifices flavour. The amateur grower can delay picking until the fruit is truly ripe, but still firm, and so gain all the subtle benefits of flavour and texture.

Mature fruit that is still green when you come to clear the crop in late autumn will ripen gradually if each fruit is wrapped in paper and stored in a cupboard or drawer; or they can be set out unwrapped in a drawer with a few red tomatoes.

Immature fruit are best used as the main ingredient of green tomato chutney.

NETTLE BOX

Another way of ripening green tomatoes is to place them in a box of freshly gathered nettles. It will also hasten the ripening of trusses on the greenhouse plants if you put nettles in a large paper bag, place over the truss and tie tightly.

Pests

Caterpillars Damage is done before you are even aware of it, particularly when the plants are at the peak of production – finding half-eaten leaves is a sure indication that caterpillars of the tomato moth are active, and there will also be droppings on leaves. They have yellow-brown bodies and pale green heads, and are usually found on young leaves. The best method of dealing with them is to pick them off by hand.

Use the biological control *Bacillus thuringiensis* (see p54) for infestation in a large greenhouse.

Greenfly Early action will prevent this sap-sucking pest from building up; it is the cause of sooty mould on the leaves, the result of its honeydew secretions and is probably also responsible for virus disease damage to plants. Look for evidence of this pest on new growth and spray with soapy water once or twice a week, or with an organic proprietary alternative.

Slugs Look for the slime trails on the inside of the glass and on leaves and for nibbled foliage. Destroy by hand, picking off the slugs early in the morning or late at night with the aid of a hand torch.

Spider mite The first indication that this pest has taken up residence is yellowing of the leaves and the presence of very fine dense webs. You might need a magnifying glass to see the tiny mites on the underside of the leaves. Hot, dry conditions favour this pest, so help to prevent an attack by misting frequently, especially during hot, sunny weather. Biological control using the predator mite *Phytosieiulus persimilis* (see p56) is very effective.

Mineral Deficiencies

These should not occur if the plants are fed regular and adequate amounts of a good liquid organic fertiliser.

Calcium shortage symptoms are blossom end rot. This is a leathery black patch at the flower end of the fruit, and the commonest cause is water shortage at some stage of the plant's growth. Plants in growing bags are particularly susceptible.

Magnesium deficiency leads to the appearance of yellow or straw-coloured patches on bottom leaves with the veins in a clearly defined green colour.

Nitrogen deficiency shows as stunted growth, spindly stems and small leaves in young plants. Flower trusses appear, but fail to develop.

Potash shortage results in greenback and uneven ripening of the fruit. There may also be a higher number than normal of small fruit for that variety.

Other Disorders

Blossom end rot. Uneven or inadequate watering causes black patches to develop on the fruit. Regular watering prevents this.

Botrytis. A greyish mould, caused by the fungus *Botrytis cinerea*, develops on leaves, stems and fruit. There is no cure, so remove all infected leaves and fruit. Botrytis can be prevented by ensuring that the greenhouse is always well ventilated, that watering is done early in the day, that pools of water are not left on paths and staging during cold, dull weather, and that plants are not overcrowded.

Curled leaves. Not strictly speaking a problem because all the leaves are curled in infancy. Any that fail to develop can be removed if you wish.

Greenback. Hard green area remains on the fruit even when the rest of it ripens. Harsh, direct sunlight and poor ventilation contribute to this condition. Don't remove leaves that help to shade the trusses.

Leaf mould. Another fungus, *Fulvia fulva*, causes a purplish brown mould on the underside of the leaves. Development is hastened by hot, humid atmosphere so, as with grey mould, always keep the air in the greenhouse buoyant and water early in the day. A sooty black mould on the upper surfaces of the leaves is a reaction to the secretion of honeydew by sap-sucking insects such as aphids and whitefly.

Oedema. Not commonly encountered, this disease shows as tiny blisters on leaves and stems. The cause is overwatering and inadequate ventilation. Remedy this and the attack will subside without further action being necessary.

Poor pollination. Symptoms are flowers that drop off or fruits that never get bigger than pea size, then fall off. The remedy is to keep the air moist, shake the plants to distribute pollen and spray them with a mist spray.

Split fruit. Irregular watering, especially if accompanied by wide variations of temperature, causes developing fruit to split. Pick any affected fruit or they will develop a mould and rot. Try to adjust watering more closely to the temperature so that if a cool, dull day is forecast, the water to the plants can be reduced. Easier said than done!

Stem rot. The stem of the plant turns black and withers away. There is no cure for this, so remove the infected plant, do not replant in the same location, and keep the atmosphere on the dry side to prevent other plants becoming infected.

Verticillium wilt. A disease caused by soil-borne fungus that is rarely, if ever, encountered by those

who raise their tomatoes in growing bags. The plants wilt, the lower leaves turn yellow, and brown streaks are seen in the tissue of the stems when they are cut open. There is no cure, so infected plants must be destroyed and the soil in which they were growing must be sterilised.

CUCUMBERS

Growing crops the organic way means rediscovering some of the techniques and skills of our forefathers, though sometimes it is difficult to know how far back one needs to go to find them still relevant; for example, providing heat for the greenhouse or conservatory throughout the winter and early spring – keeping the boiler stoked and providing the fuel for it – was taken for granted in the days when the labour for both these tasks was bought cheaply.

What the amateur gardener did with great numbers of cucumbers produced in the depth of winter is anyone's guess, although certainly earlier in Great Britain, in the days of Edwardian elegance, the well-to-do were partial to delicately thin cucumber sandwiches as part of the four o'clock ritual of tea, summer and winter alike.

Nowadays average consumption of cucumbers is 1.5kg (3¼lb) per person per year. That's only an ounce each per week and most of that takes place from mid-spring to mid-autumn.

Old varieties of cucumber included some with yellow, bronze and purple skins, such as Lord Roberts, Dr Livingstone, Long Gun, Duke of Edinburgh, Every Day and Rochford Market, but these are no longer available; however, there is still a popular pre-war variety Telegraph which is considered to be one of the straightest and most flavourful varieties even today. Butcher's Disease Resisting or Resister, another oldish variety, was bred to resist leaf-spot fungus, while Conqueror was developed to grow well in the company of tomatoes; both are still to be found in some seedmen's lists.

All the old varieties produced male and female flowers, and this was a disadvantage because cucumber plants set fruit without the flowers being pollinated. If the flowers *are* pollinated, the fruit swells at the base and the flavour becomes very bitter; so then, as now, all male flowers must be removed.

Choosing the Variety

Nowadays most commercial growers and many amateurs prefer to use all-female flower varieties of cucumber, even though the seed is costly compared with the older hermaphrodites. A point worth making is that although these may still produce a few male flowers, you don't have to watch constantly for their appearance and chase bees out of the greenhouse. Among the female varieties widely available today are:

Birgit F1, earlier and more prolific than Pepinex.
Brunex F1, low temperature tolerant and with a good degree of disease resistance.
Burpless Tasty Green F1, a dual-purpose type that can also be grown outdoors. The fruit is picked when 20–23cm (8–9in) long.
Fembaby F1, a particularly robust type that is cold-tolerant and so less demanding of warmth in the early stages.
Femspot F1, an early maturing, disease-resistant type with fruit of fine flavour.
Landora F1, a Swedish variety that is resistant to cladosporium.
Mildana F1, a high output variety with good cold tolerance and excellent disease resistance.
Pepinex F1, the grandmother of the all-female varieties that still gives a good performance.
Petita F1, this can be grown well in a large pot in the conservatory to give a moderate yield of fruit 20–23cm (8–9in) long. The plant grows to about 1.5m (5ft) tall.
Sandra F1, a high quality burpless type with exceptional cold tolerance after the first flower stage.
Superator F1, a very high yielding variety.
Sweet Success F1, a burpless variety with good disease resistance that can also be grown outdoors.
Uniflora D F1, a self-determinate variety. This means that all fruiting side growths stop short at about six inches.
Other greenhouse varieties include:
Best Seller F1, a Dutch hybrid that gives a high yield, but produces male and female flowers.
Butcher's Disease Resisting, still going strong after very many years and the seed is far cheaper than F1 sorts.
Chinese Long Green, has smooth-skinned fruit up to 60cm (24in) long.
Conqueror, bred to go well with tomatoes in the unheated greenhouse. A good cropper.
Crystal Apple, something different: this variety has fruit the shape, size and colour of large lemons.

Cucumbers share with tomatoes the need for a buoyant atmosphere, regular watering and liquid feeding.

Kyoto, a Japanese variety that produces very long, very thin fruit.
Sigamadew, good flavour and pale green very thin skin.
Telegraph or **Telegraph Improved,** a reliable old favourite with excellent flavour and high yield.
Zeppelin, this has produced some of the largest cucumbers ever grown, up to 5kg (11lb) each. What you do with them is any one's guess.

As for the taste differences between varieties, it is far more difficult to compare flavour with cucumbers than with, say, tomatoes or melons. But there *are* quite wide differences, and if you are prepared to experiment, you may well find that the old varieties such as Telegraph and Butcher's have a more pronounced traditional flavour than the new F1s, and that some of the modern varieties are distinctly sweeter.

Incidentally, many people find 'burpless' types such as Sweet Success or Burpless Tasty Green easier to digest.

Raising the Plants

Cucumber seed is expensive compared to run-of-the-mill vegetable seed such as cabbage, though membership of a gardening club or allotment association will probably allow you a considerable reduction on prices because you can order from a commercial seed firm or can secure a discount from the other seed firms.

Some people have nowhere to germinate the cucumber seed at the recommended 21–26°C (70–79°F); in this case, 'chitted' seed can be bought from several seed firms – it will arrive already germinated and ready for pricking out. However, this is even more expensive than buying F1 seed.

Chitted seed is sent out to customers with heated greenhouses, where a minimum twenty-four hour temperature of 15°C (60°F) can be maintained, from early to mid-spring. For people with unheated greenhouses, the chitted seed goes out during late spring. On arrival, the pre-germinated seed should be potted up into 8cm (3in) pots.

Growing your own plants from seed means either investing in some form of heating for the greenhouse, or buying an electric propagator, or pinching a bit of space in the airing cupboard. At 26°C (79°F) cucumber seed germinates in two or three days, at 21°C (70°F) it may take a day or so longer. Seed can be germinated by placing it between sheets of damp blotting paper in a suitably warm place; or make up paper pots (see p42) and sow one seed to a pot filled with a good peat-based (or peat substitute) compost.

Simply push the seed into the moist compost with a finger until it is about 1cm (½in) deep; then stand the pots on a plate and pop the lot into a plastic bag tied at the neck, before placing in the chosen warm place.

Remember that germination is rapid. As soon as the seed leaves have opened out fully, the seedlings must be pricked out, taking great care not to damage the long seedling root. If they are in peat or paper pots, plant them complete without destroying the rootball. Use 12.5cm (5in) pots of peat or peat substitute compost for pricking out and give them a position where there is a minimum temperature of 15°C (60°F) day and night, but preferably a few degrees higher.

When they have made five or six leaves they can be transferred to their final growing positions.

A Choice of Growing Methods

For the final stage of growing cucumbers either growing bag, straw bale, raised bed or large pot can be used. Whichever method is chosen, good hygiene is vital for success, because young cucumber plants are particularly susceptible to cold temperature shock, soil-borne disease and overwatering.

With both the raised bed and straw bale systems it is almost impossible to overwater the plants. Indeed, as the cucumber makes an extensive root system on and close to the surface of the growing medium, the greater danger with these two methods is that the roots will dry out. A good plan is to have a reserve supply of compost near at hand so that the surface growing roots can be covered, very lightly, once or twice during the growing season.

Full details on straw bale growing are given in the section on tomatoes (see p113): the same procedure can be followed for cucumbers.

The raised bed can be made on the border soil of the greenhouse, on a bench, or on the staging as long as this is strong enough. You will need a sheet of thick polythene, about two barrowloads of a mixture of equal parts of farmyard manure and sedge peat or peat substitute, plus the same liquid feed as that recommended for the tomatoes.

The peat (or substitute) can be replaced by sterilised soil to which a bucketful of coarse sand has been added, and the manure can be replaced by well-made compost.

The raised bed is prepared about ten days before the young plants are ready to be set out. Mould the bed to a neat flat top about 30 cm (12in) high with slightly sloping sides; this will give a growing area for two

plants set about 60cm (24in) apart.

Set the rootball of the plants a little proud of the growing medium as this helps to guard against fungal disease at the stem. Keep a bucketful of the growing medium nearby to add to the mound when the roots surface.

Pot-grown cucumber plants in properly drained pots are far less likely to suffer either over- or underwatering; also, this is a very convenient method when you only want one or two plants in a conservatory or small greenhouse with, maybe, a summer crop of tomatoes. A pot of at least 30cm (12in) diameter will be needed for each plant.

To avoid having to train plants up the roof of the greenhouse, choose the variety Petita, an all-female F1 hybrid that grows only about 1.5m (5ft) tall.

Get everything in position ten days before planting; use the same mix of farmyard manure or garden compost, and peat (or substitute) or sterilised soil, as for the raised method. Ensure that the drainage hole in the pot functions properly. Put a tall cane or support in position after filling the pot but before transplanting the young plants.

Growing-bags are considered by many people to be the best way of growing cucumbers in a greenhouse or conservatory. The advantages over the other methods described here are considerable and a newcomer to cucumber growing would be well advised to start off with a growing-bag and just a couple of plants. The only drawbacks are the limited space for root development and the danger of drowning the roots through overwatering. Don't put the bags direct on to the floor – put a plastic sheet down first.

Before settling the plants into the bag it is a good plan to scoop out a hole about 12.5cm (5in) deep in the compost. Work in a couple of cupfuls of ordinary sand to improve the silica content of the compost, then fill the hole with water. When it has drained through, plant the young cucumber plants and water them with just two cupfuls of water a day for seven

days. Then make slits in the growing-bag about 5cm (2in) long and about 1cm (½in) from the bottom of the bag. Once the roots have started searching through the compost for moisture you can increase the amount of water given to the bag. Once feeding starts, the rule is to feed the cues every time you water, starting about fourteen days after the plants were set out.

Management

Cucumbers like full sun and reasonable humidity, so don't tuck the plants into a dark corner at the north end of the greenhouse.

For plants growing in a raised bed or in pots, water when the surface of the compost begins to dry out; this will be at least daily at the height of the season. Because of the fairly rich bank of nutrients in the growing medium it will probably not be necessary to start feeding with the liquid seaweed extract until the first fruits have started developing.

As with tomatoes, always water and liquid-feed your cucumbers from containers kept in the greenhouse so that the temperature of the liquid is approximately that of the growing medium.

Plants in growing-bags or on raised beds need careful training. Soft string, sold as fillis, can be used to guide the developing plant. Tie it loosely round the stem of the plant, and tie the other end to a horizontal wire at head-height below the eaves. As the plant grows, train it around the string.

When the main stem reaches the horizontal wire it can be trained up the sloping roof of the greenhouse with more horizontal wires, with the side shoots tied into the wires with raffia or plastic raffia. Special fitments can be bought which fit the aluminium frame so that the horizontal wires can run from side to side or lengthways along the greenhouse.

Fruits can be allowed to develop at every leaf joint above about the first 45–50cm (18–20in) of the main stem; the side shoots should be cut back after two leaves, with the exception of the variety Uniflora D which is a self-determinate type that stops itself after the side shoots have made about 15cm (6in) of growth.

Instead of training the plants vertically up the string, they can be persuaded to grow obliquely simply by tying the string to the overhead wire at an angle of about 45° to the point where it is tied to the stem. This takes up more space in the house, but allows the fruit to hang well clear of the foliage.

Remember that if the variety is not an all-female one, the male flowers must be pinched out; they can

COSSET CUCUMBERS

Cucumbers need rather more humidity than tomatoes in the greenhouse. If you want to grow both crops together in a small greenhouse, hang sheets of clear polythene round the cucumber plants and spray inside the enclosed area regularly.

be recognised quite easily because they do not have the swelling behind the petals that is the embryo fruit.

When the bottom leaves of the main stem turn yellow, cut them off.

Harvesting the cucumbers at the right stage can be a bit tricky for the newcomer. Some varieties make fruit which is only 20–23cm (8–9in) long when it is ready for harvesting.

Don't break off the fruit, cut them off with a pair of scissors. For showing purposes the fruits must be straight, of uniform thickness with a short handle attached, and with the flowers still adhering. Show cucumbers are treated very carefully so that the characteristic bloom on the skin is retained.

Take off any ripe fruit that is surplus to your own requirements, and give them to friends; or store them for a few days in a cool place, but not the refrigerator.

The main crop of cucumbers comes in late summer, and the rate of fruiting gradually declines until, come mid- to late autumn (depending on where you live) the crop of homegrown cues has ended for the year and the plants can be removed from the greenhouse and put on the compost heap.

Cucumber Problems

As with most other crops under glass, providing adequate warmth – especially during the early life of the plants – a buoyant atmosphere and an optimum level of water and liquid feed are the best ways of preventing pest and disease problems with cucumbers.

Aphids. Take early action to prevent greenfly or blackfly getting a hold. Severe infestations of these sap-sucking insects can seriously harm a plant's development, can spread virus diseases, and cause a mess from their honeydew secretions. These secretions fall on leaves and fruit and in no time at all a sooty mould develops. Spray at the first sign of the pests – usually on new growth – with soapy water or insecticidal soap, and repeat until clear of the pest.

Bees. Not a pest, of course, but if you are growing a variety that produces male and female flowers, the bees will cross-pollinate and the resulting fruit will be inedible. Placing a fine mesh net over the ventilator or louvre will keep out potential pollinators.

Grey mould. This is *Botrytis cinera,* as distinct from powdery mildew. Stale, humid air encourages this fungus disease. There is no cure, so remove infected leaves and fruit. Adequate growing space, good ventilation and optimum watering should prevent this problem.

Mosaic. Cucumber mosaic virus produces yellow and pale-green leaves, with a mottled or marbled effect on the normal green of the leaves. There may also be some distortion and stunting of the leaves. However, nutrient deficiencies cause similar symptoms to virus diseases, particularly yellowing of the leaves, and the recognition of true virus condition is often a matter for the expert.

Virus attacks are often related to aphid activity, although hands and tools can also carry diseases from one plant to the next. There is no cure for an infected plant and it should be removed from the greenhouse, root and all, and destroyed.

Powdery mildew. Appears as a dusting of white powder on leaves. Overhot, dry air and overcrowded plants are associated with this fungal disease. If possible, cut out affected parts and dust the plants with flowers of sulphur, or spray with lime sulphur solution.

Red spider mite. Use the same control as that for the tomato crop (see p117).

Root rot. A fungus attacks the base of the stem and roots which turn black, and the plant quickly wilts and dies. There is no cure, so lift the plant with the rootball and destroy it. This disease is most frequently encountered when growing plants in border soil or in contaminated compost, and rarely when the plants are in growing bags or straw bales.

Seedling troubles. Poor germination can be due to infertile seed or too low a temperature (see p45). Seedlings that appear and then collapse or that have distorted cotyledons (seed leaves) are often the result of poor seed stock, uneven watering or bad mixing of the growing medium.

Whitefly. Biological control of this pest is very effective, and full details are given on p57.

AUBERGINES AND PEPPERS

Of the two crops, peppers are rather easier to grow than aubergines, but both are first-rate subjects for growing-bag cultivation in the amateur's greenhouse. They are relative newcomers to British gardens as well as to the kitchens, yet both crops require no more attention and bother then greenhouse tomatoes.

Aubergines

Available in several varieties including some new hybrids from Japan. Black Enorma F1 produces the largest fruit, up to 680gm (1½lb) each, and just three plants in a growing bag should keep a family of four in aubergines from mid-summer until late autumn. Long

Purple is a well-tried favourite, and the earlier, heavier yielding F1 varieties Black Prince and Short Tom are also very popular.

The seed is sown in late winter in modules or a seed tray at a temperature of 18–21°C (65–70°F) when germination takes 14–21 days. When the seedlings are large enough to handle they are transplanted to 8cm (3in) pots and given their final growing site in mid- to late spring.

Instead of a growing bag, 20 or 23cm (8 or 9in) pots filled with a mixture of loam and homemade compost can be used, setting one plant to a pot; or they can go direct into the greenhouse border where the soil should be compost-enriched.

The plants need the support of canes 1m (3ft) tall. Tie in the stems using raffia or fillis, and tie in the side shoots where the fruits develop. When the plants have made about 30cm (12in) of growth, pinch out the growing point, and when six fruits have formed, take off any further arrivals.

Once the fruit starts swelling, weekly feed with an animal manure-based liquid feed such as the brew described on p32, and continue right up to harvesting; this will ensure that you harvest plump, sweet fruit. Cut them from the plant when the purple skin shines like newly-polished glass; don't wait until the fruit becomes dull, because that indicates it is past its prime, and the flavour becomes bitter.

Red spider mite can be kept at bay by regular misting of the entire plant with tepid water. If an attack does occur, spray with liquid derris. Aphids and whitefly may also attack the plants and can be controlled by soapy water or insecticidal soap.

Incidentally, aubergines will stay in good condition for about fourteen days if harvested at their peak, then popped in a polythene bag and placed in the refrigerator.

Peppers

Peppers or capsicum are now widely used in salads, and as an item of kebabs and of ratatouille; used whole they can be stuffed and baked. The capsicum is a relative of the tomato, and as a greenhouse crop requires about the same sort of conditions for success. The two crops grow well together, with the peppers far less demanding of space.

The modern hybrid varieties of sweet pepper give excellent yields of up to ten fruit per plant, and as they grow only about 1m (3ft) tall, can be placed on a bench or staging.

Twice-weekly misting of sweet pepper plants helps the fruit to set and deters red spider mite.

Raise the seedlings in a propagator at 18–21°C (65–70°F), sowing the seed as early in the year as possible, with three seeds to an 8cm (3in) pot of compost. When the seedlings are large enough to handle, transfer in twos to their own 8cm (3in) pots; repot in further stages until the plants are large enough to go into growing-bags, three to each bag, or better still, into 23cm (9in) pots of homemade compost – worm-worked compost from a worm farm (see p38) can be particularly successful.

When the plants are in their final position, give each a 1m (3ft) cane for support and tie with fillis or raffia. No stopping or pinching out of side shoots is required. Management of the crop involves regular watering and feeding with liquid fertiliser, and misting twice weekly – more in hot, dry weather – to help the fruit to set and to deter red spider mite. If the mite does get a hold, spray with liquid derris, and if you see signs of aphids or whitefly, spray with soapy water or insecticidal soap.

Harvest the fruits when they are green, glossy and plump. Plants that were set out in mid-spring should be giving their first fruit in late summer and they will go on cropping well into early autumn.

If you like your sweet peppers on the spicy side, a fully ripe green fruit will turn red if left on the plant for about twenty days.

Good varieties are the F1 hybrids Bell Boy, Big Bertha, Canape, Gold Star (a yellow-fruited variety), Gypsy, New Ace.

Hot or chilli peppers are far less popular as a greenhouse crop. The plants are raised and managed in exactly the same way as the sweet peppers, but because chilli peppers produce an abundance of small fiery fruit, fewer plants are needed. The fruit is picked when fully mature, then dried in the sun. A good variety is Chilli Serrano.

FORCED AND OUT-OF-SEASON CROPS

Chicory, endive, seakale and rhubarb can be forced or hurried into growth in the greenhouse, especially if a little gentle heat can be supplied; while some herbs, especially mint and parsley, can be lifted and kept growing throughout the winter.

In bygone days, greenhouses and frames specially designed for forcing were fairly commonplace, and were used to produce, for example, a few helpings of very early asparagus.

Endive, an all-year-round salad plant, is blanched to make the bitter leaves a little sweeter for winter salads. Rhubarb, seakale and chicory are forced for their young shoots which must also be blanched in darkness; this means the area under the greenhouse staging can be brought into use by fixing a curtain of lightproof material over and around it.

Witloof or Belgian Chicory

Roots are used to produce the golden yellow chicons that are so delicious in winter salads. The seed is sown outdoors on an open site in late spring or early summer, and the seedlings thinned to about 23cm (9in) apart. In late autumn the roots are carefully lifted, and any damaged or forked ones are put on the compost heap. The best roots are those about 3.5cm (1½in) in diameter at the top. Cut off the foliage leaving just about 2.5cm (1in), and trim back the roots so the finished length is about 15 or 17cm (6 or 7in). The roots can now be stored in layers of sand or moist peat or peat substitute in boxes in the garden shed or garage until they are needed for forcing, a few at a time.

One recommended idea is to plant three roots close together in a 20 or 23cm (8 or 9in) flower-pot filled with moist soil. This is then covered with an inverted pot of the same size with its drainage hole blocked to exclude light. The pots are placed in a cupboard, or room, or in a propagator under the staging at a temperature of 13°C (55°F), when the chicons will be ready to eat in three or four weeks.

Seakale

Requires approximately the same treatment, although it takes two seasons to produce crowns suitable for forcing when the crop is grown from seed. Thereafter the plants for forcing can be propagated by root cuttings, or thongs. A variety such as Lily White is sown outdoors in mid- or late spring in organically-enriched soil, and the seedlings are thinned to 15cm (6in) apart.

Towards the end of the following winter, or slightly later if the soil is frostbound, the plants can be moved to their permanent position: cut off the tops of the crowns, and plant just below the surface.

For forcing, the plants are lifted and all but the main root is trimmed off. The roots are then stood upright in large pots or boxes of moist peat (or substitute) or soil, with another pot or box inverted over the top and kept in darkness at a temperature of about 13°C (55°F) to produce tender and succulent shoots – these are ready when they are about

15cm(6in) long. When the roots have accomplished this task they should be discarded on to the compost heap.

When the plants are lifted for forcing, side shoots or thongs about the thickness of a pencil can be taken; trimmed to about 15cm (6in) long they can be tied in bundles and stored upright in moist sand or peat. They are planted out about 30cm (12in) apart with the top of the thongs just below the surface of the soil.

Endive

The crisp, curled leaves are very popular on the Continent and are becoming more so in Britain and elsewhere, particularly in their blanched form. Blanching starts when the plants are fully grown, that is, about twelve weeks after sowing the seed outdoors and moving the plants into the greenhouse. The exact sowing time is dictated by when you want to start blanching, but it will be late summer or early autumn.

The seed can be sown direct or in trays or modules for transplanting. The spacing between the plants should be about 25cm (10in). When the plants are wanted for blanching it is essential that they are dry, because any rain or dew on them can cause rot to set in.

Lightly tie the leaves together with raffia, and use the flower pot method for blanching; this takes from two to three weeks to complete. Eat directly, because the blanched leaves are then at their tender best.

Rhubarb

Where forcing rhubarb is a major industry for commercial growers, specially designed forcing sheds with heat and fan-assisted ventilation enable crops of dark pink tender stems of rhubarb to reach the wholesale markets very soon after Christmas. This is a high value crop that bears little comparison to the rampant growth that most of us have for our rhubarb patch. But given warmth and darkness, even our hardy old rhubarb crowns can be encouraged to produce a worthwhile helping or two of forced stems or sticks.

Lift the crown in late autumn, split it if it is over-large, and leave it on the surface of the soil to become frosted. Then plant in a large whalehide pot or other suitable container, and either invert another container over it, or rig up a wire frame about 45cm (18in) tall covered with a black polythene sack. Water now and then, and place in the greenhouse or conservatory

OUT-OF-SEASON STRAWBERRIES

You can harvest home-grown strawberries in the greenhouse three to four weeks ahead of the outdoor ones if a little heat is provided for the crop. Use maiden plants – that is runners taken in late summer and potted up into 12.5cm (5in) pots. For 1–2lb (0.4–0.9kg) of ripe fruit, about twelve plants will be needed, depending on the variety.

Stand the pots outside until early winter, then bring them into the greenhouse and re-pot them into 15cm (6in) pots and place them on the staging where they will get maximum light. A minimum temperature of 4.5°C (40°F) is necessary, night and day, to start the plants into growth and, as the leaves develop, this should be increased to 15°C (60°F).

The plants should be in flower by mid-spring and will need to be hand-pollinated using an artist's watercolour brush. At this stage feed the plants every week with liquid organic fertiliser.

When the fruits start showing pink, increase the heat to 18°C (65°F). After fruiting the plants can be returned to the garden for growing on to crop outdoors the following year.

Good varieties for stretching the strawberry season in this way are Cambridge Vigour, Red Gauntlet and Tamella.

where there is some heat, in a cellar or garage or even in a spare room. The tender pink stalks will be ready from about mid-winter onwards: just how early in the year depends on the amount of warmth.

French Beans

Both dwarf French beans and the climbing varieties can be grown successfully in the cold greenhouse or polytunnel, and this is particularly useful in those districts where summers are short or where the growing site is exposed to harsh winds.

Dwarf beans can be grown in large pots using ordinary garden soil enriched with homemade compost or a bought-in organic version. Growing bags used the previous season can also be pressed into use, though first add and thoroughly mix in a dressing of fish, blood and bone: 4oz (113g) to the standard size bag would be about right.

Sow five seeds to each 20cm (8in) pot, or six seeds to a 23cm (9in) pot. With growing bags sow a row of seeds about 13cm (5in) apart. In an unheated

structure the seed can go in direct as soon as the growing medium temperature tops 13°C (55°F); or the seed can be sown in modules or paper pots and germinated in a propagator. Support the plants with canes or twigs and watch out for slugs.

Climbing French beans are best raised in peat or paper pots in a propagator, then planted direct into the greenhouse border where the soil has been enriched with organic material. Once the plants get away they will need support, like tomatoes – gently guide the main stem around fillis string which is tied at the bottom of the stem and to a horizontal wire under the eaves.

These plants are remarkably unfussy about conditions, but for a heavy crop of tender and succulent beans, give plenty of ventilation on sunny days and spray frequently with water at the same temperature as the greenhouse atmosphere. Remove all basal shoots, and pinch out the growing tip when the vines reach the cross-wire.

 NEW POTATOES FOR CHRISTMAS

If you save some early potatoes and chit them (allow some sprouts to develop), you can use your greenhouse to grow new potatoes for the Christmas feast.

Plant the chitted tubers in mid- or late summer direct into the border soil or in large pots or in half barrels with drainage holes. Each tuber should ultimately produce about half a pound of new potatoes.

If you are growing them in a pot or other container, use spent peat (or its substitute) from a growing-bag as the growing medium.

Plant the tubers about 5cm (2in) deep in the border soil, or cover them with about the same depth of peat substitute in whatever container you are using.

The new potatoes grow to about the size of golf balls with very little haulm, and need only occasional watering.

You can also use the cold greenhouse for a late crop of winter lettuce. Choose a butterhead variety such as Clarion, Hilde, Kwiek or Pascal.

Sow into the greenhouse soil or into growing-bags in late summer for early winter use, and in mid- and late autumn for early spring harvesting.

A Selection of Herbs

Even if you are not interested in having a few forced plants for the winter, it is well worth the trouble to have a supply of fresh mint and parsley from the greenhouse or conservatory right through the winter months and until the outdoor supply starts up again. You could also have pots or small growing bags with a wider selection of herbs, say basil, chervil, marjoram, sage and thyme, all of which can be raised from seed or bought as small plants from a herb nursery or garden centre. Many herbs, particularly in their variegated or coloured-leaf forms, are attractive plants which can be used decoratively in the conservatory as well as to provide pickings for the kitchen.

Parsley, mint and the other herbs mentioned are widely available in dried form, but the flavour is infinitely better when cut and used fresh.

Marjoram, tarragon, chives and winter savory can all be potted up and kept outside until the autumn when the pots can be brought into the greenhouse or conservatory, or placed on a sunny windowsill to give a supply of fresh leaves over the winter.

Parsley Opinions differ about which of the two most commonly grown types of parsley is the better flavoured: the curly-leaved, moss-curled type; or the French, plain-leaved one – and in my view neither is as strongly flavoured as the Giant Italian variety. There is no disputing, however, that parsley is an indispensable herb for garnishing and seasoning, and some people consider that the best plan is to use the attractive curled variety for garnishing, and the stronger flavoured French or Italian varieties for sauces and seasoning. As well as being richer in iron than any other vegetable, fresh parsley has useful amounts of vitamins A and C; and chewed slowly, it is an excellent breath sweetener.

Parsley seed is extremely slow to germinate at low temperatures and it is a good plan to soak the seed in warm water for twenty-four hours before sowing; then sow into a seed tray of peat-based or peat substitute compost, or direct into rich soil in semi-shade outdoors. This should be done in mid- or late summer. The optimum temperature for germination is 27°C (80°F), when emergence takes only about seven days.

Seedlings in the seed tray should be potted on into 8cm (3in) pots when they are large enough to handle, while those outside should be thinned to about 15cm (6in) apart. The potted plants can be stood outside in

a sheltered spot, out of direct sunlight; keep them regularly watered, and feed with liquid seaweed extract or your own make of liquid feed once a week – comfrey tea is particularly useful (see p33).

Before the first frost of the autumn the plants should be brought into the greenhouse or conservatory and re-potted into 13cm (5in) pots, or lifted from their quarters outside and potted up into pots of that size. Ordinary garden soil can be used, mixed with a generous dollop of worm compost or a peat-based or peat substitute multi-purpose compost. Parsley plants will also do well in growing bags used for a previous crop, or in wooden troughs, hanging baskets or other similar containers, providing they are well drained.

How many plants are grown in this way obviously depends on anticipated demand from the kitchen and on the available space. But they are very decorative plants and err on the side of generosity if possible because you should only take a sprig at a time from each plant.

Parsley is biennial, so the overwintered plants can be returned outside in the spring, and allowed to set seed for self-sown plants.

Mint probably beats parsley as Britain's most popular herb, a vital accompaniment to new potatoes, peas and the joint of lamb. It will grow well almost anywhere – in fact it grows too well unless kept in check by planting in a container; use an old sink, sunk in the ground with the rim slightly proud of the surface, so that the roots can't invade the whole garden.

There are many sorts of mint, although the one most commonly grown is spearmint or garden mint. Given the choice, most cooks would prefer to use Bowles mint for mint sauce, and apple mint – the round-leaved mint with its fragrant, true minty flavour – for popping into the pan of new potatoes or the home-grown peas. Try growing both types and see for yourself.

For winter use take up a few roots and pot them up into 13cm (5in) pots of ordinary garden soil, or put them into a previously used growing bag and give them a good light position in the greenhouse. All mint can be subject to mint rust, although apple mint has some resistance; watch out for the telltale orange spots on swollen stems and destroy the affected plants. Some people consider rust on mint can be controlled by spraying with an infusion of horsetail or mares tail, *Equisetum arvense*. This is the oldest species of plant still surviving in Great Britain, with an ancestry going back millions of years. The roots are wire-like

sage

thyme

mint

rhizomes that go very deep in light soil. The flowerless foliage contains tiny crystals of silica which act like fine sandpaper or wire wool, making it useful for cleaning metal; hence its old name of pewterwort. To use the weed as a fungicide, you must collect foliage, stems and rhizomes, and for each ounce pour on two pints of hot water and allow to stand for twenty-four hours. Strain off and use the liquor undiluted. It is also said to be useful for controlling mildew on strawberries and blackspot on roses.

GRAPES

Viniculture should not be undertaken without careful thought. You have to wait three years after planting the vine before picking the first bunch of grapes; the management of the vine calls for time and effort; and in a bad summer the harvest can be disappointing.

Greenhouse or conservatory culture of the grape has several advantages over outdoor growing in terms of extending the geographical boundary of where and how grapes can be grown, and there is a wider choice of varieties. But it is important to think in the long term, because a well-tended, vigorous grapevine can be productive for thirty, even forty years, over which time it may have yielded more than 300kg (660lb) of fruit for dessert or enough to make 198 litres (44 gals) of wine. Some people consider that one vine isn't quite productive enough to make a worthwhile amount of hobby wine, and that two or more are too demanding of space. Where space is restricted, many varieties of vine can be grown and fruited in pots or other containers, with the stems no more than 1–1.2m (3–4ft) tall. Good crops of high quality can be had from this method, and it is especially suited to management by gardeners confined to a wheelchair.

There are three groups of greenhouse dessert grape: sweetwater, muscat and vinous.

Sweetwater are the first to ripen and are the varieties to choose from if your greenhouse is unheated. They are high yielding with grapes that are sweet and juicy and thin-skinned, although when ripe, the grapes don't keep for more than a few weeks. There are four sweetwaters which are particularly suitable for growing in pots in the greenhouse or conservatory: Black Corinth, a very old black variety with sweet, juicy, seedless grapes; the universally-known Black Hamburgh, a reliable mid-season variety; Chasselas Vibert, a round white grape that is a consistent high yielder; and Foster's Seedling, thought to be one of the best early varieties with good-sized bunches of well-flavoured white grapes.

Also in the sweetwater category are the black Cardinal and King's Ruby; the white Chaouch, Lady Hutt, and Madeline Royale; and Chasselas Rose, a red grape.

Muscats are the next to ripen, and they require some help to pollinate and a little heat to mature. They keep better than the sweetwaters and are considered to have the finest flavour. For growing in pots the black muscat Hamburgh and the white Primavis Frontignan and Royal Muscadine are recommended.

Others in this large muscat group are Black Frontignan, one of the oldest grapes in cultivation; Black Monukka, a fine-flavoured seedless grape; Lady Hastings, an early ripening type; Madresfield Court, with large black grapes and the bonus of fiery foliage in autumn; and Prince of Wales, rather later than the other blacks with a superb flavour. Among the white muscats are Ascot Citronelle, small grapes but plenty of them; Canon Hall Muscat; Grizzley Frontignan, a very old tawny type that is a favourite for the cold greenhouse; Mrs Pearson, a late variety that can be stored until mid-spring; another good keeper, Muscat of Hungary; the very early Royal Muscadine and St Laurent.

Vinous grapes were beloved of the wealthy Victorians whose hothouses were ideal for the rather long period of heat needed for the bunches to mature; they are the last of the three groups to ripen. They will keep for several months and are still a good choice for heated greenhouses and conservatories, when they should be grown as standards in pots. After harvesting the grapes, the pots should be moved outside but protected from frost, or placed in a cold greenhouse for the necessary dormancy period.

Vinous black varieties include Alicante, Angers Frontignan, Appley Towers, Espiran, Gros Colmar, Gros Maroc, Lady Downe's Seedling and West's St Peter's. The white vinous varieties include Golden Queen; Syrian, said to be able to produce bunches up to 9kg (20lb); and Trebbiano.

Preparation and planting

Grapes grown as standards in pots are the obvious choice for the conservatory or small greenhouse. For those grown as cordons, proper allowance must be made for the space they will eventually need – up to 2.4m (8ft) length of the greenhouse for the vine, and an area of about 1–1.2m (3–4ft) wide and up to 2.4m (8ft) long for the root-run.

A time-honoured way of growing grapes was to plant the vine outside immediately adjacent to the greenhouse, and lead the main vine or rod into the structure through a hole in the wall, and this is still a sound idea. An elaborate procedure for preparing the planting site was considered essential to the long and healthy life of the vine. It included placing the carcass of an animal at the bottom of the planting hole, and although ritualistic, this probably gave a long-term steady supply of phosphates and calcium which are readily leached out in light soils. The traditional preparation of the vine border involved, first, the

SIMPLE GRAPE GROWING

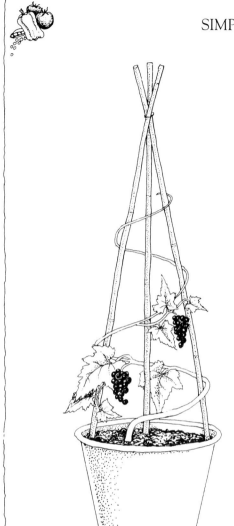

For the grape enthusiast, part of the fun is the fussing over the vine with its inescapable routine of pruning, watering, thinning, and so on. If you feel all that is too time-consuming, you could try a simplified technique; yields won't be high, and you wil have to start all over again after four years, but very little management is involved.

Buy a two- or three-year-old Black Hamburgh in late autumn or early winter and plant it in a 30cm (12in) pot. Put it outdoors for the dormancy period, and bring it into the greenhouse at the end of winter. Push three 1.5m (5ft) canes into the compost at the edge of the pot to form a wigwam. Tie at the top and train the rod spirally round the canes. Stop all lateral branches at two leaves beyond each bunch of grapes and thin these to leave a total of just six bunches.

In winter cut back the rod to half its length and stand the pot outside until early spring, when it is back in the greenhouse, give the compost a dressing of 68g (2oz) of fish, blood and bone, watered in. Then add a mulch of garden compost or well-rotted farmyard manure. In this second and subsequent years, give a fortnightly feed of liquid seaweed extract from the time the fruits form until they start to show colour.

For the simple method of growing grapes use a large pot and a wigwam of canes.

removal of the soil to a full depth of 75cm (30in). This was followed by a 15cm (6in) layer of builder's rubble or broken bricks for drainage, then a layer of old turves, followed by a mixture of five parts sifted loam, one part of mortar rubble, one part composted manure with a generous amount of wood ash, if available, and bone meal at the rate of 68–136g per sq m (2–4oz per sq yd). If mortar rubble was unavailable, ground limestone at the rate of 270–400g per sq m (8–12oz per sq yd) was substituted.

Nowadays, the planting preparation can be simpli-fied to provide good drainage and sound fertility.

Well-matured compost and well-rotted manure can be used along with a base dressing of bone meal and the ground limestone. Where you plant the vine along the outside wall of the greenhouse will depend on where, eventually, you want to train it in the greenhouse – assuming you don't intend to give it solitary occupation.

The training wires should run horizontally about 23cm (9in) apart and about 38cm (15in) from the glass. Special supports with eyes can be bought to hold the wire securely.

Container-grown vines can be planted at any time,

others are planted in late autumn. The roots should be spread out to be just below the surface and the soil firmed thoroughly. Water and mulch with compost or well-rotted farmyard manure. Dormant vines must be cut back to about 1.2m (4ft) after planting.

You can allow just one rod to develop or two or more; it depends on how much space can be spared. In the winter following planting of a container-grown vine, the main rod is cut back to 1.2m (4ft) and any lateral shoots to two buds. Pruning thereafter follows the winter pattern, where part of the new growth is cut back and the laterals are selected to match the training wires. Each spring, two shoots are allowed to form along the laterals; when it is clear which is the stronger fruit-bearing one, the other is removed. The growing point of each lateral is nipped out two leaves past the bunch of grapes, or at about the seventh leaf.

BELOW LEFT: In the first year after planting the vine train the laterals along the horizontal wires, and in the spring cut them back to five leaves from the rod (main stem). In subsequent years, when the flowers appear cut back the fruiting lateral to two leaves past the truss of flowers. For the first few years allow just one bunch to each lateral. (Below right): In winter cut back the rod by a half and laterals to within 2.5 cm (1in) from the rod.

Management

The object of training and pruning the vine is to encourage just enough foliage to maintain the health of the vine, although not too much at the expense of the fruit, and to secure the optimum number of fully-developed bunches of grapes. Given understanding care and attention, a vine in a greenhouse should go on being productive for thirty or more years, and there are records of vines of great age – for example, the Great Vine planted in 1768 at Hampton Court, London, now has a girth of 216cm (7ft 1in) and branches up to 34.7m (114ft).

For two or three years after fruiting begins, depending on the vigour of the vine, thin out the bunches to leave just one to each lateral. Every year in early spring give a dressing of a balanced organic fertiliser (see p34), teased into the top few centimetres of the soil and then thoroughly watered in, followed by a mulch of home-produced compost or well-rotted manure or a mixture of both.

Until the flowers appear, aim for a warm, humid atmosphere; when the flowers open, the greenhouse should be kept on the dry side. Pollination is aided by

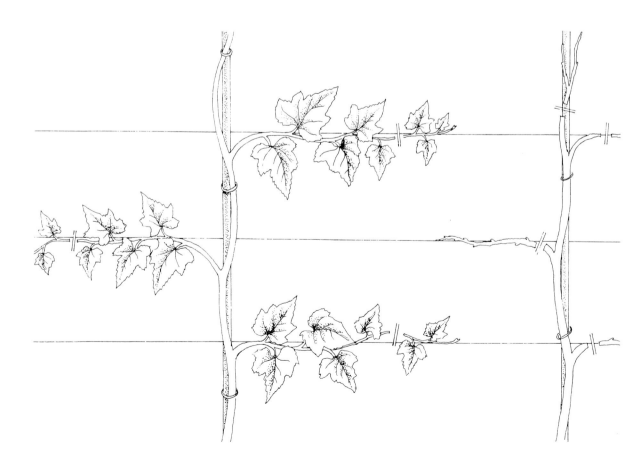

tapping the laterals, gently shaking the rod, or dusting the flowers with a twist of cotton wool.

Vines must never go short of water, and this applies especially to those growing in pots or with the root-run inside the greenhouse. Remember also that where the roots are outside even though rainfall might appear to be adequate, extra watering is often necessary, just as with climbing plants grown against a wall or fence.

From mid-summer until early autumn some shading of the greenhouse will be necessary, and later the humidity can be reduced to aid ripening. At this stage, weekly feeding with liquid manure or comfrey liquid will help to plump the berries and ensure there is a buoyant atmosphere.

Thinning of the berries in the bunches may be necessary and this can be a bit tricky. Start when the berries are pea-sized and use long-bladed scissors (special vine scissors can be bought), and repeat the process over a ten-day period so that finally the berries are evenly spaced about 1cm (½in) apart.

When harvesting the bunches, don't be in too much of a hurry. Let taste be your guide as to the ripeness. Although the grapes may appear to be ready in terms of size and colour, they will need to remain on the vine for the full flavour to mature and this might take up to ten weeks.

Cut the bunch with a handle, cradling it with the other hand, and continue to treat each bunch with great gentleness. If several bunches are ready together, those that aren't wanted immediately can be cut with a good length of stem – put this stem in a jar of water and keep the bunches in a cool, dark place. If they are cut in this way in late autumn, they will be just right for Christmas.

MELONS

Melons can be grown very well in the amateur's greenhouse and give a lot of pleasure in the process, although gardeners in colder regions face a more difficult prospect than those in climatically more favoured parts. Certainly in Great Britain, the main problem today is that, without heat and in an indifferent summer, too few fruit will ripen to make the effort worthwhile.

The melon is closely related to the cucumber, although it requires a slightly hotter and drier atmosphere. In earlier times melons were started off in a greenhouse or frame on a hotbed made up of fresh farmyard manure, and for best yields starting off in heat is still the recommendation.

 KEEP APART

Don't grow melons and cucumbers together in the same greenhouse. Both being members of the same family (Cucumis) they will cross-pollinate, and you'll have cucumber-flavoured melons and vice versa.

If the greenhouse can be heated to a minimum 15°C (60°F), melons can be started in late winter to harvest in early summer, or in early spring to pick in mid-summer. With an electric propagator you can start in mid-spring. They can also be grown successfully by starting them off in the airing cupboard at 21–26°C (70–80°F), and growing them on in pots on a south-facing windowsill; then transfer them to barn cloches outside in late spring. To keep growing, melons need a minimum temperature of 15°C (60°F) and, like young cucumber plants, any check caused by low temperature makes for a poor end product.

Choosing the Variety

Melon seeds are less expensive than the all-female cucumber varieties, although the choice is rather limited. Gaylia F1, with the grey-green varicose-veined skin, is considered to be the finest flavoured and sweetest melon of all, and it can produce very large fruits. In Great Britain, a certain Mr A. Emery won a place in the *Guinness Book of Records* with a 9lb 3¼oz (5kg) Gaylia melon, and from the same crop he had one of 8lb 1¾oz (4kg) and several from 7 to 7½lb (3 to 3.4kg), all in an 8 × 6ft (2.4 × 1.8m) greenhouse.

Ogen melons are smaller than the Gaylia, but each plant can produce up to ten ripe fruits from mid-summer to early autumn. Jenny Lind is a very old variety with a superb flavour, while two F1 hybrids, Early Sweet and Sweetheart, give medium-sized fruit that mature quickly and would be a suitable choice for growers in colder regions, although the flavour is said to be poorer than the slower-maturing types.

Raising the plants

Melon seeds are sown 1cm (½in) deep singly in 8cm (3in) pots of multipurpose compost, covered with a sheet of glass or plastic, and placed in the propagator with the thermostat set at 18–21°C (65–70°F).

Germination is rapid, taking six to nine days, and as soon as the seedlings emerge the glass cover should be removed. From then on, the seedlings need full light and when they have made four true leaves they can be transplanted to their growing site.

Growing methods

Melons are prone to soil-borne fungus disease, so unless you are entirely confident your border soil is sterile, transplant the seedlings to a growing-bag or large pots. Two plants per bag gives the right amount of root space, while for pots, each plant will want a 25cm (10in) or 30cm (12in) one, filled with multi-purpose peat or peat substitute compost. When planting, leave the rootball slightly proud of the surface of the compost to prevent stem rot.

Being vines, the melon plants must have support in the greenhouse, although under cloches or in frames this obviously isn't necessary. A sound method is to put a cane into the growing bag or pot and tie it into horizontal wires every 30cm (12in) up to the height of the eaves. In a lean-to, take the horizontal wires as high as you can comfortably reach.

Train the main stem of the plant up the cane by tying it loosely with fillis or raffia, and when it reaches the topmost horizontal wire pinch out the growing tip. This encourages the development of the side shoots which bear the flowers.

Allow the side shoots to develop so that they can be trained along the horizontal wires in either direction, but pinch out the growing points once five leaves have developed.

Each plant produces both male and female flowers, the males normally appearing first. The female flowers are easily recognisable by the swelling behind the petals. When five or six female flowers on each plant are fully open, it is time to give nature a hand by pollinating them. This means you will have that number of fruit ripe and ready at approximately the same time; staggered pollination of the same plant doesn't mean staggered ripening – it means that the first one or two fruits will develop properly, while the other female flowers will be difficult to set. However, stagger the pollination of flowers on separate plants, by all means.

The actual operation is simple, and is best done in full sunlight at high noon. Remove the male flower, take off the petals, and gently push it into the centre of the female flower. One male flower will pollinate four females.

Management

Weekly feeding with a good liquid fertiliser is important, and watering once or even twice a day is vital in hot weather, although waterlogging must be avoided. Try also to avoid splashing water on to the stem as this could lead to stem rot: a useful aid is the plastic bottle placed alongside the stem (see p112).

Melons prefer a slightly hotter, drier atmosphere than tomatoes and cucumbers, particularly during the flowering period. When the flowers have set and the fruits are ripening, increase the ventilation, reduce the amount of water and try to keep the temperature below 27°C (80°F). This isn't easy without shading, but it is quite important not to be too generous with the shade because melons must have plenty of good light.

When the fruits get to about tennis ball size, stop the feeding and give them support; various methods are used, depending on their expected size at maturity. Except for monsters, small nets made out of onion or pea bags or cut from lengths of old net curtain will do the trick, or you can use discarded tights.

The finest flavour comes from fully ripe fruit. Experienced melon growers can recognise the right stage of ripeness simply by the aroma. Otherwise a surer method is to test ripeness by touch, when the end farthest from the stalk should be slightly soft when pressed. In a normal summer the fruit ripens from late summer to early autumn.

Troubles with melons are substantially the same as those with cucumbers, but because of the hot, dry atmosphere preferred by melon plants, red spider mite can get a hold quite rapidly. Biological control using the predator mite *Phytosieiulus persimilis* is effective (see p56).

A SELECTION OF FRUIT

Peaches and Nectarines

Peaches and nectarines are virtually identical fruits except that nectarines don't have the downy skin of peaches, are rather less hardy in temperate regions, and are rather less productive. They can be grown in the greenhouse, preferably fan-trained against a wall in a lean-to structure, or with posts and wires for support in a free-standing one. You will have to accept them as permanent residents because their productive life is at least twenty years. They do not require heat during the winter, because they must have a period of natural dormancy; they will require pollinating by hand, using a soft watercolourist's brush or a ball of

cotton wool; and they will need daily spraying with rainwater during spring and summer.

The rootstock that these delicious fruits grow on is St Julien A, and all the varieties are self-fertile. St Julien A is described as semi-dwarfing, though even so, with any fan-trained peach you should allow a space at least 3.6m (12ft) wide and about 2.5m (8ft) high. When the tree is in full production some thinning will be necessary to maintain good fruit size and quality; a crop of thirty-five to forty fruit might be expected.

Prepare the planting site by digging a hole 90cm (3ft) deep and 2.7m (9ft) long; put in a 16cm (6in) layer of rubble, followed by 30cm (1ft) of well-rotted farmyard manure. Return the soil thoroughly mixed with more manure and as much of your homemade compost as you can spare. Leave a good-sized hole so that the roots can be well spread out, and erect the supports with the wires spaced horizontally approximately 23cm (9in) apart, starting at 40cm(15in) from the ground.

Planted in late autumn, the maiden tree is cut back to three buds, from which the shoots will emerge to start the fan of branches. In early spring give a top dressing of fish, blood and bone fertiliser at the rate of 85g (3oz) to the sq m (sq yd), and lightly tease it in; repeat this each spring for the next three years. In the

following winter after planting, the central shoot is cut back and the other two are tied to canes that, in turn, are tied to the wires. In the third and fourth years the fan training continues by selecting shoots from the two main branches and tying them into canes and wires. Until the tree has reached maturity it is advisable to remove the blossom, although some experts recommend allowing a few fruits to develop in the third year, then double that number in the fourth year. When the tree is mature, an annual spring dressing of well-rotted manure or compost, and a couple of foliar feeds with seaweed extract, will keep it in sound condition. Fruits will be carried on the shoots of the previous season, and the pruning regime is aimed at stimulating this process, with the fruit-bearing laterals shortened to about six leaves.

Kiwi Fruit

For the more adventurous, Kiwi fruit make a challenging crop for the greenhouse owner. The small 1.8 × 2.4m (6 × 8ft) greenhouse will happily accommodate three female and one male plant, but as they will be in occupation for years, a spare greenhouse will

Fan training a peach or nectarine involves cutting back the central shoot in the winter after planting. Then tie in selected branches to canes and wires.

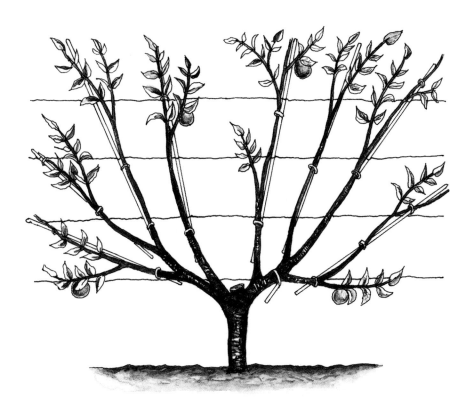

OPPOSITE: *Pollinating peaches by hand is necessary for proper setting of the fruit.*

ABOVE: *A lemon tree can be grown from a pip (see p137), but quicker and more reliable results are obtained from young plants raised by a specialist nursery.*

be needed – and a great love of this still-luxurious fruit.

Kiwis are a vine fruit, and the stock plants can be bought from a nursery. They can be grown outside in warmer regions, but are better given year-round protection under glass.

The soil should be deeply fertile with a high humus content and slight acidity, say pH 6.5.

A good variety is Hayward and one male to six female plants will be needed. Outside a spacing of 5.5m (18ft) apart is about right, but in the greenhouse, plants should be spaced at 1.5m (5ft), so three females and one male would occupy the 6ft by 8ft house.

They are vigorous climbers and their vines need both vertical and horizontal supports. The main stem of each plant is taken to a horizontal wire under the eaves at eye-height, and the main stem is then trained one way and a main shoot is trained the other. As shoots develop from these two main leaders, they are trained along parallel wires.

The female flowers have to be hand-pollinated by a male flower, one male providing enough pollen to fertilise four females.

The fruits develop rapidly and will have reached a mature size by late summer. However they must remain on the vine for at least another twelve weeks for the sugar content to reach an optimum level. Once ripe, they can stay on the vine for weeks without loss of flavour or quality and can even withstand quite hard frosts.

The fruit will keep for up to twelve weeks if stored in a cool place. You can expect to harvest about 13.5kg (30lb) of fruit from each fully grown plant and the vines will go on bearing for fifteen or more years – or until you lose interest.

Obviously they will need to be controlled, so pruning and trimming are important. Basically, it is necessary to shorten the lateral stems to six to eight buds during the winter. A further light pruning in mid-summer should leave just a few buds of the current year's growth. In early spring the vines should be given a mulch of well-rotted farmyard manure or compost preceded by a blood, fish and bone dressing.

PINEAPPLE PLANT

When next you buy a pineapple and cut off the top, save it. Cut away the soft flesh and leave it to dry for 48 hours, then place the crown of leaves with its fibrous core in a 13cm (5in) pot of soil-based compost. In time the core will make a tiny root system and the handsome rosette of leaves will continue to grow. Treat it as a bromeliad by giving it a small pot, a minimum of water and an occasional foliar feed.

In the main pineapple producing countries, the plants are propagated vegetatively from the shoots that grow from the base.

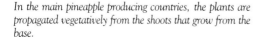

PLANTS FROM PIPS AND STONES

Citrus

Young children and those who are still young at heart can have great fun growing citrus plants from pips. However, don't expect to gather the fruits unless you are very patient, because lemon, lime, orange and grapefruit trees do not come into bearing until at least seven years after sowing the seeds. They are sub-tropical evergreens and are frost tender, so they will need to be regarded as fairly permanent residents of the conservatory or even the cool greenhouse. Most parents opt to enjoy growing them as interesting and instructional houseplants.

Simply soak the seeds in water for twelve hours or so, then sow them about 1.5cm (½in) deep, three to an 8cm (3in) pot of a peat substitute compost. Pop each pot into a plastic bag to retain moisture, and place in the propagator at 21°C (70°F) or in the airing cupboard.

Examine the pots after fourteen days and every other day until the shoots appear; then, move them to a warm, sunny position in the house, greenhouse or conservatory. The seedlings should be re-potted into separate 8cm (3in) pots when they are about 10cm (4in) tall.

The plants can be stood outside in a sunny, sheltered spot for the summer, but must never be allowed to dry out; feed with a dilute liquid seaweed fertiliser. The growing tips should be pinched out to encourage bushiness. In the conservatory or greenhouse the plants require plenty of light and a minimum winter temperature of 5°C (40°F). Draughts and sudden changes of temperature should be avoided, but try to maintain a buoyant, fairly humid atmosphere.

An alternative to growing citrus fruits from pips is to buy young bushes or specimen plants from a specialist nursery.

Dates

Germinate quite readily at 21°C (70°F), although they take up to fourteen weeks. Save a few stones from the Christmas stock and plant them three to an 8cm (3in) pot of soil-based compost with extra sand in it. Push the stones vertically into the compost so that their tops are about 1.5cm (½in) below the surface. Cover with a plastic bag and place in the propagator or airing cupboard.

POT GROW A FIG

As a greenhouse or conservatory plant the fig has a lot to commend it, and especially suitable is the variety Bourjasotte Grise. It is both ornamental, with handsome foliage, and edible, with delicious fruit. Moreover, it is easy to grow in a large pot or tub and is seldom troubled by pests or disease. With winter warmth of 10°C (50°F) it is possible to gather two crops a year, because both the current and the previous year's shoots yield fruit. Plant in a free-draining, soil-based compost in a pot or tub no larger than 38cm (15in) diameter, as root restriction is important. The plant can be fan-trained against a south-facing wall or left as a bush, when it is preferable to give it a summer holiday outdoors in a sheltered spot in the garden. Throughout the growing season the plant should be given plenty of water and a fortnightly feed of an organic liquid fertiliser, preferably seaweed based. Do *not* overfeed as this can induce sappy, tender growth. In winter in the unheated greenhouse the embryo fruits and new shoots should have protection against frost.

PEACHES FROM A STONE

It is quite possible to grow peaches from seed, although the resulting tree is seldom up to the quality of one grafted on to a suitable rootstock. Save the stones from peaches bought at the greengrocer during the summer, and put each one in a fifty-fifty soil and sand mixture in a flower-pot; bury it in a shady part of the garden or a cool cellar throughout the autumn and winter. In early spring sow the seeds singly in 15cm (6in) pots of soil-based compost, and place in a propagator to give bottom heat of about 19°C (66°F), or put them on a sunny windowsill. When the roots of each seedling have filled the pot, pot on to a 23cm (9in) pot and feed regularly with liquid fertiliser. Tie the central shoot to a cane, removing any laterals below the 30cm (2ft) mark. In the third year plant the young tree in the autumn, and cut back the centre leader to about 75cm (2ft 6in).

When the seedlings are large enough to handle, pot them up individually, potting on as the plants outgrow their pots. However, date palms will inevitably grow too large to accommodate indoors.

Avocado pears

Can also outgrow their welcome, making about 30cm (12in) of new growth each year, although with pruning it is possible to restrict the height to about 1m (3ft). The mature plant is not particularly attractive, though the seed, about the size of a hen's egg, is great fun for children to germinate. Blunt end first, it is pushed into a 13cm (5in) pot of compost, covered with a plastic bag and given a place in the propagator at 21–24°C (70–75°F) or airing cupboard until the stone splits and the shoot appears.

Alternatively, stand the stone in a jar of water with a narrow neck so that the blunt end is just touching the water; or balance it by pushing a cocktail stick through the stone, as in the illustration. This is the more interesting way, because the children can watch the fleshy fang-like roots develop. When the shoot has emerged the seedling should be transplanted to a 13cm (5in) pot of soil-based compost.

When the seedling avocado pear has grown like this it can be transplanted to a 13cm (5in) pot of soil-based compost.

OPPOSITE:

An annual crop of tomatoes can be grown in a greenhouse where the permanent residents are nectarine or peach trees.

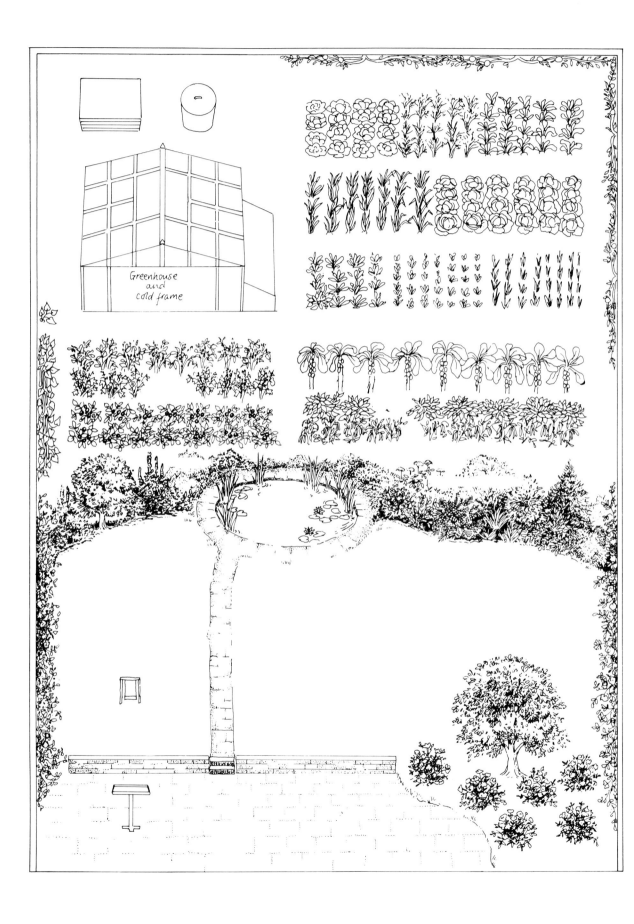

Greenhouse
and
cold frame

THROUGH THE YEAR CHECKLIST

Too many tomes on gardening are far too precise as to when seeds should be sown, bulbs planted or shrubs pruned. Although well intentioned, such advice suggests inflexibility, whereas every gardener knows that an unpredictable climate can throw the best laid plans completely haywire. Raising plants in the greenhouse and conservatory does have a great advantage over outdoor activities in that the environment is controlled. Nevertheless, in the following pages allowance has been made for regional variations and personal choice. Hence, the reminders are based on seasons rather than the months of the year.

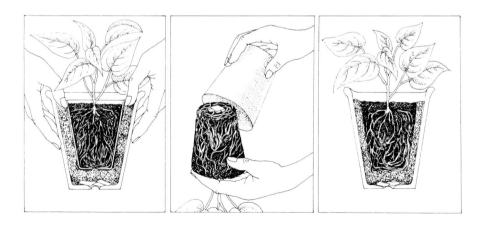

MID-WINTER

- Overwintering plants in pots may need extra protection from hard frost. Bubble film insulation, newspaper or polythene sheeting spread over and round the staging is often sufficient, or paper or plastic bags over individual pots will keep out several degrees of frost. If frost penetrates the greenhouse or cold frame, remember that a quick thaw does more damage than freezing of the plants. Keep insulation in position or the frame covered and let the temperature warm up gradually.
- Ventilate on fine days, but be sure to close down before dusk.
- Check dahlia tubers in store for signs of rot.
- Check all cuttings of geraniums and pelargoniums for mildew and remove any affected leaves. Water cuttings only when the growing medium has dried out.
- Water pot plants with care. Over-watering kills faster than giving too little.
- Bring bulbs into the light.
- Cut down stems of late-flowering chrysanthemums after flowering, clean up debris and towards the end of the period start taking cuttings (see p102).
- Sow early carrots, winter lettuce and radishes in growing-bags to harvest in mid- to late spring.
- Pot up schizanthus sown in late summer into 13cm (5in) pots and pinch out growing tips.
- Some plants can be brought in from the cold outside for earlier flowering. These include primroses, lily of the valley, pansies and wallflowers which should be potted up into appropriate size pots and given a position in full light.
- Dead-head flowering plants and remove any dead leaves.
- Perpetual flowering carnations need a minimum temperature of 7°C (45°F) and ventilation whenever possible. Water sparingly.
- Propagator: Sow hardy annuals, such as calendula and godetia at 16–18°C (61–64°F), and later in the month antirrhinums, gloxinia and streptocarpus. Sow seed of sweet peas in individual tubes or paper pots (see p42), and perpetual flowering and annual carnation seeds at 16°C (61°F). Sow onions and leeks in boxes at 12°C (55°F). Sow cauliflowers and Hispi or Primo cabbage seed at a temperature of 16°C (61°F) for planting out in mid- to late spring.

    Take cuttings of perpetual flowering carnations and place in the propagator or heated frame at 13–16°C (55–61°F). If using a mist propagator, maintain a temperature of 21°C (70°F).

LATE WINTER

- Shorter nights and marginally warmer days will see the overwintering fuchsia plants making some growth. Give them more water as growth increases and the benefit of an occasional spraying with tepid water. Other pot plants will need more watering as this period progresses, but always do so in the morning and never give too much.
- If the job hasn't already been done, wash all empty pots and trays with a mild sterilising solution, leaving them outside the greenhouse to dry off.
- Shrubby plants in containers should have a little of the old compost removed from the surface. Replace with fresh potting or worm-worked compost.
- Continue to propagate perpetual flowering carnations by cuttings, and pot on rooted cuttings into 8cm (3in) pots. Give plants their first stopping when they have made nine pairs of leaves.
- Bulbs that have finished flowering should be kept watered sparingly until conditions are ready for them to be finished off by planting outside.
- Take root cuttings of appropriate alpine plants.
- Pot up lily bulbs for forcing as pot plants. Allow three small lilies to a 15cm (6in) pot and three medium-size ones to a 20cm (8in) pot.
- Take cuttings of late-flowering chrysanthemums.
- Early potatoes can be chitted (sprouted) in trays in the greenhouse but be prepared to cover them if frost could penetrate. Spray the tubers with tepid water every so often.
- Overwintered geraniums, pelargoniums and coleus cuttings can be potted on into 13cm (5in) pots.
- Sow broad beans in trays or individually in peat or paper pots for planting out in early spring.
- Start shallots and onion sets into growth by placing them on trays of moist peat. Plant out when they have made about 2.5cm (1in) of root growth.
- Propagator: Sow the first of the half-hardy annuals, including African marigolds, antirrhinums, dahlias, geraniums, petunias and salvias. Sow summer-flowering pot plants, such as gloxinias, hibiscus, Morning Glory and streptocarpus. Sow tomatoes if you can provide a minimum temperature of 10°C (50°F) for growing them on (see p112). Gladioli flower earlier if sprouted in the greenhouse. Place the corms on peat in a tray and place in the propagator at 10°C (50°F).

    Sow Brussels sprouts, cabbages, cauliflowers, leeks and onions in the propagator at 15°C (60°F), but move to the staging in full light when the seedlings have emerged.

EARLY SPRING

- A wide variety of seeds can be sown at this time in the cool greenhouse and propagator. Prevent damping off by using only sterile equipment. Water with a proprietary compound if you are doubtful of your anti-damping-off measures.
- Seed sown earlier may now be ready for pricking out, using the technique described on p44, while tomato plants sown in mid-winter will probably be ready for transplanting to growing-bags, pots or the greenhouse border. They need to be grown on at not less than 13°C (55°F). Seedling tomatoes and cucumbers should be pricked out individually into 10cm (4in) pots
- Liquid feed plants in pots once a good root system has grown. The rule with liquid feeding is little but often. Young plants should only have feed at half the normal strength.

- Make sure your automatic vent openers are working properly. This is a period when mid-day temperatures in sunny weather can hit 22°C (80°F) in a closed conservatory or greenhouse.
- Overwintered fuchsias, begonias and gloxinia tubers can be started into growth by restrained watering.
- Cuttings of chrysanthemums, coleus, dahlias, fuchsias, geraniums and hydrangeas can be taken (see pp48–9).
- Early potato varieties that have been chitted in the greenhouse can be planted out in favourable areas.
- Sow celery, French beans and lettuce.
- Top dress shrubs in containers by replacing the top few centimetres of compost with fresh compost.
- Bring the capillary matting out of store and into use.

In early spring the greenhouse staging may well be packed with trays and pots of seedlings, and some shading may be necessary.

MID-SPRING

- Plant out in growing bags or pots aubergines, cucumbers, peppers and tomatoes that were sown in early spring.

Make your own growing bag out of a strong plastic bag, but make sure it is not bio-degradable.

- Sow tomatoes, melons for outdoors, and ridge cucumbers, courgettes and marrows.
- Sow celery, celeriac, French beans, if not sown earlier, and sweetcorn in 8cm (3in) pots.
- Frost is still likely to strike. In the unheated greenhouse be prepared to protect peach blossom and seedlings with newspaper and netting.
- Pinch out the growing points of fuchsias and geraniums to encourage bushiness. Pot on as necessary.
- Hanging baskets for outdoors can be prepared. Stand the basket on a bucket to fill it with compost and plants and give it at least ten days in the greenhouse or conservatory before gradually introducing it to outside.
- Stop late-flowering chrysanthemums, according to the variety (see p105).
- Watering, ventilation and shading need extra attention at this time.
- Prick out bedding plants sown earlier and continue sowing annuals and half-hardy annuals that will flower in mid- and late summer.
- Towards the end seedlings intended for outdoors can be hardened off. Place them outside for longer periods each day over a fortnight, but remember to bring them in before sundown.

LATE SPRING

- Hanging baskets prepared earlier can be hung outside.
- Sow cucumbers, melons and sweetcorn for outdoors and cineraria for indoor plants to flower from mid-winter onwards.
- Shading should be applied to the exterior of the greenhouse. Young seedlings are particularly liable to scorching from direct sunlight.
- Gradually harden off frost-tender plants.
- Sow French beans, runner beans, courgettes and marrows for planting out later in early summer.
- Sow winter-flowering pot plants, including calceolarias, capsicums, cineraria, primulas and schizanthus.
- Pinch out the growing point of fuchsia cuttings when about 10cm (4in) high to encourage bushiness.
- Tomato plants can be planted into the border soil, growing bags and other containers. Use fillis string as support by tying one end to the base of the stem of the plant, the other to a horizontal wire along the eaves.
- Provide shade for all plants in flower and increase both ventilation and humidity as a preventive against disease and red spider mite.

A good way to prepare a hanging basket is to stand it on a bucket as you fill it with compost and plants.

EARLY SUMMER

- Many under-cover plants can be moved to a sheltered position outdoors for the summer, but remember they will need watering and checking for pest attacks.
- Shading, ventilation and watering in the greenhouse and conservatory may need attention twice or more daily unless automatic controls are installed.
- Tomato plants need regular feeding with a liquid seaweed extract, and removal of side shoots. At the first sign of whitefly hang up yellow sticky traps.

Yellow sticky traps will control mild attacks of whitefly.

- Dead-head begonias and gloxinias.
- Thin dessert grapes, retaining only well-shaped large bunches.
- Pollinate melons using a soft watercolour brush. Pinch out the growing tips on the two leaders once seven leaves have formed.
- Cucumbers should be kept tied in and fed with liquid manure. Pick off male flowers unless growing an all-female variety. Top dress with compost when the roots appear on the surface.
- Pot on late-flowering chrysanthemums.
- Perpetual flowering carnations should have side buds removed for large bloom production, central bud removed for sprays.
- Take leaf cuttings of saintpaulias and *Begonia rex*.
- Plant out French beans, courgettes and marrows as early as possible during this period.

MID-SUMMER

- Plants in the conservatory will need extra attention to avoid stress from overheating. Provide as much general humidity as possible. Local humidity can be given by placing open containers of water near the plants on hot, sunny days.
- In the greenhouse damping down by spraying the pathway, staging and borders with water will help to increase humidity and lower the temperature during the hottest part of the day.
- Tomatoes and cucumbers should be in full production. Regular watering should prevent blossom end rot and split fruits on the tomato plants.
- Unless capillary matting is in use or another form of automatic watering, plants will require watering once or twice a day. Fill the watering cans and stand in the greenhouse or conservatory so that the water is applied at about the internal temperature.
- Pots and trays should be scrubbed after use in a mild disinfectant and stored in a shed or garage.
- Take cuttings of acacia, hydrangea, escallonia, lavatera, regal pelargonium and viburnum (see p45).
- Sow dwarf hyacinth-flowered larkspur, *Phlox drummondii* and *Clarkia elegans* for flowering in the winter conservatory.

MAKE FRIENDS WITH FRONDS

Ferns aren't everyone's choice of indoor plants, but they are happy to have a home in a west-facing part of the conservatory out of direct sunlight. An average temperature of 16°–22°C (60°–70°F) suits most ferns, although it can be a little lower in winter. Generally, the large ferns with strong foliage are easier to raise than the small-leaved types. Use a peat-type compost and keep it moist, preferably by watering from below, but keep it a little on the dry side over the winter. Remove all fronds that become brown and brittle to allow new growth to develop, and repot when necessary in early spring.

LEFT: *Even if your greenhouse or conservatory is not as large as this one at the Cambridge Botanic Garden, it is quite possible to create a colourful indoor 'garden'.*

ABOVE: *A variety of containers can be filled with plants raised under glass for a long-lasting patio display.*

LATE SUMMER

- Sow schizanthus, the butterfly flower, *Cyclamen persicum*, *Exacum affine*.
- If you leave the door of the greenhouse open on the hottest days, use netting to keep out birds and cats and to keep in any biological control predators or parasites.
- Continue damping down, but maintain a buoyant atmosphere.
- Dry off amaryllis (hippeastrum) bulbs and store them in their pots under the staging. Plant freesia corms for flowering in mid-winter.

CARRY ON GROWING

As the days shorten and the nights get longer, extra light for your indoor garden means that some of your plants will remain in active growth. Tungsten bulbs are unsuitable, but fluorescent tubes with special reflectors, on units that can be raised and lowered, are ideal. The lighting unit should provide about 20 watts per 30sq cm (1sq ft) of plants and be positioned about 30cm (1ft) above flowering plants such as saintpaulia, cineraria and begonia, and double that distance for foliage plants. Special types of lighting units can be bought for DIY assembly or as complete kits.

- Start sowing winter lettuce in growing-bags or the greenhouse border. Choose a variety such as Charlene, a butterhead, or Marmer, an iceberg type. Sow an early carrot, such as Early Nantes, Suko or Gregory, to harvest in early or late winter.
- Take cuttings of fuchsias and geraniums for overwintering, pinks, bougainvillea, calceolaria and *Campanula isophylla*.
- Prick out seedlings of plants sown in mid-summer.
- Take cuttings of rock plants. They can be rooted in a shaded cold frame.
- If the greenhouse tomatoes are to be succeeded by late-flowering chrysanthemums, stop the tomato plants by pinching out the growing point above the topmost truss. Towards the end of summer gradually reduce watering and stop feeding. A brown paper bag tied round the last truss will speed ripening.

EARLY AUTUMN

- Pot up prepared hyacinths for Christmas flowering, and winter-flowering bulbs for the conservatory and place in a plunge bed or cool, dark cellar. Pot up arum lilies, cyclamen and lachenalias.
- Take a few roots of mint and pot up into 15cm (6in) pots for forcing over the winter.
- Disbud late-flowering chrysanthemums (see p105). Move the plants into the greenhouse as the tomato plants finish cropping.
- Frost-tender plants from the borders and beds can be lifted and planted in large pots or boxes for overwintering in a frost-free greenhouse, conservatory or light, cool spare room.
- Rest summer-flowering bulbous and tuberous-rooted plants by reducing the watering and allowing them to dry off.
- House plants that have spent the summer outdoors should be returned to their usual positions having first checked them for insect pests.
- Sow annuals for spring flowering. Sow thinly in trays at 13–16°C (55–61°F) and prick out into 8cm (3in) pots when large enough. Overwinter in a cool greenhouse.
- Take cuttings of fuchsias, *Campanula isophylla* and geraniums if not taken earlier. Other cuttings to take at this time include coleus, impatiens, heliotropes and *Plumbago capensis*.

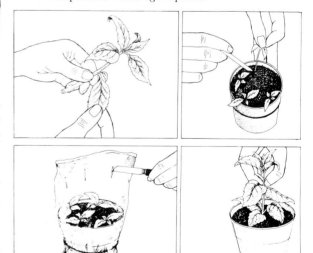

This is the time to take fuchsia cuttings. For details see page 50.

- In northern districts the shading can be removed towards the end of the month but be prepared to provide some protection from direct sunlight for seedlings.

MID-AUTUMN

- Pot up cuttings of fuchsia, geranium, pelargonium, plumbago, and so on, which were taken earlier in the autumn, and pot up a few hardy items from the garden for growing on indoors. Helleborus, pansies and polyanthus are suitable. Select a few good impatiens plants, trim them back and pot them for flowering over the winter in the conservatory or indoors.
- Cherished border perennials, such as chrysanthemums and delphiniums, can be lifted from the garden and packed into boxes of a sand/soil mixture. They can be overwintered under the staging and cuttings taken from them in the spring, while the parent plants can be restored to the border.

 ## GET PLANNING

With the memory of the season's successes – and failures – still fresh, use this relatively quiet period to plan for the coming year. As well as giving the greenhouse a thorough cleaning (page 53), check the structure for any repairs that might be needed and the glass for cracked panes. Heating and lighting equipment should be serviced, along with the propagator. Check also that there are enough undamaged pots and trays for the new season's activities.

- Three key features of greenhouse management from now and throughout the winter are frost protection, watering with care, and ventilating whenever possible. In districts where early frosts are normal it is a wise plan to secure the greenhouse insulation a little later this season.
- Remove all dead and diseased leaves from the late-flowering chrysanthemums and other plants.
- Better to under-water rather than over-water from now until the warmer days of spring, and try to give some roof ventilation on all but the damp and foggy days of the autumn and winter.
- Spring-flowering bulbs can be potted now for display in the conservatory or indoors (see p95).
- Use the propagator for more cuttings of evergreens.
- Prick out annuals sown earlier and cyclamen seedlings, pot on cineraria and calceolaria.
- Sow a short-day variety of lettuce, such as Charlene or Marmer, for planting out into a cold frame or into the greenhouse border.

LATE AUTUMN

- Dull, damp days with very little activity in the garden make this an excellent time for spring-cleaning the greenhouse (see p52). Don't forget to wash the capillary matting, dry it and then pack it away until needed again in the early spring. It is better to use a watering can very sparingly over the winter rather than any automatic method because the big danger in the unheated greenhouse from now until the warmer weather of spring is stagnant air, and over-watering leads to puddles, mildew and grey mould.
- Wash all empty pots and trays with a mild sterilising solution and leave them outside the greenhouse to dry off thoroughly.
- Overwintering plants should be kept as near to the glass as possible; evergreen foliage plants should be kept almost bone dry.
- When the late-flowering chrysanthemums have finished flowering they can be used to provide cuttings for next year (see p104, Storing your stock chrysanthemums).
- Bulbs in the plunge bed can be brought into the cool greenhouse before being taken indoors for flowering.
- Mid-autumn sown sweet peas should be stopped when the plants are about 10cm (4in) tall.
- Calceolarias, cinerarias and primulas can be potted on.
- Prune grape vines when the leaves have fallen (see p130).
- Overwintering lettuce plants sown earlier can be planted into the border or into growing bags.
- Provide ventilation whenever possible. Fix insulating material to the structure later in this period, whether your greenhouse is heated or not.
- Winter-flowering pansies in pots will be happy in the cold greenhouse. If there are frost-tender plants maintain a minimum temperature of 5°C (42°F). It will be necessary to cover such plants with newspaper or bubble polythene if deep frost is forecast.

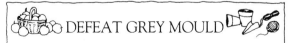 DEFEAT GREY MOULD

Botrytis (grey mould) can strike at any time, but is most likely to occur in cool, damp conditions. The best control is to ensure that plants are not overcrowded and that air can circulate freely.

EARLY WINTER

- Fit bubble polythene insulation to the interior of the greenhouse early on.
- Schizanthus sown in the summer can be potted on and the growing tips pinched out. Primulas, primroses and pansies can be potted up and brought into the conservatory for early flowering.
- Sow Winter Density or a similar winter hardy variety of lettuce for planting out in a cold frame or under cloches. For exhibition size onions and leeks, sow now at 10–12°C (50–55°F) in trays and place in the lightest position in the greenhouse.
- Late-flowering chrysanthemums should be cut back to within 15cm (6in) of the compost after flowering. The stools can be labelled and stored in boxes of moist spent peat or peat substitute, bark or soil.
- Winter-flowering plants and bulbs can be gradually introduced to warmer conditions.
- In the greenhouse water sparingly and avoid splashes. Ventilate whenever possible, except on damp, dull days.
- To ensure a supply of berried holly for Christmas decoration, cut the sprigs early on, and stand in a bucket of water in the greenhouse.
- Container-grown fuchsias and hydrangeas can be brought into the greenhouse or conservatory for the winter.

FURTHER READING

Ayres, Alistair, ed., *Successful Propagation* (Consumer Association 1988) Boniface, Priscilla, *Garden Room* HMSO 1982)

Buczacki, Stefan, and Harris, Keith, *Pests, Diseases and Disorders* (Collins 1983)

Clements, Tony, *African Violets* (David & Charles 1989)

Davidson, William, *Illustrated Directory of House Plants* (Salamander Books 1983)

Hessayon, D.G., *Flower Expert* (PBI 1984)

Kelly, John, *Sowing a Better Garden* (Unwin Hyman 1988)

Lacey, Roy, *Green Gardener* (David & Charles 1991)

Lacey, Roy, *Organic Gardening* (David & Charles 1988)

Pople, David, *Technique of Growing from Seed* (Eric Bruton Associates 1985)

Randall, Harry, and Wren, Alan, *Growing Chrysanthemums* (Croom Helm 1983)

Readers Digest Association, *Encyclopaedia of Garden Plants and Flowers* (The Readers Digest 1978)

Robinson, G.W., *Cool Greenhouse* (Penguin 1959)

Shellard, Alan, *Geraniums for Home and Garden* (David & Charles 1981)

Walls, Ian G., *Complete Book of the Greenhouse* (Ward Lock 1988)

Wells, George, *Fuchsias* (RHS Wisley Handbook 1987)

Wright, John I., *Propagation* (Blandford 1985)

ACKNOWLEDGEMENTS

I am indebted to Thompson & Morgan for the use of many of the colour photographs of plants; to Tricia Newell for her line drawings; and to *Gardening from Which?* magazine for reference material on which the drawings of watering, shading and ventilation methods are based, together with the diagram on compost on page 32. I am grateful also to John Glover for the use of his photographs on pages 11, 18, 54, 78, 114, 119, 134, 135, 138, 146, and to Amdega Ltd for the photograph reproduced on the back of the jacket. Finally, the help and encouragement given by my editor Sarah Widdicombe is here most gratefully recorded.

R.L.

INDEX

Entries in *italic* refer to illustrations

SUPPLIERS

GREENHOUSES

AGL, Birmingham Road, West Bromwich, West Midlands B71 4JY (Aluminium free-standing in various styles to 12ft 3in long)

Alitex, Station Road, Alton, Hants GU34 2PZ (Aluminium free-standing and lean-to, some with curved eaves, bespoke made models to order, any length)

Alton, PO Box 17, Banbury, Oxon OX17 3NS (Cedar free-standing, lean-to and octagonal, up to 20ft 7in long)

Baco Aluminium Products, Middlemore Industrial Estate, Smethwick, Warley, West Midlands B66 2EE (Aluminium free-standing and lean-to to 12ft 3in long)

Baco Leisure Products, Windover Road, Huntingdon, Cambs PE18 7EH (Aluminium free-standing, only to 12ft 4in long)

Banbury Homes & Gardens, PO Box 17, Banbury, Oxon OX17 3NS (Aluminium free-standing, lean-to and extra height with double door)

Bernhards, Bilton Road, Rugby, Warwickshire CV22 7DT (Aluminium free-standing, double doors, choice of polyester finish, to 12ft 6in long)

Cambridge, Comberton, Cambridge CB3 7BY (Aluminium free-standing to 15ft by 16ft)

Clear Span, Greenfield, Oldham OL3 7AG (Aluminium curvilinear free-standing and lean-to, maximum 10ft 2in by 24ft 8in)

Cotswold, Standlake, Oxon, OX8 7QG (Cedar free-standing, lean-to and octagonal to 18ft 11in long)

Crittall, Crittall Road, Witham, Essex CM8 3AW (Aluminium free-standing, straight or curved eaves to 12ft 7in long)

Europa Manor, Appletree Road Trading Estate, Chipping Warden, Oxon OX17 1LL (Aluminium free-standing and lean-to to 12ft 5in long)

Garden Relax, Bridge Works, Little Hallingbury, Bishops Stortfordt, Herts CM22 7RP (Polythene-covered tunnel, steel frame to 10ft wide by 30ft long)

Halls Homes and Gardens, Church Road, Paddock Wood, Tonbridge, Kent TN12 6EU (Aluminium free-standing and lean-to, max 8ft 5in wide by 12ft 7in long)

Headen, 218 High Street, Potters Bar, Herts (Aluminium free-standing and lean-to to 12ft 5in long)

L.B.S. Polythene, Cottontree, Colne, Lancs BB8 7BW (Polythene-covered tunnel, steel frame to 10ft wide by 40ft long)

Lewes Road Sawmills, Glencoe, Church Road, Scaynes Hill, West Sussex RH17 7NZ (Cedar free-standing to 12ft 8in long)

Midland, Lye Head, Bewdley, Worcs DY12 2UX (Whitewood free-standing or lean-to, max 8ft by 13ft 1in)

N.H.M., Chiswick Avenue, Mildenhall, Suffolk IP28 7AZ (PVC-covered, steel-framed free-standing, lean-to and octagonal to 14ft 9in long)

Edward Owen, Stanhope Road, Camberley, Surrey GU15 3AU (Aluminium free-standing to 12ft 6in long)

Park Lines, Park House, 501 Green Lanes, Palmers Green, London N13 4BS (Cedar or whitewood free-standing and lean-to, max 10ft 5in by 20ft 2in)

Pounds, Hopleys, Bliss Gate Road, Rock, Kidderminster, Worcs DY12 2UX (Whitewood free-standing and lean-to, to 13ft 1in long)

Pratten, Charlton Road, Midsomer Norton, Bath, Avon BA3 4AG (Cedar free-standing to 15ft 3in long)

Regal, Cromford Works, Cromford Road, Langley Mill, Nottingham NG16 4EB (Cedar and whitewood free-standing and lean-to to 19ft long)

Robinsons, Robinson House, Winnall Industrial Estate, Winchester, Hants SO23 8LH (Aluminium free-standing and lean-to, some with double doors, max 10ft 7in by 12ft 8in)

Rosedale Engineers, 9 Bridlington Road, Hunmanby, Filey, Yorks (Dome-shaped PVC on steel or aluminium, max 19ft 6in diameter)

Serac, Nyton Road, Aldingbourne, Chichester, West Sussex PO20 6TU (Aluminium solar design, plastic double glazing, extended south roof, max 10ft by 12ft)

Silver Mist, Security House, 58 London Road, Horsham, West Sussex RH12 1AY (Whitewood free-standing and octagonal, max 8ft 9in by 16ft 2in)

Sun, Sears House, Bailey Industrial Park, Kepler, Tamworth, Staffs B79 7UL (Aluminium free-standing and lean-to, some with double doors, max to 12ft 5in long)

Waytogrow, Unit 8, Westfleet Estate, Robert Way, Wickford, Essex (Aluminium multi-sided free-standing to 8ft 2in diameter)

Wernick, Lindon Road, Brownhills, Walsall, West Midlands WS8 7BW (Cedar and whitewood free-standing, lean-to and octagonal, max 10ft 5in by 20ft 2in)

Whitehouse, Buckhurst Works, Frant, Tunbridge Wells, Kent TN3 9BN (Cedar free-standing, lean-to and hexagonal, max 12ft by 40ft)

BIOLOGICAL CONTROLS

Agralan Ltd, The Old Brickyard, Ashton Keynes, Swindon, Wilts. SN6 6QR

Chase Organics (GB) Ltd, Coombelands House, Coombelands Lane, Addlestone, Surrey KT15 1HY

English Woodlands Ltd, Burrow Nursery, Cross-in-Hand, Heathfield, East Sussex TN21 0UG

Oecos, 130 High Street, Kimpton, Herts SG4 8QP

Steel & Brodie, Stevens Drove, Houghton, Stockbridge, Hants SO20 6LP

GREENHOUSE EQUIPMENT

Access Garden Frames, Crick, Northampton NN6 7XS (Frames, heaters)

Aeromatic-Barter, Kynoch Road, Eleys Estate, London N18 3BH (Heaters)

AL-KO Britain Ltd, No 1 Industrial Estate, Medomsley Road, Consett, County Durham DH8 6SZ (Shredders)

Ambi-rad, PO Box 30, Engield Works, Micklow Hill, Halesowen, West Midlands B62 8DS (Heaters)

Autogrow Products, North Walsham, Norfolk (Propagators)

Autoheat, Findley Irvine Ltd, Bog Road, Penicuik, Midlothian EH26 9BU (Heaters)

S. Brannan & Sons Ltd, Cleator

Moor, Cumbria CA25 5QE (Thermometers, pH tester, humidity meter)

Dimex Ltd, 116 High Street, Solihull, West Midlands B91 3SD (Disinfectants and cleaning fluids)

Chronar Ltd, CP House, 97–107 Uxbridge Road, London W5 5TL (Solar-powered lighting)

George H. Elt, Eltex Works, Bromyard Road, Worcester WR2 5DN (Heaters)

Fyba Pot Company, Malvern Road, Knottingley, West Yorks WF11 8EG (Biodegradable pots, capillary matting)

Geeco, Gore Road Industrial Estate, New Milton, Hants BH25 6SE (Heaters, propagators, plant holders)

Green Brothers (GEEBRO) Ltd, South Road, Hailsham, East Sussex BN27 3DT (Polythene insulation)

Grosfillex (UK) Ltd, 10 Chandos Road, London NW10 6NF (Conservatory furniture)

Hotbox Heaters, Unit 7, Gordleton Industrial Park, Sway Road, Lymington, Hants SO41 8JD (Heaters)

Jemp Engineering, Canal Estate, Station Road, Langley, Berks SL3 6EG (Heaters, propagators)

R.A. Lutter Ltd, 16–18 Stenson Street, St James, Northampton NN5 5ED (Heaters)

Metro Products, Eastman House, 98–102 Station Road East, Oxted, Surrey RH8 0AY (Frames, compost bins, watering equipment)

Keith Newmark Ltd, Victoria Works, Institute Street, Padiham, Lancs BB12 8BB (Planters)

Novatech Products Ltd, Pearce House, Acrewood Way, St Albans, Herts AL4 0JY (Mini greenhouse, selfwatering growing bag)

Olive Tree Trading Co Ltd, Twickenham Trading Estate, Rugby Road, Twickenham, Middlesex TW1 1DG (Terracotta containers)

Quantum Electronic Systems (Cupar) Ltd, Baird Avenue, Dryburgh Industrial Estate, Dundee DD2 3XA (Computer-controlled environment)

Richard Sankey & Son Ltd, Bennerley Road, Bulwell, Nottingham NG6 8PE (Propagators, water butts, watering cans)

Thermal Tempest Heating Equipment Ltd, Yaxley, Peterborough PE7 3H5 (Heaters)

Two Wests & Elliott Ltd, Unit 4 Carrwood Road, Sheepbridge Industrial Estate, Chesterfield, Derbyshire S41 9RH (Range of greenhouse equipment)

Wilson Grimes Products, Corwen, Clwyd LL21 0DR (Soil and pH test kits and meters)

ORGANIC COMPOSTS AND FERTILISERS

Camland Products Ltd, Fordham House, Fordham, Cambridgeshire CB7 5LN

Cowpact Products, Adstock, Buckingham MK18 2RE

E.J. Godwin (Peat Industries) Ltd, Meare, Glastonbury, Somerset BA6 9SP

East Anglian Organic Products Ltd, Green House, Timworth Green, Bury St Edmunds, Suffolk IP31 1HS

Fertosan Products (Wirral) Ltd, 2 Holborn Square, Birkenhead, Merseyside L41 9HQ

Fisons Horticulture, Paper Mill Lane, Bramford, Ipswich, Suffolk IP8 4BZ

Goldengrow Ltd, Court Farm, Llanover, Abergavenny, Gwent NP7 9YD

Humber Fertilisers plc, PO Box 27, Stoneferry, Hull HU8 8DQ

E.W. King & Co Ltd, Monks Farm, Coggeshall Road, Kelvedon, Essex CO5 9PG

Leggar Organics, Knapp Farm, Chadshill, Cannington, Bridgwater, Somerset TA5 2BR

Maxicrop Ltd, 21 London Road, Great Shelford, Cambridge CB2 5DF

Norfolk Farm Composts Ltd, Docking Farm, Outlon, Norwich NR11 6BR

Organic Concentrates Ltd, 3 Broadway Court, Chesham, Buckinghamshire HP5 1EN

Organic Worm Products, 43 Francis Road, Ashford, Kent TN23 1UP

Skirza Horticultural Products, Roadside, Skirza, Freswick, Wick, Caithness

Stimgro Ltd, Bridge House, 97–101 High Street, Tonbridge, Kent TN9 1DR

Uza Frenly Organic Gardening, Stallard Common, Great Ellingham, Attleborough, Norfolk NR17 1LJ

Warner Knowles, 67 Queensway, Great Cornard, Sudbury, Suffolk

ORGANIC PESTICIDES

Chase Organics (GB) Ltd, Addlestone, Weybridge, Surrey KT15 1HY

Cumulus Organics and Conservation Ltd, Two Mile Lane, Highnam, Gloucester GL2 8DW

Dig and Delve Organics, Fen Road, Blo Norton, Diss, Norfolk IP22 25H

East Anglian Organic Products Ltd, Green House, Timworth Green, Bury St Edmunds, Suffolk IP31 1HS

HDRA (Sales) Ltd, Ryton Gardens, Ryton-on-Dunsmore, Coventry CV8 3LG

Pan Britannica Industries Ltd, Britannica House, Waltham Cross, Herts EN8 7DY

Koppert (UK) Ltd, PO Box 43, Tunbridge Wells, Kent TN2 5BY

SEEDS

*Denotes suppliers of organic seeds

J.W. Boyce, 67 Station Road, Soham, Ely, Cambridgeshire CB7 5ED

*****Chase Organics (GB) Ltd,** Addlestone, Weybridge, Surrey KT15 1HY

Samuel Dobie & Son Ltd, Broomhill Way, Torquay, Devon TQ2 7QW

Mr Fothergills Seeds, Kentford, Newmarket, Suffolk CB8 7QB

*****HDRA (Sales) Ltd,** Ryton Gardens, Ryton-on-Dunsmore, Coventry CV8 3LG

Hursts Seeds, Stepfield, Essex CM8 3TA

W.W. Johnson & Son Ltd, Boston, Lincs PE21 8AD

*****Kings Crown Quality Seeds,** Grange Hill, Coggeshall, Essex

S.E.Marshall & Co Ltd, Regal Road, Wisbech, Cambs PE13 2RF

W. Robinson & Sons, Sunny Bank, Forton, Preston, Lancs PR3 0BN

*****Suffolk Herbs,** Sawyers Farm, Little Cornard, Sudbury, Suffolk CO10 0NY

Suttons Seeds Ltd, Hele Road, Torquay, Devon TQ2 7QJ

Thompson & Morgan Ltd, Poplar Lane, London Road, Ipswich, Suffolk IP2 0BA

Unwins Seeds Ltd, Impington Lane, Histon, Cambs CB4 4LE

Van Hage Seeds, Great Amwell, Ware, Herts SG12 9RP